Loving Relationships
Self, Others, and God

Loving Relationships
Self, Others, and God

Robert L. Shelton

Foreword by David W. Augsburger

BRETHREN PRESS
Elgin, Illinois

Loving Relationships
Self, Others, and God.

HM
132
.S517
1987

Copyright © 1987 by Robert L. Shelton

BRETHREN PRESS. 1451 Dundee Avenue, Elgin, Illinois
60120

Cover design by Kathy Kline

The A-H-M Frame on p. 141 is from James Crosby, *Illusion and
Disillusion* © 1976 by Wadsworth Publishing Company, Inc. Used by
permission. The chart on p. 167-168 is from *Getting to Yes* by Roger
Fisher and William Ury, Copyright © 1981. Reprinted by permission
of Houghton Mufflin Company. The "rebuilding blocks" chart on
p. 214 is from *Rebuilding: When Your Relationship Ends* © 1981 by
Bruce Fisher. Reproduction by permission of Impact Publishers, Inc.,
P.O. Box 1094, San Luis, Obispo, CA 93406. Further reproduction
prohibited.

Library of Congress Cataloging-in-Publication Data

Shelton, Robert, 1934–
    Loving relationships.

    Bibliography: p.
    1. Interpersonal relations.   2. Love.   I. Title.
HM132.S517   1987   306.7   86-26828
ISBN 0-87178-542-0

Manufactured in the United States of America

to

DAVID and MICHAEL

HEIDI and WENDI

and, especially, to

CAROLYN

*in our ongoing pilgrimage
toward a love-filled life*

ITEM CHARGED

P.Barcode:

Due Date: 4/17/2019 10:30 PM

Title: Loving relationships : self, others, and God / Robert L. Shelton ; foreword by David W. Augsburger.

Author: Shelton, Robert L., 1934-

CallNo.: HM132 .S517 1987

Enum.:

Chron.:

Copy: 1

I.Barcode:

Non-reserve items can be renewed by logging into your library account at www.jkmlibrary.org. All library materials are subject to recall.

Contents

Foreword

Love, the emotion reputed to be natural, inevitable, automatic, is not innate. Love is learned.

We learn to love from our first experience of being enfolded by loving arms to the final hand clasp of life. Intuition, observation, instruction, participation and the reception of affection all teach us to give and receive love. Yet the love we learn is often more confusing than calming, more complex than simple, more ambivalent than constant, more distorted than direct. Often the love learned is only a fragment of authentic loving relationship enlarged to become everything, a part pretending to be the whole.

So love takes as many forms and faces as there are family patterns and family values. Human families are bound together by a wide variety of understanding of what is central in connecting with and caring for others. Let me list a few of these forms of "loving relationship" which one observes in single, marital, familial and friendship contexts.

Love is control
If you love me
you will do what I want
and act as I prescribe.
(Love and power are confused)

Love is agreement
If you love me
you will not differ from my position
because to differ is to reject.
(Love and harmony are combined)

Love is understanding
If you love me
you will know what I need or want
without my telling or asking.
(Love and magic are blended)

Love is conformity
If you love me
your behavior will fit perfectly
with everyone around you.
(Love and pleasing others are eclipsed)

Love is obligation
If you love me
you owe me your loyalty
and respect for me is your duty.
(Love and duty are seen as synonymous)

Love is denial
If you love me
you will hear no evil,
see no evil, say no evil about me.
(Love is transformed into a defense mechanism)

Love is anxiety
If you love me
you will be anxious when I am anxious,
feel the fears I feel.
(Love is regressed to basic anxiety avoidance)

Love is rescuing
If you love me
you will let me dedicate my life to rescuing, saving,
taking care of your dependency needs.
(Love is projection of one's own weakness on another.)

Love is closeness
If you love me
you will always be close,
you will never act, feel, be distant.
(Love is converted into a need for security and support)

Love is availability
If you love me

you will always be present, open,
willing to match my schedule.
(Love is usurping of the other person's freedom)

Each of these forms of "love" is highly conditional, it is love given if one conforms, when one performs, because one is matching the lover's demands. Such "love" invites low self-esteem, low trust, low intimacy. It blocks the growth of both the lover and the loved.

Love is all these and none of these. Love, as commonly expressed, masquerades as one or many of these ways attachment may be expressed, yet it is not love. It is astounding how unloving the many forms of love can be when the heart of valuing, prizing and caring for the other equally with the self is missing.

What is this central, crucial, essential nature of the loving relationship? For over a decade, Robert Shelton has been teaching university courses on the loving relationship, on its nature in singleness, marriage, family, community, and helping relationships. His concern for authentic caring throughout the whole life cycle challenges both the way we think about loving and the many ways love energizes and transforms friendships and covenantal relationships and redirects the tensions and conflicts of living with one another.

As a resource for group or classroom exploration or as a guide to personal reflection and study, this book will stimulate the kind of inner discovery that sets relationships free to deepen in intensity, to broaden in inclusiveness, to lengthen in fidelity, to open themselves to the loving power and presence of God. This spiritual sensitivity to the unconditional love of God makes this book a welcome and needed addition to and alternative to the current literature on loving relationships. The integration of affection and respect and commitment to self, other and God centers love in our relatedness as fully human beings, not in ourselves as narcissists, in others as either saviors or servants or in God in private religiosity. In love we can be truly *with* others *before* God. Let this book be a profound invitation to love, because caring is our highest calling.

David W. Augsburger
Professor of Pastoral Care
Associated Mennonite Biblical Seminaries
Elkhart, Indiana

Introduction

Relationships.
Loving relationships.
Everyone wants and needs them. We describe them in various ways:

"We have a *wonderful* relationship!"
"I'm in this new relationship . . ."
"My relationship with my mother is lousy . . ."
"I'd sure like to improve my relationship with my boss, but . . ."
"My relationship with God is the most important thing in life to me . . ."
"Our loving relationship will lead to marriage, I'm sure . . ."
"Our relationship with Russia has taken a definite turn for the worse . . ."
"I know it sounds weird, but my cat and I have the neatest relationship."
"What I want most is a really *meaningful* relationship, you know what I mean?"

This book is about loving relationships. About loving and being loved. It assumes that nothing is more important than being able to relate to others, God, and to oneself in ways that are loving.

The very word, "loving," or "love," implies a "relationship." We have lots of different types of relationships. Thus, we experience "love" in many different ways. Obviously, the term "loving relationship" often seems to suggest a romantic arrangement. In fact, many persons automatically assume that an affectionate attachment with sexual involvement of some sort is what is meant when they hear or read that term. Romantic love does, of course, form the basis for *one* kind of loving relationship, although many who are caught up in romances discover that they are not experiencing a very *loving* relationship. We also have relationships involving love of some kind with friends, family members, fellow human beings in the community, and with many aspects of nature.

Most of us resist the notion that loving requires knowledge and practice. We prefer to think that it "just happens," that it is a natural part of living. Loving may well be "natural" for human beings; included in this book are the ideas of some who are convinced of that. Although it may be a part of our nature to be loving and caring, the experience of many of us, however, indicates that we don't know nearly enough, that our attempts at loving are often frustrated or unsatisfactory. Thus, we may be willing to learn more about what is involved in "loving"—to *unlearn* some things that have become a regular part of our living for a long time and to practice what we are learning as we would practice anything else that is important to us. Through this willingness to unlearn and relearn, the relationships we have with ourselves, with others, and with our total environment can be enriching and productive.

The approach used in this book is basically the approach that I have found to be helpful to hundreds of persons in university classrooms, in workshops and seminars, in community groups and church school classes, and in contacts with individuals through a correspondence course. The major sources for our understanding are found in Jewish and Christian scriptures and tradition, in contemporary existential and humanistic psychology, and in reports of experience from the daily lives of persons. These provide helpful ways of understanding what love is and how we go about the process of loving. We have a "tradition" in Western religious and philosophical thought that has heavily influenced the ways in which we have learned to think about loving. We do our loving in a complex of experiences—the experience of self-love, of loving and being loved by others (including other-than-human environment), and the experience of being loved and cared for by the transcendent power in which we are grounded. The transcendent dimension, of course, is called God by many of us. This circle of loving—self, other, transcendent—is basic to our experience, and various interpretations of it have influenced our thinking about what we are doing, whether we have consciously paid attention to it or not. In addition, this tradition of the interaction among love of self, neighbor and God has conveyed values to us that shape what we think to be "good," "true," or "real" love.

I have also been aided by the ways in which Erich Fromm and Rollo May have combined their psychotherapeutic backgrounds with insights from history, scripture, theology, philosophy, Greek mythology, literature—and daily life. Fromm's book, *The Art of Loving,* is now a "classic," and its influence is clearly seen in this as well as most books of recent vintage having to do with love. May's *Love and Will* pushes us to consider the need to reunite sex and eros, meaning and decision, the constructive and destructive aspects within our own psyches—to reunite love and will. I have utilized these sources in the pages that follow, as well as Milton Mayeroff's *On Caring* and Sam Keen's playfully profound analysis of "stages of loving," *The Passionate Life*—along with dozens of others.

We begin by looking at some samples of loving and establishing a theoretical grounding for the work of loving. Although our conditioning inclines us to assume that "loving relationships" are romantic duos, our reality is that we live out our lives in a wide variety of relationships that involve intimacy, caring, nurturing, and activity for growth. The contexts that I've chosen to discuss are friendship, ways of living together including marriage and family, community, and the larger world of "nature" and the Divine. In the discussion of these selected contexts, it is my intention to "expand our consciousness" of the types of circumstances in which we give and receive caring and/or intimacy with others.

In the second half of the book, I focus on particular problems, issues and opportunities encountered in our attempts to love. Within such considerations as the struggle with the self, possessiveness, dependence, conflict, sexuality issues, and loss of relationship, we discover ways in which we frustrate and impede our potential. We also learn ways to enhance the possibilities of achieving more productive relationships. How shall we test our capacity for loving? In the last chapter, on loving the enemy, I am suggesting a special model of loving which is recommended in the New Testament, as well as other significant sources. Jesus' suggestion that the love of the *enemy* is the real challenge followed his assertion that there is no big deal in loving those who love us. We recognize that loving those within our usual circles of positive feelings is often anything but easy. Nonetheless, we take seriously the challenge to consider the love of the enemy as the real test for loving relationships, and I have ventured into a particular way of looking at the concept of enemy which may be a bit unusual. Assuming that persons are placed in "enemy status" whenever we put them outside the normal bounds of human interaction, I wrap up this book with an application of loving to our special relationship with persons who are forced outside the circle of "us" into the outlying territory of "them."

At the conclusion of most chapters, there is a section on "Shared Experiences and Insights." I have asked hundreds of persons in my courses to write on their personal experiences and feelings related to many of the topics in this book. Many of these deserve to be shared with others, and I included a few selections because I am certain others will appreciate them. For a variety of reasons, most of these statements are not identified by name. These insights and experiences are presented, however, in exactly the words in which they were given to me.

In this discussion of loving relationships, I make no claim for a new and original theory. We have centuries of contributions by others which we are still trying to understand and implement in our lives. I do hope to bring insights together and add a number of my own in a way that helps us to think and act—to better understand our experience and to integrate that understanding into more productive and satisfying ways of living and loving. My writing is intended to help the reader rethink some assumptions and ways of doing things, and to introduce approaches that may be new or unfamiliar. Our common goal is to both understand and improve our ongoing interaction of experiences with self, with others, and with transcendent meaning.

This book is enriched by the experiences and insights of untold numbers of persons who have looked into their own relationships and shared their observations. Among those whose contributions have found their way into these pages are: Robert Bacic, Jim Beaumont, Linda Beckcom, Wanda Boone, Jane Buttenhoff, Marygene Perry Fagan, Peggy French, Marianne Gowen, Matthew Grove, Gail Hamilton, Julie Hammond, Lori Hoffman, Ursula Huelsbergen, Don Hufford, Kathy Hulyk, Billy Johnson, Pat Kehde, John Marquis, Sara Jane McNeive, David Merriweather, Maureen Monaghan, Linda Muth, Jerry Neuner, Paula Richardson, Theresa Saltsman, Aprylisa Snyder, Sylvia Stone, Betsy Topper, Elaine Vick, June Weatherwax, and Joan Wittmer.

In a long evening's conversation more than ten years ago, Mary Jasnoski told me of her concern, as an undergraduate student, that the academic study of "loving relationships" was not available on our campus. The course that has now touched thousands of lives grew out of that conversation, and now Dr. Jasnoski, clinical psychologist, is happily recognized as a major stimulus for this book.

Hoy Steele, a longtime friend and colleague, critiqued part of the manuscript and was especially helpful to me in the section on conflict management. I also appreciate the very special contribution of Donna and Frank Shavlik in sharing what a loving relationship looks and feels like.

Early in my campus ministry days, a bright freshman from another campus caught my eye and ear in a state meeting, demanded my attention, and stretched my intellect. Some twenty years later, Dr.

Carol S. Robb, increasingly known for her work as a feminist social ethicist, has contributed immensely to this work by a careful critical reading of the entire manuscript. She provided the incisive response that comes from a caring friend and, at times, pushed my foundational thinking to its roots while insisting on hearing my unique voice with more clarity.

Hours, days, weeks spent in conferences, workshops, class sessions, and personal conversations with unique, precious human beings have played their own special part in bringing this book to life. The University of Kansas provided the sabbatical leave during which much of the manuscript was prepared, and I am grateful for the opportunity that only that kind of uninterrupted time provides for the reflection and writing. The Kansas Committee for the Humanities, through its Public Research Grant program, supported my work on loving the enemy. My long affiliation with their efforts to engage the public in consideration of personal and social values has influenced many of the ideas emerging in these pages.

I am deeply indebted to professor David W. Augsburger for his kind foreword. He well represents the historic peace church tradition, a tradition which has long sought to put into practice "loving the enemy" (chapter 12).

The transfer from my typewriter to this printed page was facilitated through the joyous competence of Ann Heinrich, Sandee Kennedy, and Pam LeRow at the University of Kansas, as well as the skillful staff of Brethren Press. For all their efforts, I am deeply thankful.

1

What Do Loving Relationships Look and Feel Like?

Life is full of loving relationships. We know what they look like. We're sure we know—or "will know"—what they *feel* like.

Or, life may be *empty,* when it comes to relationships that are loving. We think we know what they look and feel like, but don't have much of that experience.

Before we consider how we "think about" loving relationships, as we shall do in chapter two, it is useful to examine first some special descriptions of relationships. The first is a kind of fairy tale, rather poetic in its profound observations. The others are self-descriptions of actual relationships. I do not suggest that any one of these descriptions—or all of them—have all the truth about loving relationships. Within each there are, nonetheless, many insights that may help us to search out the truths in our own experience.

The Friendship Of The Little Prince and The Fox: "Taming"

In *The Little Prince,* Antoine de Saint Exupéry has spun a tale that touches on some of the deepest aspects of life and love. You may have seen some of his ideas on posters, or read them in popular books on love. The book is about an encounter with a visitor from a faraway asteroid. Among its profound insights are some observations regarding love and friendship that are shared with the visiting prince by a fox.

The narrator of this story tells us that, when flying alone, he happened to crash his airplane in the Sahara desert. While attempting repairs on the plane, he is suddenly joined by a "most extraordinary small person" unlike anyone he ever met before. In the course of time, he learns that this is a prince who inhabits a very small planet, no larger than a house. He shares his asteroid with three volcanoes (two active and one extinct) and a rose which he considers to be unlike any other flower in the galaxy. The prince left his planet in search of friends elsewhere, and has visited a number of planets, now including Earth. One of his experiences on Earth was the discovery of a rose garden, where he was startled to learn that there are thousands of flowers just like his flower at home. Because he had been led by his flower to believe that there were no others like her in the universe, he was "overcome with sadness." As he reflects on this great disappointment, he realizes: "I thought that I was rich, with a flower that was unique in all the world; and all I had was a common rose."[1] As he lies in the grass, crying, a fox appears and greets him.

Once the unhappy little prince sees how attractive the fox is, he proposes that the fox come and play with him. The fox replies that he cannot play, because he is not *tamed*. The prince does not understand. "Tame" is not a familiar word to him. He asks the fox what "tame" means. After clarifying that the prince is indeed searching for friends, the fox is willing to tell him what "tame" means. It isn't done often enough, he explains, but its meaning is "to establish ties."

The prince is intrigued, but doesn't understand. They don't yet really mean anything to each other, the fox goes on, and they don't need each other. He is indistinguishable from all the other foxes, and the prince looks like any other little boy. In "taming," or establishing ties, they begin to need one another, and each becomes unique to the other.

Then the fox gives a magnificent description of what it will mean if the prince will tame him:

My life is very monotonous. I hunt chickens; men hunt me. All the chickens are just alike, and all the men are just alike. And, in consequence, I am a little bored. But if you tame me, it will be as if the sun came to shine on my life. I shall know the sound of a step that will be different from all the others. Other steps send me hurrying back underneath the ground. Yours will call me, like music, out of my burrow. And then look: you see the grain-fields down yonder? I do not eat bread. Wheat is of no use to me. The wheat fields have nothing to say to me. And that is sad. But you have hair that is the color of gold. Think how wonderful that will be when you have tamed me! The grain, which is also golden, will bring me back the thought of you. And I shall love to listen to the wind in the wheat . . .[2]

Establishing a tie will bring sunshine into his life! Whereas the steps of others are the source of fear, their sound driving him to hide in his burrow, the sound of his friend's steps will bring him joyfully out of his hiding-place. Furthermore, formerly meaningless aspects of his surroundings will now become symbols of deep meaning for him. The color of the wheat field is the same color as the little prince's hair. Not only will he be reminded of his friend whenever he sees the wheat, but the activity of their love will sing to him through the sounds of the wind in the wheat. After contemplating some more on the wonders of such ties, the fox again implores the prince to tame him. The prince, in turn, assures him that he would like to, but he has much to do, and little time. He wants to find new friends, and there is much he still wants to understand. The fox's reply is powerful:

> "One only understands the things that one tames," said the fox. "Men have no more time to understand anything. They buy things already made at the shops. But there is no shop anywhere where one can buy friendship, and so men have no friends any more. If you want a friend, tame me . . .[3]

Taming is a new experience for the prince, and he asks what he must do to tame the fox. Saint Exupéry here relates what he considers to be two of the most important components in establishing ties: patience and rituals. He also underlines the importance of non-verbal communication and the problems of verbal communication.

> "You must be very patient . . . First you will sit down at a little distance from me—like that—in the grass. I shall look at you out of the corner of my eye, and you will say nothing. Words are the source of misunderstanding. But you will sit a little closer to me, every day . . ."

The next day the little prince comes back.

> "It would have been better to come back at the same hour," said the fox. "If, for example, you come at four o'clock in the afternoon, then at three o'clock I shall begin to be happy. I shall feel happier and happier as the hour advances. At four o'clock, I shall already be worrying and jumping about. I shall show you how happy I am! But if you come at just any time, I shall never know at what hour my heart is to be ready to greet you . . . One must observe the proper rites . . ."[4]

The little prince doesn't understand about rites, either, and he is told that, like taming, they are acts "too often neglected." Rites, the fox explains, are what makes one day, one hour, different from another.

The fox gets his wish. He is tamed by the prince. We are told no more about it, nor what followed. We only learn that the time comes for the prince to depart, and the fox says he will cry. The prince doesn't know how to deal with that. After all, the fox *asked* to be tamed; he certainly intended him no harm. Since the fox is now going to cry, the prince concludes, the taming must not have done any good. The fox agrees that he asked for the taming, and he disagrees that it has done no good: "It has done me good," says the fox, "because of the color of the wheat fields." Establishing ties with another not only has meaning in that relationship, but it brings new meaning to otherwise insignificant parts of our surroundings. The new meanings remain after the person is gone.

At this point, the fox helps the prince understand something important about his rose. He instructs him to go back and look at the thousands of roses in the garden; when he returns to say goodbye, the fox will share a secret with him. The prince follows the suggestion and discovers that the roses are not at all like his flower, because they have not been tamed. His rose is more important because he has watered her, put her under a glass globe to keep her warm at night, sheltered her with a screen, and kept the caterpillars from her. In addition, he has listened to her, whether it be grumbling, boasting, or just silence.

Upon his return to the fox, he is given a threefold secret:

—"It is only with the heart that one can see rightly; what is essential is invisible to the eye."

—"It is the time that you have wasted for your rose that makes your rose so important."

—"You become responsible, forever, for what you have tamed. You are responsible for your rose . . ."[5]

There is great depth, as well as romance and sentiment, in Saint Exupéry's tale. The establishment of ties is often neglected. It takes time and must be a priority. It concentrates on the uniqueness of the other, and contributes to that uniqueness by the attention and devotion given. "Taming" shatters the monotony of life and provides alternatives to the fearful responses that have become routine. Aspects of the other person are enlarged into symbols of meaning and fuller joys in life. Rites and rituals make it more possible for the "heart to be ready" for greeting and loving activity. They provide ways of incorporating anticipation of the other into the routine of daily experience.

Loving is something that one does as a part of the orientation of the whole personality. Saint Exupéry put it in terms of seeing rightly only with the heart, being in touch with what is otherwise invisible. All those things we do for the other that are such a "waste" of time . . . feeding, watering, sheltering, protecting . . . those are the things that make the other so important. (Washers of diapers, take note!) The permanency of commitment, a notion that is troubling in a time of such tenuousness of ties, is affirmed by the assertion that one is "responsible forever" for what or who is tamed. The tie that is established is something to which one will always respond, in one way or another.

"Gramp" and His Family: Preservation of Dignity

What does a family do when an eighty-one year old man removes his false teeth and announces that he will no longer eat or drink?

One answer is documented in *Gramp* (1976), a photo-essay by Mark Jury and Dan Jury. It is, as the cover of the book states, an account of how "a man ages and dies." It is also "the extraordinary record of one family's encounter with the reality of dying." We can also call it a set of loving relationships within a family, a network which actively preserves the dignity of a loved one.

The family of Frank Tugend, a retired Pennsylvania coal miner, had been through a three year "ordeal" of arteriosclerosis—sometimes called senility—with him. Although it was painful to do so, they respected what they knew was a decision on his part, and stayed with him in his final three weeks.

Millions of American families are faced with the pain of watching the slow deterioration of a person who has been physically and mentally alert all of her or his life, with the loss of control over both physical and mental capacities. Families respond to such circumstances in widely differing ways, depending on resources, geographical availability of family members, and strength of family ties. Many members of the Tugend family had been close for years, centered around Frank and "Nan" and their country home. Since one of the daughters lived with them, and two grandsons lived nearby, they determined to answer the question of whether to keep "Gramp" at home or put him in a nursing home by mobilizing their energies to keep him at home, in the house he had built years before with his own tools. In his last few weeks, they had to make the decision whether to have him hospitalized and sustained by intravenous tubes. They "chose to let him die at home, with some dignity intact."[6]

Frank Tugend had been an unusually healthy man; during his first seventy-eight years, his only visit to a physician had resulted from a sprained wrist. Friends and family began to notice his "failing." He stopped going to his favorite hangout, a friend's garage. He parked his car and never drove it again, after experiencing a severe state of confusion. He underwent an extensive personality change, from a shy, polite person to "an outspoken lion." Increased states of confusion led him to admit to one of his grandsons, while planting the garden, that he "didn't know who the people around him were, and that he was scared." Dan Jury reported that, "when he asked me to stay near and not leave him alone, I said I'd stay near him."[7] Gramp became more and more dependent on others for personal needs, such as shaving and trimming his hair. He began to develop an imaginary world, inhabited by a variety of creatures with delightful names. His dressing habits, in Mark Jury's words, "became more and more creative." Some of his behavior became both childish and childlike. His comments in public led others in the community to shy away from him and from the family. Many who had regularly called on them stopped coming by. "Most people who had known Frank Tugend as a respected, proper pillar of the community just couldn't take being around him as he shuffled about in his wife's velvet housecoat or blew his nose loudly on a pair of Nink's underpants that he'd found and decided to use as a handkerchief."[8] On the other hand, younger friends of the grandsons, who had never known him in earlier days, found him to be interesting company: "While a Gramp phrase like 'Come to me with a cap in your can and a devil double whatchacall with a horse in your hands' spelled anguish to those who had sung with Gramp in the Dalton Community Minstrel Show, to another group it was pure poetry."[9] One of Dan's friends, an outsider, observed that she often had the feeling that Gramp was playing a game with those around him—but had become involved in the game and couldn't get out.

Difficulties for the family increased as Gramp encountered new problems. His behavior became more bizarre, from washing his hands in the toilet bowl to dismantling and hiding various objects around the house. He seemed to get his days and nights mixed up, and would often be extremely active through the night. Twenty-four hour care, which often creates the necessity for nursing home placement, became the norm for the family. Eventually, he entered a new stage in which he withdrew to his room. The loss of bowel control was as bewildering to Gramp as it was troublesome to those around him: "In one incredible day, the Tugend house became a military-like operation of diapers, rolls of toilet paper, and a well-orchestrated platoon system for getting him cleaned off before the next 'accident' happened."[10]

The family decided against a nursing home, mainly by not deciding; the expense, and the knowledge that he would often be strapped to his bed to quell his wanderings, were more than they could accept. Once he took out his teeth and refused to eat, he began to deteriorate rapidly. Several failures at efforts by family members to induce Gramp to take liquid nourishment led them to admit that they were doing it for themselves, and not for Gramp. In his last few days, it was clear that he wanted someone with him, although there was no other communication: "His bony but still strong fingers clutched the hand of whoever was with him."[11] A final deep sleep of ten hours culminated in a moment of arm movement and a low moan, and then he was dead. At least three members of the family were nearby at the time.

Mark Jury recorded his feelings after Gramp's body was taken away:

> After the funeral director left, I looked at the empty bed and for the first time it hit me: the ordeal was finished. For three years—through babysitting, "accidents," hassles, and diapers—much of our lives had revolved around this room.
>
> Now it was empty.
>
> Surprisingly, I felt no overwhelming sense of relief that Gramp was gone; instead, a tinge of emptiness, a feeling that we would miss the craziness he brought into our lives—but, most of all, I felt an enormous amount of respect for this tough old coal miner. "You pulled it off, Gramp," I thought. "You really pulled it off."[12]

There is more here than simply the story of a man's death, as important as that is. This is also the story of a group of relationships, among persons whose lives are intertwined and focused around their concern for one member of the family. From seventy-eight year old Nan, Gramp's life partner for fifty-seven years, to baby Joshua, the lives of five adults and two small children were greatly influenced by the interactions of those three years. "During that time," the grandsons Mark and Dan Jury wrote, "we learned a lot about Gramp, and about one another. All of us, though, learned even more about ourselves."[13]

It is obvious in the examination of this story that Nan could not have taken care of Gramp alone. The twenty-four-hour demands of his circumstances were more than one person could handle. It is questionable whether it would have been possible, even, for Nan and "Nink," their daughter who lived with them, to have done it without the help of others. Nink was a school teacher and had to keep up her work. Apparently the two grandsons, whose parents lived a considerable distance away, had chosen to live near their grandparents as they began their adult lives. They, too, had their own work, as did the spouse of one, but all three chose to devote a good deal of time to Gramp's needs and support of each other.

Hillary, who was four at the time of her great-grandfather's death, was close to him and had a special understanding of him. Not so far from learning the skill of bowel control herself, she seemed to understand Gramp's loss of that skill: "He's so old he forgot how to do it himself." She delighted in his imaginary world and shared it with him.

His "chillysmiths, rupes, Michigans, and bugeyes" were not imaginary at all, she insisted later. "They're not pretend. They moved over to our house," she confided to her father. "They tied strings together and made themselves into a mobile in my room. They look like fish now. They remind me of Gramp."[14] Hillary now has an acceptance of aging and death which the adults around her find healthy and admirable. On Gramp's last day, Hillary sat with him and held his hand, because he like her to. "I thought he was pretty nice and lovable," she remarked as she looked at the photograph of her sitting by Gramp's bed, holding his hand. "This is the last day. He died that night."

By now, thousands of persons have read this photo-essay on Frank Tugend and/or seen the filmstrip made from it. It is not uncommon for persons to react with some guilt, thinking of a family member in their own lives who suffered Gramp's malady, but were removed from their homes to finish their days in a nursing home. A very normal question arises: "does that mean we aren't loving, that we didn't do the loving thing for our relative?" That is an agonizing question that many of us have to face, and often more than once. There are no simple answers. My purpose in relating the story of Gramp is not to assert that this is necessarily the *norm* for love. It is, however, an illustration of the response which arose in the lives of one particular family, and in that response we can see a number of things happening that reveal loving relationships at work.

The family accepted change, rather dramatic change, in the behavior and capacities of the loved one.

They committed themselves to continue to interact, even though the patterns of interaction with which they had been familiar for a long time were no longer useful.

They found ways to express concern while at the same time sensing what was necessary to help Gramp maintain some dignity.

As persons who shared love for each other, they mobilized that love in a common task. They supported each other in supporting him.

What might be "convenient" seemed much less important than what was necessary to protect the quality of Gramp's life—and death.

Relationships across generations brought special resources to their experience. Their remaining open to outside relationships added even more resources.

Photographs tell a great deal about relationships. On the back cover of this book is a picture of Frank Tugend holding his small grandson (less than a year old) in his arms. The photo next to it was taken twenty years later: the same grandson, now a sturdy twenty-one year old, is holding in his arms the frail body of his grandfather shortly before his death. Dan Jury's journal recorded his feelings: "Of one thing I am sure. No matter how many times I have to clean Gramp, or feed him, or blow his nose, or care for him in the middle of the night when my body only wants to ignore him, I will always remember the good times with Gramp before I recall the bad."[15]

Self-love: "Don't You Think You Deserve To Be Served By Me?"

How does it feel to love yourself? What does self-love look like? Here are some answers from a waitress, reported by Studs Terkel in his book about the working lives of hundreds of persons. Dolores Dante, he tells us, is a waitress who refuses to be demeaned. When we read her words as he has recorded them for us, we encounter a person who finds creative and dignified ways to serve others because she cares about herself.

> I have to be a waitress. How else can I learn about people? How else does the world come to me? I can't go to everyone. So they have to come to me. Everybody wants to eat, everyone has hunger. And I serve them. If they've had a bad day, I nurse them, cajole them. Maybe with coffee I give them a little philosophy. They have cocktails, I give them political science. . . . I can't be servile. I give service. There is a difference . . . I'm called by my first name. I like my name. I hate to be called Miss. Even when I serve a lady, a strange woman, I will not say madam. I hate ma'am. I always say milady. . . .
>
> It would be very tiring if I had to say, "Would you like a cocktail?" and say that over and over. So I come out different for my own enjoyment. I would say, "What's exciting at the bar that I can offer?" I can't say, "Do you want coffee?" Maybe I'll say, "Are you in the mood for coffee?" Or, "The coffee sounds exciting." Just rephrase it enough to make it interesting for me. That would make them take an interest. It becomes theatrical and I feel like Mata Hari and it intoxicates me.
>
> . . . When somebody says to me, "You're great, how come you're *just* a waitress?" *Just* a waitress. I'd say, "Why, don't you think you deserve to be served by me?" . . . I don't feel lowly at all. I myself feel sure. I don't want to change the job. I love it.
>
> . . . I tell everyone I'm a waitress and I'm proud. If a nurse gives service, I say, "You're a professional." Whatever you do, be professional.[16]

"Don't you think you deserve to be served by me?" Delores's question is worth thinking about. She points out in her discussion with Terkel that the question put to her, about being *just* a waitress, implies that she is in a lowly status. She doesn't accept that, and frames her question in a way that puts things into perspective, potentially calling into question the status of the inquirer: If you have seen the musical production of "Working," you know how delightful this waitress really is, and are left with the feeling that it is, indeed, an honor to be served by her. Her question raises an important point: do I love myself enough to be served by someone who clearly loves herself? Doesn't the acceptance of her self-love help me to feel good about myself, as well? That kind of love looks good *and* feels good.

Respect and Growth: Self-description Of a Relationship

I had just begun teaching a course on loving relationships, when I visited with some long-time friends. They, too, have been close friends for years and are also married to each other. The idea of describing what makes a relationship loving intrigued them, and they began to talk about the elements of their own relationship which they considered to be loving. I took notes on the scraps of paper I could find in my pockets.[17]

In considering their description, it is well to keep a few things in mind. First, they have known and loved each other for over twenty years now. They have had time to work through a vast array of experiences—to grow. A number of things in their description would undoubtedly not have occurred to them during the first year or two of their relationship. Further, in our discussion, they were concentrating on those aspects of their relationship which seem *loving* to them; it is not the whole story of all aspects of their relationship. In addition, they emphasized that much of what they described is the result of work, of effort, of conscious decisions and willful actions, undergirded by a real affection for each other. They are willing to work at their relationship because they have fun with each other.

Two basic expectations seem to be a foundation of the loving nature of their relationship. They expect *respect* from each other; thus, they expect to give respect as well. They also expect that their individual *growth will involve each other.* Each assumes that she or he will grow, and so will the other. They consciously seek growth from time to time, and they have also learned to involve the other in the experience. Sometimes this simply means talking about what is happening, how that feels to the other, and what it might introduce to the other as new options for personal development. At other times, this expectation will involve shared experience, planning, and coordination.

"I feel accepted." This was characterized as a lack of stereotyped expectations of how the other person will be or behave. Each person experiences a "free to be me" feeling, with the freedom to change. During one period of their lives together, the man took a year's leave from his job in order to stay home and complete his doctoral dissertation. In a neighborhood in which the persons who were "at home" during the day were "housewives," he was cast in the role of "house-husband." That was OK.

"I don't need to 'explain' him when we are with other people," she asserted. Neither needs to feel responsible for the way the other is. In many relationships, we may feel uneasy with another's behavior, and feel pressed to explain, "she is tired tonight," "it's been a bad day," or "he gets like this after two glasses of wine." These lovers find that they both have more freedom in not becoming interpreters—or definers—of the other's life. It is worth noting that this ability had been there all along with one partner but had developed and grown for the other in the course of their relationship.

"We have a whole lot of trust." Their professions require them to spend a great deal of time apart—usually living in two different cities during the week. Each also travels often without the other. Thus, each of them has a number of friends and co-workers whom the other doesn't know. They trust each other to function in those circumstances without negative assumptions or fears. They treasure a card, given to them by a friend, that carries the motto, "I don't want to give you reasons to stay—only reasons to return."

"Through the years, we have legitimized doing things by ourselves." They don't "own" each other. As friends and lovers, they do many things together. Their growing trust, respect, and acceptance has also increasingly allowed doing things separately. Some of their separate experience can find ways to be shared, some cannot. They return to each other, not because they are owned, but because they want to be together.

"We have lots of genuine caring." Much in our human "caring" is actually sentimentality. That is, we do caring things, go through caring motions, because we care about "caring," and that is what we are supposed to do. In "genuine" caring, the person cared for *feels* cared for, knows that the care-er is concerned about the care-ee, not just about doing something care-ing.

"I feel understood." I asked what that means. "I rarely feel misunderstood," he responded. Sounds simple, doesn't it? Stop and think about that. If you were to describe what it feels like to "feel understood," what would you say? Is it a little hard to pin down? Would you be able to give recent specific examples? Now, turn it over. If you are asked about feeling *mis*understood, I suspect that you know what *that* feels like. More than one recent example probably comes to mind rather easily. When I feel misunderstood, the feeling can be located—in the stomach, or in the chest—as a knot or a dull ache. It results from a variety of causes. I may be suddenly aware that I didn't say what I really meant, that I have clearly given the other person an inaccurate perception. Or, I may be relatively confident that my message is basically accurate, but the listener is placing assumptions regarding my motivations on the message. An event from the past may be coloring the other's perception of my statement or my behavior. I may say nothing at all, and the other may take my silence as an indication of no concern or no desire to discuss it. In many of our relationships, we may feel misunderstood. In a loving relationship that experience is less common. One listens with respect for the other's feelings and experience. The temptation to attribute motives is set aside in an acceptance of the partner's basic integrity. A general "tone" exists in the relationship that allows one to ask what the other is feeling when nothing is said, or encourages one to be supportive of the other's need to be quiet while remaining open to discussion as soon as possible. Feeling understood is feeling received and accepted.

"Unconditional Positive Regard." This concept from Carl Rogers had been a major influence in one partner's intellectual and emotional growth. In Rogers' approach to counseling, the therapist or counselor accepts the other person without conditions or evaluation of behavior or background. Behavior doesn't alter the basic positive regard for the other. This couple sees this to be true in their love relationship, just as it is advocated for counseling or other helping professions. Obviously, in a relationship of intimacy, it is not always easy to separate "regard" from behaviors. At the same time, both partners find freedom in a decision to maintain one's basic regard (love) for the other without it being conditional on specific behaviors. Such freedom contributes to more real sharing in the relationship and—in the long run—encourages positive and growthful behavior.

"I am proud of her accomplishments, of the things she is doing. The things she does are things I value." Her response was significant: "He respects me, and that is very important to me. Respect, as I experience it from him, is something I can't give to myself." Don't be misled by that last statement. She is not saying that she lacks self-respect. She *is* expressing a basic truth of human experience: Some of the richness of human interaction is found in the reality that we can give certain things to each other in ways that are different from what we give ourselves. I can cook a good meal for myself, preparing something that I know I like, and can be sure that it is put together just the way I like it. Likewise, someone else can prepare a good meal for me, something she or he knows I like, in a way that is different from my way, and it is wonderful! The gift of respect given to another is a special gift because it is something one can't give oneself in the same way, experienced with the same quality.

This "pride" is enhanced by the lack of possessiveness. He *values* what she does, and that is important, but it is not what *he* does. She does it, and does it in her own way; it is a source of joy to him.

"The things we value in life are not very different, especially the way we spend our time and our commonality of motivation to give to other people." There are, of course, differences in the ways these values are expressed in their behaviors and priorities, but their style of interaction with others is similar enough to be described as "compatible." This compatibility of styles led to another insight: "We talk about stuff when it happens and don't stew over it." For each of them, it is a priority to talk when something is a felt issue and not wait until later. Neither would be able to wait until another "gets ready" to talk something over; their similarity of "styles" her is important to them.

"We both value having a job that is rewarding and satisfying." In their circumstances, this has led in recent years to their working in different cities, and being together primarily on weekends, special occasions, and vacations. Every night apart they are on the telephone; they probably have as much or more real communication with each other, and real presence with each other, as do many couples who eat and sleep in the same house seven days and nights per week. Because of their values regarding significant work, the "next stage" in their lives may be difficult, not wanting to give up what they are now individually experiencing. At the same time, they are aided by their commitment to grow together.

"We have a commitment to move ahead at a similar pace." This has made major transitions in their life experience—moving from one locale to another, graduate study, change of jobs, being without work—a matter of choices emerging from growth and changes going on in both of them. They have renewed and reshaped this commitment along the way, while recognizing that fluctuations occur, and variations in pace are inevitable. Thus transitions can be new adventures, rather than situations in which one has gained a new opportunity while the other has lost something of irreplaceable value.

"I don't think we have ever fought unfairly." Whether this is a case of selective memory or is indeed accurate, the point is a crucial one: They *do* fight, *and* they try to be fair about it. What would be unfair fighting? "If we shot at tender spots or tried to embarrass the other." They are not afraid to tell each other if they are hurting, or express anger, unhappiness, or disappointment. Their goal in doing so, (as we discuss in chapter nine), is to decrease distance and increase intimacy; thus there is nothing to be gained by wounding the other in the process.

"I trust his style as being an alternative to mine, and not as competition." He agreed. The other is not put in the position of being "wrong" because of having a different style of decision-making, behaving in groups, approach to household tasks, etc. They have different ways of doing things, of seeing things, and these differences are alternatives, rather than competitive approaches vying for some kind of victory. Is one way a better way to do things than another? In a mutual relationship, no one is in a position to be an objective umpire for determining an answer to that question. What is "better" or "right" is relative to many factors, most of which are secondary to the quality of the relationship itself. To describe these persons as simply noncompetitive would be inaccurate. They are able to pursue competition in their work or other activities, when that is appropriate. It is not appropriate, as they see it, to their relationship: "We haven't developed competitive things." Because they are not in a competitive mode within their relationship, they do not compete with others for each other's affections; they can allow intimate, meaningful relationships with others, and be supportive to each other in that.

The friends who described their relationship in these preceeding paragraphs may have something unique; I'm not sure. When I have presented these descriptions to classes or groups, listeners have often protested that they are too "ideal" and thus can't be real. The reader should remember that I have described *their* experience of what is *loving* in their relationship. They were concentrating on that quality and did not take time to go into descriptions of specific points of tension or sadness. Furthermore, they emphasized repeatedly that they have worked to get to where they are now; it has been a process of growth and change. If they are "unique," it does not mean they are any less real. It simply means that M. Scott Peck is correct in saying that many of us are "lazy," not choosing to make the kind of decisions and commitments that produce love in relationships. I would also have to recognize that background and choices of friends or partners make a real difference. These persons learned to be the way they are in their families of origin. Their community backgrounds were similar, and the values which they share have long-standing roots. The shape of their growth, change, and development, however, is a product of their two basic expectations, which they have learned to articulate and have expanded in meaning throughout their relationship.

One further note: Although these persons are married to each other they are not parents. Unable to physically have children, they have chosen against being adoptive parents in order to be more free to extend their concern for growing human beings through their work and other activities. To what extent their self-description would be modified were it necessary to include children and parenting in their daily lives can only be a matter of speculation. Undoubtedly there would be some differences. The basic persons remain, however, as do the elements of loving described by them.

Shared Experiences and Insights

One of my students wrote this about her daughter:

Cats have never appealed to me, but my daughter adores them. It was love at first sight as she would bring home one after another—some gasping for breath as she half-squeezed them to death—anything from mangy, one-eyed, battle-scarred tomcats to sweet, purring, little balls of fluff. Her motherly instinct came out in full force as she tried to bathe, powder, dress them in doll clothes, bandage their wounds, and completely deplete the family's milk supply.

Now she's grown but hasn't changed. An excited phone call came the other day when she informed me that she had found a black and white cat who seems to be quite retarded and she intends to teach him how to be normal.

Many warm, loving thoughts of my daughter have crossed my mind as I've written this paper.

Another wrote about her son and his friend:

My son and his friend are eight years old. Recently I heard them talking about their friendship after my son's friend had come home from a visit with his grandmother. The friend told my son how much he had missed him, and that he never had such a good friend as him. My son said, "I missed you a lot too, and I'm sure glad you're home." They continued talking about living in the same house when they were grown. They decided that their wives would think it would be fun, too.

These two boys really care for one another and express their feelings very honestly to one another. They show their sensitivities easily to each other. It is just delightful to watch. It's sad, too, because I know they won't stay this way. Perhaps I'm wrong—I hope so.

One reported a story about a teacher:

A teacher looked back into his memories and told us about an experience he had as a young teacher, which he considered the most valuable one for his whole teaching career:

During recess he came by a classroom and saw an older teacher sitting at her desk. All the children were playing outside. She was moving her head as if looking to one pupil's desk, then over to the next one, again to the next, then even stretching out her arms toward the empty chairs—toward one after the other—somewhat in a rhythmical manner, and slowly. The young teacher was puzzled, a little worried at the same time, and asked her hesitantly and urgently what in the world she was doing there? "I am sending out love to my students!" she said.

2

Thinking About Loving Relationships

"If Love is the Answer, What is the Question?" With this question as a book title, Uta West confronts us with a fact of life and love: if we want to understand, we have to ask the right questions. Or, to put it differently, we may need to be alerted to the many wrong questions we've been asking. We are nurtured to insist that love can solve all problems. Like me, you probably realize that often we don't understand our problems well enough to know how it would feel to have them "solved." What *is* the question, or what *are* the questions, that so many well-meaning persons assure us will be answered by "love?"

Our "Human Condition"

In his classic, *The Art of Loving,* Erich Fromm contends that there is a basic question to which love *is* the answer. To him the question is about a *problem:* "What is the answer to the problem of human existence?" Our problem as human beings is that we have self-awareness. We are aware of ourselves as *separate* entities. Having left the security of absolute togetherness at birth, we are thrust into life on our own and in isolation from others. We may be overwhelmed by our separateness from each other and from our "ground of being." We long to overcome that separation. We strive to gain union with ourselves, with another, with all others, and with the source of our life. Thus, our question is how to overcome our condition of separateness, how to transcend our own individual lives, how to achieve oneness with persons and other realities that are important to us. His answer is mature love, allowing union, or fusion, between separate persons while preserving individual integrity. The *active* power of love breaks through the walls separating human beings from each other and unites them. The "sense of isolation and separateness" is overcome. In *immature* love, one self is absorbed into the other, or integrity is in some way sacrificed. In *mature* love, however, "the paradox occurs that two beings become one and yet remain two."[1]

We often speak of "falling in love." I like Fromm's insistence that love is an *activity*. It is not something we "fall into," or "fall for." Instead, we "stand in love" or "stand *with*" another in loving. Fromm further emphasizes that, generally speaking, love is more a matter of giving than receiving. I would certainly not want to overlook the fundamental importance of the act of receiving as a part of a loving relationship. For many persons I know, and certainly at times in my own life, the ability to *really receive* the gift of another, has had to be learned and relearned. Nevertheless, Fromm's point is crucial. As an activity, love is producing something. It involves "potency," the capacity for and practice of productivity. The act of giving is producing something in the life and growth of another being. Although the emphasis is on "giving," there is no suggestion that we are "giving *up*" something. Productive love, the "highest expression of potency," is an expression of one's aliveness and personal strength and power, and is thus anything but a deprivation. Rather, it is a "joyous experience of heightened vitality," expanding the claim that "giving is more joyous than receiving." The beginning of our exploration of what it means to be "in" a loving relationship, then, is to consider what we are about as human beings, in our feeling compelled to develop a comfortable, satisfying union with another or others.[2]

Another perspective on our "condition" (to which love is seen as the "answer") is offered by Rollo May. In *Love and Will*, this psychoanalyst tells us that we have a strong tendency, both as individuals and as a (Western) culture, to be "schizoid." This condition is described as: "out of touch;" "alienated;" "detached;" "apathy;" "indifference;" "feelinglessness" (or inability to feel); "avoiding close relationships." Much in our individual and community lives contributes to our succumbing to these states. They are certainly understandable responses to the predicament which Fromm has described as being our lot. At the same time, May sees a combination of love and will to be inherent in much of our "reaching out, moving toward the world, seeking to affect others or the inanimate world." Such reaching is an opening of the self, inviting others to take part in our forming and molding. It is an attempt to relate to the world, or require the world to relate to the self.[3] The temptation to let go, to not be involved, to withdraw feelings is a threat to relationships that are loving. The daily newspapers remind us of this grim truth about ourselves. Each of us has the capacity to stand on the apartment balcony and listen or watch while a young woman is murdered below; it is within us to stand back and watch a young teen-age girl being raped by a group of older teen-age boys in a public fountain; we could urge on the gang-rapists at the pool table; we regularly ignore the rape and murder of the planet earth and its life around us.

The lover, however, is actively involved with the loved in a process that is shaping their world while remaining open to being shaped by it. For May, we humans have "alternative possibilities for good and evil"; we may destroy or we may enhance our "humane, life-giving qualities." If we choose enhancement, we choose to *care*. That is, we choose to recognize others as being human beings like ourselves; we choose to identify with another in pain or joy; we choose to be aware of a common humanity from which each of us draws our life. The lover *cares,* insisting that *"something does matter"* . . . what we care about is what constitutes the "good life."[4]

Recovery of Passion—Reunion With Our Source

Basic to our tendency toward alienation, as described by May, is our loss of an adequate sense of "eros." We *think* we know what "erotic" means: Most cities of any considerable size have a block or two set aside where one can gawk at or purchase "erotic" books, movies, stage performances, or gadgets. A term rich with meaning has been distorted in our vocabulary by the consignment of "eros" to a confused and often perverse fascination with things sexual. Furthermore, something important may well be missing from our understanding of the erotic. "Eros" describes a special perception of reality held by the classical Greeks. Life was created on earth by Eros, according to early Greek mythology. Thus, the "spirit of life" is given by eros. "Eros" had to do with passion, the experience of delight and joy in achieving a union that continues to pull one toward greater and deeper dimensions of experience. Some, including St. Augustine, have considered eros to be what drives humans toward God.

The recovery of eros as basis for more complete loving has a more recent interpreter; Sam Keen, in *The Passionate Life* (1983), demonstrates how our separation from each other reduces our "Erotic Quotient," or "E.Q." Our potential for truly erotic experience and expression is systematically reduced, according to Keen, in the process of maturing into adulthood. Our "tribal" inclinations separate the world into "them," the enemy, and "us." Modern forms include nationalism and racism. An automatic reduction of 50 percent is thus made in our potential for love and passion, for caring, for identifying with others. The combat between sexes and the division between masculine and feminine traits and roles further reduces our potential, or "E. Q." Closely related is the separation between nature (usually perceived as female) and controllers of nature (usually male). Finally, women are separated from women, and men from men, over the fear of homosexuality. The result is that an extremely small portion of our original potential for erotic love—the passionate union with others, with nature, and with the universe—remains open to us. By moving beyond the socially conforming "adult" stage of loving, through the expanding openness of what he calls the "outlaw" stage, one is able to develop to the full status of "lover." The lover's identity is characterized as "spirit": "Spirit is the capacity to transcend the encapsulation of personality . . . Spirit is the realization that we are embodied within a continuum, that we are alive only when a universal life force flows through us like breath through lungs, like wind through the evergreens."[5] The passion of Eros thus involves opening oneself to life that is both within oneself and beyond the self. *In our separateness we are at the same time in unity with all that is, and love is the power at work in that unity.*

That concept is important as we explore the sorts of relationships we experience in our everyday lives. Briefly stated, we are more than we usually think we are. There is power in us that isn't limited to us, but is nonetheless at our command. We feel that power, that excitement, that quiet urging toward some unidentified fulfillment, at important moments in our lives. Often that feeling is focused on a specific object—person, pet, flower, or task—and we are compelled toward that object, to become immersed in it, or her, or him, or them. When this happens, we are experiencing what some have called "eros." Our ability to have loving relationships is directly related to our recovery of that sense, that "Erotic Quotient," in our experience.

In our human journey, we have been surrounded through the centuries by persons who have had insights similar to those we have been describing. The ancient Hebrews developed stories of creation that picture all of life as an expression of the being and love of the eternal life spirit. This source is something beyond human description, while at the same time it is intensely central to the human experience and being. The name given to this source, known to us in English transliteration as "Yahweh," is in its very formation a recognition and affirmation that there is no adequate name or description for God, that it is human blasphemy to so speak the name of God as to claim full knowledge or relationship with that power. The ease with which moderns say "God" was foreign to the biblical writers who warned against taking the name of God "in vain." Rather than being worried that someone might be so offensive as to say "damn" after "God," they were concerned with the vanity of human beings who tried to restrict and manipulate the source of all Life by the familiarity—even arrogance—of speaking a name for an ultimately unnameable reality. At the same time, they celebrated their oneness with this reality.

The Bible struggles with a recognition that, although humans are separated from their source and each other, we were not always that way, and do not always need to stay that way. In the Garden of Eden, the bliss of unquestioned unity is broken by eating the "forbidden fruit" of self-awareness and knowledge, leading to complexity, ambiguity—and individuality. The rest of the Hebrew and Christian scriptures contain descriptions of ways in which the Creator reaches out to the created, the created reaches out to the Creator and to other creatures, attempting to regain a vaguely remembered but sometimes clearly envisioned unity. Our forebears, not only in the Jewish and Christian traditions, but in other religions as well, saw, in Keen's words, "that there is a bond between the self and the cosmos, that every being is within Being, that human consciousness is interior to the consciousness that informs all things."[6] The gaining (or regaining) of that bond is the quest described in the Bible, just as it is basic to the problem described by Fromm: the closing of the chasm between self and self, self and others, self and the universe. The message perceived by so many through long centuries of human struggle is rather clear: The kind of relationship which closes that chasm, overcomes the alienation, opens vast possibilities for growth and productivity, is the loving one.

How "Natural" is Love?

Is it "natural" for us to overcome the isolation we feel? Is it within our human nature to experience union with what is most important to us, including the body/spirit of another human being? The concept of "eros" has captured imaginations and intellects for centuries of human history. It asserts that the union we seek is a central, fundamental part of our reality. We are capable, of course, of so separating ourselves from our own inner being and from others around us that our activity then varies between meaningless non-productivity and destructiveness. That is a very real part of our story. Just as real is our capacity to open ourselves wide for others to enter, to penetrate tenderly and with care into another, to so identify with another or with "nature" that we feel what the other is feeling and want what is nurturing for the other.

Willard Gaylin argues that it is our *nature* to care: the biological and social truth about human beings is that "goodness" is inherent in our being, and we have survived because we care and are cared for.[7] A similar position is taken by Michael Zwell: "Love is the way people naturally feel toward each other in the absence of painful emotion."[8] We feel love toward persons we know, *if* those feelings are not blocked by feelings of hurt, anger, fear, or embarrassment. Love, the most basic of our emotions, can be released by gaining control over those "painful emotions."

If it is our nature to be loving, why do we seem to spend so little of our time and energy doing it? One answer, of course, is that all those who've said that love is "natural" are wrong, that we are at best depraved (at least since the time that some Christians call "The Fall") and at worst downright evil. I am much more convinced by the argument that our nature includes many diverse capacities—as May put it, "alternative possibilities for good and evil." Given that we have such choices, why do we decide so often against love? M. Scott Peck answers: *laziness.* Peck's examination of *The Road Less Traveled* (1978) leads him to the conclusion that the human capacity to love is nurtured in large part by "grace" (the love of God). Many of us resist this grace due to what he calls laziness, or "entropy."[9] Although we are pushed to move up the ladder of evolution, we nonetheless prefer the comfort of the *status quo,* or even back down a rung or two, rather than meet the demands we are facing. Love is a form of spiritual power that involves responsibility, and we are often reluctant to choose such power and responsibility.

Many have analyzed our condition, and theories abound on how we got this way. I agree with our biblical ancestors and such contemporaries as Fromm and May, that our basic problem is one of alienation, of separation from self, others, and the source of our own being.[10] This statement of the problem is a statement about relationships. I also agree with them that our "problem" is not the whole story of our reality, and that our relationships can be, and often are, loving ones. For our basic nature to dominate in our patterns of living, we have a lot of work to do, energy to expend, debris to clear away . . . and joy to be experienced. *Loving* relationships are always an option for us.

Relationships in Interaction: Self, Other, Transcendent

How do we experience love in relationships? Loving is known in a pattern of interacting, interlocking, interdependent relationships—love for self, for others, and for the transcendent dimension of our experience. We can see this interaction in a story that is central to the Christian Gospel.

The story appears in varying forms in all three of the "synoptic" Gospels: Matthew, Mark and Luke. An incident is reported in which Jesus is asked about the greatest commandment in the "Law," or what is required to inherit eternal life. In each version of the incident, Jesus first refers the questioner to the great "Shema" of the Hebrew tradition: "Listen, Israel: Yahweh our God is the one Yahweh. You shall love Yahweh your God with all your heart, with all your soul, with all your strength." (Deuteronomy 6:4–5)[11] Jesus' answer, of course, does not end there. The Torah is again his source: "You must love your neighbor as yourself."[12] Together, these two "commands," to love God, and to love the neighbor as yourself, make up what is known to New Testament scholars as the "Double Commandment." The "greatest," or most central and important of the commandments of God is actually a combination of two commands. The way to "inherit eternal life," or "enter the Kingdom," is to follow these two commands, and to live them as a unity.

It is important to notice what is being called for in this "double commandment." The Shema (Deuteronomy 6:4–9) was an affirmation of a crucial claim made by the early Hebrew people. "Yahweh," the God they worshiped and followed, is the *one* God, the only God worthy of their total obedience and commitment. Where others around them claimed to have access to a variety of gods, these people insisted that the God of their experience is so all-encompassing as to claim *all* one's "heart, soul, mind and strength." That is an overwhelming kind of power, and the way in which they were to relate to that enormous power was by *love!* Jesus, a skilled student and teacher in this tradition, reminds his listeners that there is no separation between loving this God and loving one's neighbor as one loves oneself.[13] This dual command has a fundamentally *moral* quality. The emphasis is not on "cultic" practices, having to do with forms of worship, or even on attitudes. What is stressed, rather, is action, behavior, ways of being in relation to the other.

Loving the Neighbor

This emphasis on loving behavior comes out in Luke's version of the story. Not satisfied with being reminded to love the neighbor as one loves the self, the questioner persists with "and *who is my neighbor?*" Jesus' response is to tell the story of the "Good Samaritan" (Luke *who v. doing*

10:30–36). A man beaten by robbers and left injured in a ditch is first ignored and avoided by religious officials of his own people. He is then aided by a Samaritan. Although they were geographical neighbors, Samaritans and Jews did not get along at all. By his use of the Samaritan as a central character in the story, Jesus introduced new ways of thinking about the identity of the neighbor. The fact that the Samaritan saw the Jew lying in the ditch as *his* neighbor could not be ignored by Jesus' hearers.

Two important aspects of this story stand out. First, for those who followed the "Law," the neighbor was usually understood rather narrowly, as one who is part of the group. The Samaritan would be more "enemy" than neighbor to those in Jesus' audience. To his listeners it was made clear that the status of "neighbor" has to do with deeds, action, performance. Jesus didn't define "who" or "what" a neighbor *is;* he told what a neighbor *does.* He described an act of neighborly love. The neighbor is one who is cared for. The one giving the care is also neighbor. The second aspect of the story comes out in the relationship of self-love and neighbor love. As Victor Furnish has noted, the command to "love your neighbor as yourself" is not a *command* to *love the self.* It is presumed that one already loves the self without being commanded to do so. Rather, the focus is on what this says about the other person:

> . . . the best exegesis of "as yourself" comes in the parable of the Good Samaritan which artfully causes each hearer of the parable to identify himself with the hapless victim by the roadside. Finding yourself in that place, one really discovers what "as yourself" means. It means that the neighbor can be no more avoided than one's own self, that the neighbor is as present and as real as one's own ego . . . the point is that the neighbor must be no less an object of our loving concern than our own life inevitably is.[14]

The interactional framework of love in relationships is seen through these biblical accounts: love of God, love of neighbor, and love of self are inextricably tied up with each other. As Pheme Perkins points out, Jesus appealed to his listeners to "look at others the way God does and not the way they think God ought to." How God looks at the world is perceived by Christians as demonstrated in Jesus' ministry: "he was open to sinners and outcasts, to anyone who wanted to approach him . . . Act like that and you find the rule of God."[15] Guidance for loving the neighbor is found in knowing how one is loved by God. Likewise, one knows something of the love of God and one's own value in being loved by the neighbor.

Loving Relationship With God

How does God love us? "Unconditionally," we are often told. That concept, summed up in the word *Agape* is dominant in much of Western religious thinking about the ideal forms of love. The fundamental claim of the Christian gospel, of course, is that God has first established a relationship with all beings through Creation, and has restored that relationship from its distortions and fallenness through the life, death, and resurrection of Jesus the Christ. Whether or not we accept that claim, whatever our theological stance (or non-stance), most of us have some sense of the power of being valued simply for being. This is central to the notion of Agape love. In this unconditional form of love, we are loved simply because we exist, not because of anything we have done or can do. There is no reciprocity assumed in Agape love. The loved may not love in return; this may produce pain for the lover, but it does not stop the love.

Conditional love is also a part of religious experience. The God who makes rules and says, "If you keep my commandments, then . . ." is expressing conditional love. God is presented in the Bible as a parent—a Creator—who is to be loved by obedience to the expectations of the parent. This parent gives directives to the children about how they are to live with each other. Parental love for the children, however, far surpasses the children's willingness or ability to meet all the parent's expectations. This biblical God often continued to give love to the disobedient and apparently unworthy children. The testimony of human experience through the ages is that God's love is given both unconditionally and conditionally; it seems to have its greatest power when it is experienced as unconditional.[16]

And how do human beings love God? In the Jewish *Talmud,* a delightful answer is related by the rabbis. When a king is confronted by subjects who want to express their love for him, he asks what gifts they could possibly give him. After all, *he* is the King, the ruler of all! But he has an answer. If the subjects wish to show their love for this king, they should do so by going out and serving his "children—their fellow subjects. It is possible, of course, to express love to God by certain kinds of worship and prayer. Real depth of love, however, is best expressed in "loving kindness and service" to the children of "God the Father"[17] Are there other ways of "loving God?" The mystics in many religions, including Judaism and Christianity, have spoken of gaining *unity* with God, certainly a form of love which meets some of our basic needs. In many traditions this striving for union often involves giving up the self in order to be absorbed in the Other. Within the union, however, the Creator shares creative power with the creatures, allowing them to participate in the great joy and deep pain of loving and being loved, of producing and not producing, of not loving and not being loved. This God gives and receives love, both conditionally and unconditionally.

Many of the values of our culture, including what it means to love and be loved, were shaped by a way of thinking which accepts this interactional perspective of relationships. In this view, one experiences the value of one's self through the grateful acceptance of the gift of one's own life and its fantastic array of possibilities. Thus, one chooses to say, "I know that I am loved, that I am important—even precious—to the Being from which life has been breathed into me." One usually receives the first parts of this message in the experience of being cared for and loved by others. With maturity, the interaction process is understood to be incomplete without the giving *of* and *from* oneself to others. One loves the neighbor as one loves oneself, a being who is loved by God, by the transcendent power of creation and ongoing life.

Loving the Self

Many of our spiritual parents have affirmed the power found in recognizing that "God loves *me;* I'll give thanks for that, celebrate it, and nurture it!" The experience of reaching to the transcendent (or, for many of us, the immanent) dimension of our lives is an experience of loving, and being loved. It is also an experience of knowing the wonder of one's self and the importance of loving the self already loved by another.

But what about self-love? Isn't that being selfish and self-centered? Isn't that *wrong?* Most of us have certainly grown up confused about the proper location of "self" in a hierarchy of values in relating to others. That confusion is expressed in an old slogan (taken up by a title of a popular book), "I am Third"—first God, then others, and, third— me. These relationships, however, are not *hierarchical* at all, but exist together in a pattern that defies any rank ordering, each part being necessary and integral to the other. A careful reading of biblical insights supports Fromm's insistence that self-love is in fact the opposite of selfishness. Selfishness involves the grasping of whatever one can get for oneself; self-love frees one from the need for such grasping.

If it's OK to love myself, how do I do it? For many, this is a deeply troublesome question. Recent claims that we are in a time of "narcissistic" concentration on the self confirm a widespread observation that we have a *problem* with loving ourselves, and we need some help in getting over that problem. If the loving relationship we need with our self is to thrive and grow, we have to recognize that need and perhaps do some work on it. John Powell outlines three forms of action involved in loving another person, and then asserts that self-love requires us to turn these three actions toward the self. First, you are asked to esteem and affirm your unconditional and unique value. Second, acknowledge and try to fulfill your recognized needs. Third, forgive your failings.[18] That is a big order, pushing us to careful examination of our loving capacities. The person caught up in "narcissism" simply will not be able to be that open to self. Narcissus, the Greek mythological youth, became infatuated and pined away with an image of himself, his reflection, rather than his actual self.[19] The narcissist is left to fulfillment of that image and mask, conforming to the perceived expectations of others and refusing to look beneath the surface of her or his own experiences and feelings. On the other hand, one who knows the experience of being loved without condition is free to both accept and examine what is under the surface, in order to more fully and creatively participate in the flow of life.

A healthy model of self-love is found in the Hebrew and Christian understanding of Creation. The activity of creation is seen as an act of love by God, and the products of this act are declared as being in "God's own image." According to the story, once the creation has been completed (at least for the time being), God looked at it and said, "that's good." The extension of self in productivity and creativity was judged as *good*. This is an act of self-love, acceptance, and approval. Human self-love enters into this creative process. Human beings are empowered to be a part of the ongoing acts of creation; the power that enlivens that process is love. Having entered into creativity, the individual extends the self and all that preceeded the self, and in joy, declares "that's good." When I love my creations, I love myself, my Creator, and others who create.[20]

However we describe it, it is basic in my approach to the contexts and issues of loving relationships to assume this interactional framework. We experience loving, we learn to love, we practice loving, in a "circle" that includes self, others (both human and other-than-human), and the transcendent power that we know to be both beyond and within us as the source of our existence and power.

What the Words Mean

Love and Loving

We have managed to discuss "love" and "loving" thus far without ever defining these terms. Love, to say the least, is hard to define. We are inclined to say that it needs no definition—we all know what it means! Ordinary comments heard in daily experience lead us to conclude, however, that much usage of the word "love" does not qualify as a basis of loving relationships. From "I just *love* Corvettes!" to "let's spend the night making love," we find a considerable range in the experience being described. Common in many of the books written about love is the reminder of different words used in other languages, especially classical Greek, to describe differing forms of experience of love. It is worthwhile, of course, to know that the Greeks recognized differences between "family," "brotherly," "erotic," and "divine" love. *Storge* is family affection, describing love between parent and child; *Philia,* the attraction between friends, as well as the feeling for another human being within the universal family; *Eros,* a passion pulling us to create and procreate; *Agape,* concern for the welfare of another without any concern for oneself. I am helped by Rollo May's assertion that these forms of love, along with sex, are all found in any authentic human experience of love. They are blended together, and vary in their proportions in different relationships. As I try to sort out my feelings in a friendship, or a family relationship, in a work setting, or an intense attraction to someone I've recently met, I am less confused when I accept the fact of all forms of love being present, with one being more dominant than the others in a particular relationship. Given the multiplicity of meanings of love, how can we reach some useful definition?[21]

As background for the ideas discussed in the chapters that follow, I recommend a definition offered by M. Scott Peck. Love, he says, is: *"The will to extend one's self for the purpose of nurturing one's own or another's spiritual growth."*[22] The component parts of the definition can be "charted" in order to begin to tap its richness:

> Will
> Extension of self
> Purpose
>   Nurture
>   self and other
> Spiritual growth

What is going on here is not simply a *desire,* nor can it be limited to *action,* as important as that may be. "Will" transcends the distinction between those two. It chooses to act in a certain way, to actualize intentions and respond to meaning. This action has a goal or purpose.

Loving requires the extension of one's own limits. Effort is involved. As in learning an art form, the self is extended through mastery of its theory and the kind of practice that requires discipline, concentration, and patience.[23] Pushing out the limits simply produces a "larger" be-ing, a fuller, more extended self.[24]

Loving has a purpose, or a goal. It doesn't "just happen," when the "electricity," or "chemistry" (both beyond our control in the common usage) are right. An essential ingredient in May's understanding of "will" is what he calls "intentionality," the "structure of meaning" which informs our thinking and action. Values, interpretations, and commitments underlie our willingness to extend ourselves. In this case, the "purpose" has to do with *nurture*.

Nurture is caring. It supports, it feeds, and it opens opportunities. Some nurture can be done "naturally." If I am to aid in the nurture of a child, however, I must learn enough about that child and the process of its development to be sure that I do not get in the way. Nurture may involve removing obstructions to development, as well as positively contributing to the growth process.

What is being nurtured? What is the purpose of this active process of loving? Surely the answer is "spiritual growth." There is no distin-guishing "mental" and "spiritual" in Peck's understanding of human experience. Spiritual growth is, for him, the "evolution of conscious-ness," the ultimate state of which is unity with God. Peck goes so far as to say that in this unity, we "become God," in the sense of having the "capacity to make decisions with maximum awareness."[25] This is to exercise great spiritual power and responsibility, and the resistance to loving is based in a resistance to accepting that power and responsibil-ity.

Whose spiritual growth is nurtured? This definition includes self-love with love for the other: "not only do self-love and love of others go hand in hand. . . ultimately they are indistinguishable." Expansion of one's own spiritual power and consciousness takes place as one nur-tures the consciousness expansion of another, and vice versa.[26]

John Powell provides a similar "working definition" in his descrip-tion of communication and dialogue as "The Secret" of being and staying in love. Borrowing from Harry Stack Sullivan, he proposes: "When the satisfaction, security, and development of another person become as significant to you as your own satisfaction, security, and development, love exists."[27] Again, the love of the other and the love of the self are inseparable. The goal of the activity is development and growth, with the added dimension of security. Consciousness and awareness are necessary, if I am to know what is "significant to" the one loved. I shall certainly need to "extend the limits" of my self if I intend to assure that others experience satisfaction, are secure in their self-knowledge, and have the same freedom to grow as I intend for myself.

Some have suggested that love cannot, or ought not, be defined or explained.[28] Such a position is tempting. I have often shown a preference for asking students to work on their own definitions. Henri Nouwen expresses this inclination: "What is most obvious, most close, doesn't need an explanation. Who asks a child why he plays with a ball; who asks a tightrope walker why he walks on his rope—and who asks a lover why he loves?"[29] It is, however, necessary to resist that temptation. Perhaps a child will not tell us *why* she plays with a ball, other than "it's fun." There will come a time, though, when that child will want to play soccer, or baseball, or basketball, with as much personal skill as possible. At that point, she will want to know why certain ways of handling the ball aren't as useful as others in getting the ball to where she wishes it to go. She will need to practice ways of maneuvering the ball with her hands or feet if she is to move it with satisfaction. She will learn those things from others, and will spend hours in practice, trying out her own variations.

We may have some difficulty in adequately defining love, but there is much we can learn about it if we want to have the kind of loving relationships that are potential for human beings. We don't have to conclude with Charlie Brown (after an unfortunate round with Peppermint Patty), "you not only can't explain love . . . actually, you can't even talk about it." Nor do we need to join with Senator Proxmire and his "Golden Fleece Award" in opposing funds for research about love because we "want to leave some things in life a mystery," and really "don't want the answer."[30] We *can* "talk about it," and learn from those who have done research and have thought about their own experience. We can also reflect on our own experience, and develop more and more guidelines for our reflection. The tightrope walker may be rather poetic if he even attempts to answer *why* he walks that rope; you can be sure, however, that he knows a lot about *how* he does it. Furthermore, I suspect that as he practices it more and more, tries out exciting variations, learns from his mistakes and enjoys the exhilaration of his successes, the answer he might give to "why" will change. His developing experience will lead him into new insights about the ways in which his tight-rope walking fit into his total growing perspective about life, about other people, and about the nature of the universe. So it is with the practice of love.

Relationship

Loving takes place in relationships. Just as it is often assumed that everyone knows what "love" means, the word "relationship" usually goes without definition. Even a scholarly study into the relationships of liking and loving, done by competent social psychologists, will use the term dozens of times without defining it. They seem to assume that "relationship" is so common as to need no clarification of its meaning.[31] Perhaps that is a safe assumption. I find it informative, however, to consult some dictionaries. There we discover that most definitions of human "relationship" tend to assume a familial connection, either by blood or marriage. This suggests that our common usage assumes that a "relationship" is something tying persons together in a "kinship." Either we are "relatives," or we have begun to make commitments to each other that set "us" apart from other connections that we experience. When we hear someone begin a sentence with "This relationship I'm in now . . .", we assume they are not talking about a "relative," but about a *chosen* contact with another in which there is a growing bond of intimacy, shared experience, and expectations. We can probably also assume, with safety, that the model for expectations about that "relationship" is found in the participants' own family background and/or cultural values and standards about ways of being together that move toward marriage.

As we explore this topic more fully you will find relationships that do not fit into the assumptions implied above. Certainly a broader definition of "relationship" than one tied to family or marriage connection is required. It is helpful to consider the way in which the word "relation" was used in English during the seventeenth century:

> The position which one person holds with respect to another on account of some social or other connexion between them; the particular mode in which persons are mutually connected by circumstances . . . The aggregate of the connexions, or modes of connexion, by which one person is brought into touch with another or with society in general.[32]

The language is somewhat stodgy, but it does help us by suggesting a broader understanding of ties than those confined to marriage and/or family. A "social or other connection between" persons is a relationship. A "mutual connection" between persons by circumstances is, or may be, a relationship. Patterns in which persons are brought into contact with one another, or with society in general, form relationships. They may or may not be "loving." Let's look at some examples.

Sorority sisters and fraternity brothers in a college or university setting have a social connection between them. The relationship between them may be loving. Certainly their rituals and traditions speak of mutual love. They participate in practices designed to cement bonds of affection, loyalty and commitment. Sentiment, however, is not the same as love, and these ties may be more sentimental than loving. On the other hand, many persons in this setting find that they do establish relationships with others that can best be characterized as "loving."

Two recruits into the Marine Corps are "mutually connected by circumstances." They have no family ties, and their social and economic backgrounds are such that under other conditions they would probably never be attracted to each other. Their assignment to an international "peace-keeping force" in a distant land brings them into an arrangement of dependency on each other for life and death matters. They talk with each other about topics they've never discussed with anyone else, and they share experiences of such emotional depth that they could only discuss them with each other, because no one else could possibly understand. They know that they would literally die for each other. They have a "relationship" which is, in many significant ways, a "loving" one.

An infant is the child of a particular set of parents. An "aggregate" of connections, or "modes of connections," also exists by which the infant is brought into touch with others and with "society in general." Born in a hospital, the infant is in contact with physicians, nurses, technicians, janitors, and administrators. Also involved are vast numbers of unseen employees of companies who make hospital supplies and equipment, blood donors, and a physician's friends who accepted her abrupt need to leave a birthday celebration and rush to the hospital for the delivery. The child is "related" to members of the hospital board of trustees who accepted the staff proposal to have a "birthing room" and allow other family members to be present for the birth and during the hospital stay. These are "modes of connection," ways in which the child is "related" to others, and those modes may be loving or not.

Power is not often mentioned in the discussion of loving relationships, but is nonetheless important as an ingredient in a "position which one person holds with respect to another." A relationship is a particular structure of power. Persons influence each other, exercise forms of control (direct or indirect) over the way others think, act, grow, and develop. That is simply a reality of human existence. Every relationship is in one way or another a power relationship, in fact, it can be said that there are tiers, or levels of power in each relationship, with alternating expressions of these tiers as various functions of the relationship are experienced. Crucial to the relationship is the awareness of the power involved and the care exercised in the use of power in the relationship. Love does not mean the giving up of power. It is the conscious utilization of power in a way that enhances the goals and potentialities of the relationship, the growth and flowering of the persons in the relationships.

Loving is an *activity*. In any kind of relationship, and certainly in one which is "loving," something is going on, things are happening.

Fromm emphasizes that loving activity *produces* love in the loved person. This means that the relationship is productive, and it is just. The loved person, in response to feeling "more loved," will likewise produce love, or loving activity. We usually assume that a loving relationship is a reciprocal one; that feelings of caring, respect, affection, etc., are acted upon, and somewhat similar actions are received in return. Parents and teachers, among others, know that this is not always the case. The product of one's loving may very well be that the recipient is better enabled to be loving toward another or others, without turning much—or any—back to the initial giver.

Loving As Art

There is no better interpretation of what is involved in becoming a lover than in Erich Fromm's claim that loving is an *art*. Learning an art requires that we follow certain steps: We must first master theory, then we must practice and master the ways of doing it. Overarching this understanding is the recognition that no artist succeeds in a very satisfying way unless her or his art is a matter of ultimate concern.

At various times in my life I have thought I'd like to play the saxophone. I can play the piano, and I know some chords on the ukelele and guitar. The saxophone, however, is a quite different instrument. Knowing something about music and having a strong feeling that I'd like to play the saxophone, however, isn't going to make me a saxophone player. If I get serious about it, I'll have to learn about the physical structure of the instrument and the theory behind its structure and forms of expression. I'll have to learn a lot more about music theory in general than I now know, in order to apply it to the mastery of this instrument. I'll need to learn to recognize the difference between tones of quality and those more easily acquired tones that do not draw on the real potential of the instrument. And, I'll have to practice. I should learn how to practice, however, from those who have been successful in their efforts at it, lest I end up practicing wrong or inadequate techniques and developing unuseful habits and methods. If I want to be *really good*, playing the saxophone has to be more important than anything else.

The central core of Fromm's theory, the four "elements of loving," offer us a basis for careful thinking about our own relationships. Those elements are *care, responsibility, respect,* and *knowledge.* Each element is a quality that stands on its own. These elements are also interdependent, interacting with, and affecting each other in any form of love. Each will be found, in varying degrees, in any of the many ways of experiencing authentic love.

CARE. The experience of caring can be described in many ways. Fromm's discussion centers around an "active concern for the life and growth of that which we love."[33] There is power in that very short phrase. The idea is *active* concern; not just sentiment, or feeling good about it, but *doing* something. This is no simple demand for affection. Life must be protected and nurtured, and growth must be allowed, even encouraged and assisted. A similar understanding is Milton Mayeroff's notion of "caring as helping the other grow." In so doing, he says, "I experience what I care for . . . as an extension of myself and at the same time as something separate from me that I respect in its own right."[34] A further elaboration of what "care" means is offered by Mayeroff:

> To help another person grow is at least to help him to care for something or someone apart from himself, and it involves encouraging and assisting him to find and create areas of his own in which he is able to care. Also, it is to help that other person to come to care for himself, and by becoming responsive to his own need to care to become responsible for his own life.[35]

Some growth in understanding of "caring" was demonstrated to me in two visits to an institution separated by about ten years. The first visit came while I was still in high school, and I was on a tour of a state institution which was then called "the State Institute for the Feeble-Minded." The residents of this institution were obviously receiving, at best, custodial "care." The tour guides seemed comfortable in pointing out to us various oddities of each of the individuals, and no expectation of change or desire for growth was mentioned. When I returned some ten years later, in the early 1960s the institution was now called a "State Training School." At the beginning of the tour, I learned that the institution was operating on a philosophy that assumed that every human being had the right to grow beyond where he or she was at that moment in life. The life and work of the institution were organized around that principle. About this time, behavioral research was showing increasing correlation between motor and mental development. Persons whose motor development improved to the point that they were able to climb stairs were given rooms on the upper floors of the dormitory as a symbol of their growth, as well as a stimulus for further growth. The staff/resident ratio was increased, as more attention was given to discovering ways in which each individual could make even the smallest amount of progress. *Care* had changed from custodial functions to active concern for growth.

RESPONSIBILITY. Fromm's use of this term is somewhat different from our common usage. It is best written: "response-ability," the ability—as well as the readiness—to respond to the needs and growth of another or others. Much of our more common understanding of "responsibility" involves such things as "taking charge," "obligations," or "duty." Responsibility often looks and/or feels "heavy"; a person with "a lot of heavy responsibilities" often has stooped shoulders to show for it. Readiness to respond to the needs of the other, however, requires an openness to what is really going on in the other. Our usual meanings of responsibility feel much more closed; we know what others need and we set out to provide for it. Or, we assess our obligations and make sure that we fulfill the obligations. Fromm makes a crucial point in directly connecting this element with the next: "responsibility could easily deteriorate into domination and possessiveness, were it not for a third component of love, respect."[36]

RESPECT. The other person is seen as she or he is. Exploitation or domination are not needed or desired. The unique personality of the other is recognized and appreciated. One's concern is "that the other person grow and unfold" according to that person's own being. I can exercise respect for another only if I respect myself and am thus sufficiently independent as a person to want independence for the other. My freedom to be who and what I am lead me to want that for the other.

The combination of responsibility and respect is certainly an issue for parents, as well as for any in a role requiring others to be dependent on them for physical and/or psychic needs. Many parents are so locked into their "responsibility" that they cannot allow the freedom required by the uniqueness of an individual child. The delicate balance in this relationship is a challenge to the most skilled lover. A person who has "responsibility" for a temporarily disabled adult will need to respect that unique individual's need and right to return as quickly as possible to independent activity, and provide the kind of care that encourages it. Responsibility for the permanently disabled will so recognize precious individuality that as much freedom as possible is nurtured and maintained.

KNOWLEDGE. Again, Fromm is applying a somewhat different meaning to this word from what is commonly assumed. Rather than having facts and information or learning secrets, "knowing" here refers to an active penetration of the other, an "entering into." A once popular song expressed it: "I'm in you and you're in me." This understanding takes into account the meanings in the ancient Hebrew word, both "to know" and "to have intercourse with." Knowing another involves being open to the central core of the other; being known requires taking the risk of opening the self, allowing another in. The "communion of consciousness" is May's term for building consciousness *in* and *of* the other. One enters into, or knows, the other, while at the same time making it more possible for another to do that with one self. In other words, I am more able to "tune in" to the feeling another is expressing to me, if I have been willing to let my real feelings be known to that person. Thus, I know myself better and more deeply in allowing myself to know another. In the act of loving, one takes a "daring plunge into the experience of union."

The interdependence, the interaction, of these four elements may be obvious, but I want to emphasize it. Real respect requires knowing; the openness in knowing is built through caring; responsibility is balanced by respect; any number of combinations can be worked out. Altogether, these four elements as described by Fromm provide a strong foundation on which to build deeper understanding of relationships that are loving.

How do we *practice* this art? The first of Fromm's "general requirements" for the practice of loving is *discipline*. Not only must one have a regular and orderly way of going about the practice of this particular art form, but one must be a disciplined person. That is, a loving person is a person who is disciplined in *all* of life. Such discipline is not imposed from outside. This is not something *done to us* by teachers, police, or parents. Discipline is a way of living, worked out *by* oneself (although certainly influenced by others) and regulated within oneself.

A second requirement for practice is *concentration*. Somewhat rare in our culture, this requires the ability to be alone with ourselves, to function without external stimulation. In concentration, the activity of the moment is all that is important. If one is living fully in the present, "in the here and now," one doesn't need to be thinking about what wasn't done awhile ago or what is to be done in the next few hours. In concentration, one is sensitive to oneself, and thus able to be sensitive to another. One who concentrates with others is able to listen, is in a "state of alert equilibrium," able to receive whatever is coming from another person. Thus, the paradox: "The ability to be alone is the condition for the ability to love."[37]

A third requirement is *patience*. Ah, patience, where have you gone? At least three streets in my home town are testimonials to our societal lack of patience: every other business is fast-something-or-other. It is no longer sufficient that we do not have to wait for a meal to be prepared, and can pick it up immediately at a counter and eat it. Now, we don't even have to leave our automobiles, but can "drive-thru" and have our orders handed to us through a window. There *is no* "drive-thru" for learning an art. Learning to love takes time. Howard Thurman, who recognized the necessity of a "sense of leisure" in the development of discipline, reminds us that "we cannot be in a hurry in matters of the heart."[38] Trial and error, relearning, experimenting, listening to response, meditating on experience, learning more, experimenting—all take time. The lover has time—a lifetime.

Discipline, concentration, and patience must be practiced in all facets of one's life if they are to be applied usefully to our loving relationships. "I'm not a disciplined person," you say? You can become one. I suspect that there are any number of things that you couldn't do several years ago that you do rather well now . . . drive a car, operate a computer, type on a typewriter, perhaps play a guitar. If so, you learned to do it because it was important to you; you accepted enough discipline to get it done. You see, you *can* be a disciplined person. If it is important to you—more important than anything else—to be a loving person, you will become a disciplined person. The same is true with concentration and patience. They are not simply congenital attributes, no matter how "naturally patient" some acquaintance of yours seems to be, or what "powers of concentration" another seems to possess. You can develop them.

The final points I want to borrow from Fromm have to do with faith, courage, and risk.[39] In brief, *faith,* as he means it, is a rational process necessary to the practice of love. Not a belief in something, but a "conviction which is rooted in one's own experience of thought or feelings," is what is meant by faith. It has to do with the "quality of certainty and firmness" in our convictions. Our faith in ourselves finds a core within our personality which can be depended on, is persistent and relatively unchanging in the midst of changes going on in our lives. When one has faith in one's own love, one is confident of one's "ability to produce love in others," and the reliability of that trait. One who has faith in humankind as an extension of faith in a few others, sees the potential in all persons to contribute to an order based on justice and equality. Far from an idealistic dream, this faith is based on a rational examination of history, recognizing the expressions of this potential in the achievements of the human race. The expression of such faith is seen in living productively.

Courage is required for such faith and productive living. This courage is "the ability to take a *risk,*" even being willing to accept pain and disappointment. What is the risk? I might be wrong. The love I give may not be returned to me. We take such risks, through faith, every day. We are willing to go to sleep, an act of faith; we are willing to begin difficult tasks, having no assurance of how they will turn out; we have enough faith to reproduce and to bring up a child. "To love means to commit oneself without guarantee, to give oneself completely in the hope that our love will produce love in the loved person."[40]

Learning to Love

I am firmly on the side of those who insist that we *learn* to love. This is not to disagree with the perspective that says that love is a part of our nature. However "natural" it may be for us, there are many things that can impede our putting it into practice, and there is much we need to learn about doing it in a way that is productive and satisfying.

We begin to learn to love by *being loved.* An impressive amount of scientific research with primates, as well as careful observations of human infants and children, reveal the close connection between the experiences of being loved (nurture, hugging, other forms of touch, expressions of physical and emotional warmth, tenderness in taking care of needs) and the developing capacity of the infant both to survive and to interact productively and meaningfully with others. "Feelings of love," Ari Kiev reminds us, "are initiated with the child's experience of being loved by the parent. When all the child's needs are attended to, when the gratification of its desires is not unduly deferred, when it is among caring and affectionate people, it experiences the feeling of love in its most primitive form: It feels good about itself."[41] Reports from both institutional and private therapy indicate that persons who were not provided such warmth of care in their early childhood have great difficulty in developing self-esteem and worthy self-concept, as well as the trust and risk involved in loving others. As our self-consciousness and conceptualization develop in human growth, we are able to *practice* loving others on the basis of how we have experienced being loved; there is continuing growth in the interdependent process of loving/ being loved. This is emphasized by Willard Gaylin in his study of nurture and caring:

> Survival itself requires feeding, but feeding alone only guarantees the sur-
> vival of something, not necessarily a person. For a full development into
> personhood, with sensitivities and sensibilities, with capacities to commu-
> nicate and relate, a broader sense of nurture is necessary. It is necessary to
> be loved in a specific, caring way; it is being loved in this way that initiates
> in the child the capacity to give love to others.[42]

He further points out that the "protective, parental, tender aspects of loving" learned by the child from parent's love is extended to relation-ships "among peers, child to parent, friend to friend, lover to lover, person to animal, and multiple other patterns."[43]

Just as the beginning of our learning about loving is based in being loved, our growth in this learning comes by doing, by practicing loving. Our experience teaches us much about how loving is done, what it feels like, what the risks are, and what rewards or results will follow. Be-cause this is an ongoing process, it is possible to intervene in it with new information, with new experiments, with decisions to make changes. As Leo Buscaglia puts it, the person who "wishes to be a lover . . . must start by saying 'yes' to love."[44] With increased aware-ness, we recognize deeper levels of ways in which we are loved, and

can thus give love. The true artist grows and changes; continuing encounter with life and reflection on such experiences lead to new perceptions and restructured visualizations of the meaning of experience.
Likewise, the one whose relationships are loving relationships learns
and relearns in those relationships, and expands in the capacity for
loving.

3

Friendship: A Loving Relationship

Friendship is a chosen relationship. It is a gift that we choose to give and choose to receive from another. As such, it is one of the most basic of loving relationships. From all the evidence, friendship appears to be a deep human need. Robert Brain considers it an "imperative":

> Friendship must be taken as seriously as sex, aggression, and marriage . . . The lack of loving is a key to the new but almost universal problem of anxiety. We have become estranged from the simple human tendency to cling together, which is taken for granted in other cultures . . . For long, we have turned a blind eye to friendship needs, to the pain of loneliness and separation, and the psychological damage it can cause; being alone is *not* "good for you." Complete self-reliance makes for sterile pride and isolation and hence it is universally held that it is good to make friends, sharing common experiences and interests . . . We must learn to forget the way personal relations worked—or did not work—fifty, or ten, years ago. As human beings we are capable of myriad variations in mood, belief, and social practice; in our fields of friendship and love, changes may be expected as the stale fabric of our old society is worn away. I have no qualm, therefore, in elevating friendship into an imperative.[1]

For many in contemporary society, friendship seems harder and harder to come by. It is not unusual to hear someone say, "I don't have many *good* friends," or, "I wish I had at least one really good *close* friend." With increased mobility and rapidly changing social structures, many persons grow into adulthood inadequately prepared to find, develop, and enjoy close friendships. We hunger for them.

Consider the following example. Debbie leaves behind her friends of childhood years when she graduates from high school and goes off to college. Within a few weeks, however, she establishes a close friendship with a new acquaintance in her dormitory, and they room together two of the three remaining years of her undergraduate days. At graduation, however, the friend gets married and moves to Dallas with her new husband. Debbie moves to Kansas City to an exciting new job, full of intentions of maintaining contact and close ties with her good friend. After a few long-distance calls, decreased regularity in letterwriting, and an aborted attempt to make a long weekend trip to Dallas, it is apparent that it simply isn't possible for Debbie and her friend to share experiences as they had for three years. Besides, Debbie has begun to spend a lot of time with two "just friends" in her apartment complex, modified by a developing romance with Brad. Although there was a desire to test the friendships with her apartment mates, in an attempt to replace the depth of communication which had characterized the college relationship, the energy required was drained off into the demands of the growing commitment to Brad. Debbie and Brad are soon married and, in less than a year, decide to move to new jobs in St. Louis, leaving behind friendships that had just begun to develop. The couple from Dallas did come to their wedding, but Brad and the Dallas husband didn't hit it off. There was a bit of strain in the conversation as Debbie and her old friend attempted to "pick up where they left off." The move to St. Louis included the purchase of a home in a suburb, and before long, Debbie and Brad are spending a lot of time with some neighbors about their age. Their evenings playing bridge often lead into lengthy conversations in which, increasingly, there is personal disclosure. They find that they are able to reveal some of their conflicts and talk together about ways of deepening their marriages; in so doing, they also notice an exciting strengthening of their friendship. Their friends, however, are about to become parents. Even though Debbie and Brad rejoice with them and are involved in preparing the baby's room and all that goes with it, it is clear that there is now less time for the four of them to talk with each other without interruption. Also, their friends often have little energy left for them. Just as they are beginning to want to talk that over and see what can be done about it, their friends are transferred to Seattle for a job promotion.

The scenario continues. We could add Debbie and Brad's own move a year later, the beginning of their family, the year of isolation in a new neighborhood where there are no other young parents at home during the day, the attempts to meet new couples, the experiments with developing non-couple friendships, and so forth. These events are all part of living in the fast-paced, rapidly changing society of which we are a part. The impact on our ability and opportunity to make and develop friendships is often devastating, increasing the reluctance to start again, for the losses of those friendships are too painful. The time required to start new ones may be more than we are willing to invest when we fear one more upheaval in something that is so precious.

There is, of course, another side of this story. We have all experienced enough of a friendship at some time in our lives—often at a relatively young age—that we know how important it is to our humanhood. You may, in fact, be thinking as you read this, that this description does not fit you—that you do, indeed, have one or more close friendships that have prevailed through any number of changes in your lives. Whether your story is like Debbie's, or is a more settled and satisfying one, it is clear that friendship is something we want, and the desire for it is recognized in every culture.

Historical and Cultural Significance of Friendship

Perhaps you went through a ritual with a young friend, hidden in the basement or behind the garage, in which you each cut or pricked your finger and allowed your blood to flow together. If so, you were not simply indulging in silly childhood play. You were involved in an ancient practice, carried on by persons in diverse racial and cultural traditions. Often accompanied by solemn rituals and observed by elders, the blood of two friends flows together as a symbol of the new unity of their lives, a unity that flows even more deeply than a family blood relationship. Such friendships in many cultures are assumed to be lifetime ties of intense interpersonal commitment, and many cultural supports are provided for the maintenance of these friendships. The violation of such a relationship is a matter of extreme personal pain and potential social severity.

One of the more beautiful expressions of such friendship is that of David and Jonathan in the Old Testament. The young David is admired by the son of King Saul, Jonathan, and their love for each other is publicly demonstrated. The relationship is culminated when Saul and Jonathan are killed in battle, and David's lamentation over their death is especially moving because it expresses both passion and pain in its poetry.

> How are the mighty fallen
>   in the midst of battle!
> Jonathan lies slain upon thy high places.
> I am distressed for you, my brother Jonathan;
>   very pleasant have you been to me;

> your love to me was wonderful,
> passing the love of women.
> How are the mighty fallen,
> and the weapons of war perished!

(2 Sam. 1:25-27)

Although we know relatively little about these two young men, several things can be learned from their friendship. One aspect is the "civic" or "political" role of friendship in the ancient world. From the great Greek and Roman writers, as well as from more recent literary and anthropological studies, we know that in many settings a political tie was often involved in close friendship. This tie was demonstrated in public acts and often was connected with one's public identity; thus, it was not only a strictly personal relationship. The permanence of such a bond was strengthened by social and cultural traditions and rituals. In David's case, there is sorrow over the loss of a close friend and the friend's father, and an ingredient in the sorrow is a loss of some of his own identity in the process.

Another important aspect of their friendship is revealed in the proclamation by David that the love shared by these two men surpassed their experience of the love of women. Throughout the traditions of many peoples, it was expected that close friendships would be more satisfying and meaningful between persons of the same sex than would marriage or a friendship with a person of the opposite sex. Many writers have suggested that the introduction of romantic love in certain elements of the Western European middle class, in recent centuries, has produced our widespread expectation that the deepest intimacy of full human sharing will be with a romantic partner of the opposite sex. Throughout human history and even to this day in some cultures, it has been assumed that such sharing takes place with a close friend, usually of the same sex, selected for the special purposes of friendship. This made possible the kind of experience described by Francine du Plessix Gray: "Friendship is by its very nature freer of deceit than any other relationship we can know because it is the bond least affected by striving for power, physical pleasure, or material profit, most liberated from any oath of duty or of constancy."[2]

The friend described by Gray is a person selected on some *preferential* basis. Although there are variations at different stages of cultural development, the most consistent fact about a friend is that she or he is chosen, is preferred over others. Furthermore, the relationship, if it is to be friendship, rather than some other form of love, must be *reciprocal.* Many centuries ago, the philosopher Socrates established through dialogue with Menexenus that friendship is reciprocal, or mutual, love.[3] Throughout Western history, particularly that portion influenced by Christian thought, tension has developed between the self-giving recognized in friendship and the reciprocity and preference normally assumed in friendship. It is clear, however, that fundamental human needs are at stake in the desire for and experience of friendship. What are some of those needs? What do we *expect* from friendship?

Expectations of Friendship

In their fascinating and rich study, *The Heart of Friendship,* Muriel James and Louis Savary list the expectancies most of us seem to hold for friendship:

Availability
Doing things together
Caring
Honesty
Privacy
Confidentiality
Loyalty
Understanding
Empathy[4]

When asked to write on what she expected from friendship, one of my students presented a somewhat similar list:

Honesty and truthfulness
A reciprocal process
Humor
Freedom for each of us to be who we are in the way that is best for each of us;
Awareness of needs and feelings, care and concern to find out if there is a misunderstanding or a feeling of not knowing what is going on;
Willingness to spend time with each other
Ability to work through conflict without defensiveness
Care and affection, including hugging, touching and playing
Support, encouragement, and pleasure when we're "flying high" and feeling successful
Support, encouragement, and empathy when we're feeling down
Time with others, both together and separately
Respect for "alone time," or privacy
Give and take. Neither of us have to have our own way.[5]

Friends enjoy each other. They want to be with each other; they have common interests and feelings. Friends will spend time with each other, at the exclusion of others, and consider it time well spent. They have learned that they would rather do certain things with each other than with anyone else; likewise, they are likely to turn to each other to explore new interests as well. Friends have decided to admit their vulnerability, their fears, to each other, and have found those fears much less threatening within their relationship. Friends insist on being honest, sharing feelings about self as well as observations about the other. Through their honesty, they allow each other a high degree of personal authenticity, or "freedom to be." They respect and protect each other's privacy; they look to each other for such protection. Friends tell each other things they tell few or no others. They "stand by" each other, and inconvenience is seldom an issue. Most friends recognize the need to be with others, and allow "space" for that, even though jealousy sometimes creeps in.

Andrew Greeley suggests that we human beings build up walls to separate us from each other, and that friendship is a way we break through those walls. He asserts that human society is characterized by fear and terror; friendship is our attempt to "transcend the boundaries of terror." As such, it involves invitation, gift and promise.

> It is first of all an *invitation*. Friendship says to the other, "Come with me. There's nothing to be afraid of. Let us put aside our foolish fears and terrors. Let us tear down the barrier between us. Let us pledge ourselves not to destroy or mutilate one another but rather to comfort, challenge, and support. Let us speak honestly and openly with one another. Let us trust. Let us set up bonds that will hold us together. Let us make a commitment to one another. Let us establish very clearly the conditions that we both will honor in our friendship."[6]

Greeley is convinced of the depth of fear that lurks within all of us. He further suggests that in friendship we are willing to "act as though we are not afraid" of each other, even "to acknowledge to one another the fears when they are especially powerful." This invitation includes the assertion: "I will actually let you see me afraid of you if you will let me see you being afraid of me."[7]

This element of fear, or terror, is also recognized by Martin Marty. He draws on his skill as a historian, as well as his intensely sensitive human individuality, to observe that "We have friends, or we are friends, in order that we do not get killed."[8] We survive by having—and being—a friend. "Buddies" in war try to keep each other from being killed. Persons who live in urban apartments face problems of emotional and, sometimes, physical survival. Children, in the process of growing up, encounter enormous threats to identity survival from the viciousness of peers and the thoughtlessness of adults. In turning to another for "survival," we learn truths about ourselves, about others, about the world. We may also learn ways to live as a friend in and to the world.

In addition to being an invitation, friendship, according to Greeley (and a host of others), is a *gift*.

> In order that we might persuade the other to accept our invitation, we offer him an inducement, that is to say, we offer him ourself. We say to the other, "I will give you me, I will not hold back, I will not hide, I will put myself at your service, will be willing to listen and to support, to run the risk of being hurt. I am yours to do with as you want, but my faith in you is so great that I know I have nothing to fear from you."[9]

Giving friendship is not something most of us do just once, but we are constantly renewing it. It often becomes easier through practice, although the risk and potential terror always remain.

Another perspective on friendship as "gift" is offered by Marty. Not only is being a friend something that is offered as gift by one human being to another. It is also (and first) a divine gift, something given to creatures who are sorrowing, reminding us of the joy that is our real destiny.[10] Living in a world that includes sorrows as well as joys, the gift of another and the capacity to be with the other opens up new joys in the midst of sorrow, disappointments, and fears.

"Finally," Greeley tells us, "friendship is a *promise*." A promise of, or to, what? "It is a promise to ecstasy, a dream of pleasure and joy, a utopian vision. It is a promise of a wonderland in which we shall forever play together." The "forever," we learn from experience, is often limited by the vicissitudes of life and change. Yet, the *promise* of "forever" is important.

> When I offer myself in friendship to you I promise that the best in me will become better and better and that I will demand of you that the best in you become better and better. As the fear and the anxiety, the suspicion and distrust in the two of us melt away, the world in which we live will grow more splendid, and together we shall frolic in that world. It is not merely myself that I promise to you without condition and without limit but it is a whole environment in which the two of us will become happier and happier that I offer to you, and of course you make the same promise back to me.[11]

There are lots of wonderful things we can expect from friendship, if we surrender ourselves to the experience. Realism demands that we also recognize some problems. Many friendships don't last "forever." They fade, and die, from lack of nutrition and attention. Some friends disappoint us, even betray us. Others simply move away. Friendships that are sustained also have problems. They take time, often when we'd rather be doing something else. When there is a falling out, it takes work to get it back together. Criticism is necessary in a friendship, but figuring out how to do it is not easy. Recognizing that a friend "is one who warns us," we have to learn how to take—and give—warnings. There may be temptation to respond to the natural feelings of sexual attraction, thus changing the status of the relationship. Since friendship is based on integrity of two unique individuals, there will be differences and conflict—making that a creative experience is a challenge to friendship. So it is with anger and jealousy. Perhaps one of the most puzzling problems of friendship is that discussed at some length by Marty— envy. As much as friends want the best for each other, they do not always want it if success for one's friend suggests lack of success for one self. Not so puzzling is the common experience of what Marty calls "insatiability." Some of us seem not to be able to get enough of another. "Availability" is crucial, but it must have limits. If the demand for availability is actually an expression of dependency and inability to be alone with oneself, it is a sign of dis-ease and unhealthiness in the relationship.

We expect a great deal from friendship, and often find that we receive what we were expecting, along with some surprises—some happy, some not. Since friendship is very important to us, and we want to invest ourselves in such experience, how does friendship come about?

Stages in Development of Friendship

Assuming that we *choose* a friend, how does it happen? If it is true that there is an "invitation," a "gift," and a "promise," can we describe how that takes place? A few observors of our behavior have formulated some descriptions, and it is worthwhile to check our own experience against their observations.

Gerald Philips and Nancy Metzger have described stages common to the development of "bonded" relationships in their study of "intimate communication."[12] They suggest six stages that may help us to understand what happens as we develop a friendship.

1. They call the first stage, *acquaintanceship*. The term is obvious, describing the fact that we become acquainted with someone, learn a name, have some common interest, or at least a common context, through which we meet or become aware of one another. We often speak of our meeting someone who becomes a friend as "accidental"— it "just happened" while at work, or sitting in a park, in a class, or on an airplane. This first stage, however, suggests that such meetings are

not entirely "accidental." We *choose* our activities, the places we go, and the means of transportation for getting there. Furthermore, we are more open in some settings than in others for conversation and letting another know who we are. I suggest, therefore, that we have some control over the making of acquaintances, and can exercise that control more creatively than we often do.

2. *Temporary accommodation,* their second stage, comes with the two parties agreeing to *do* something together. Having done the activity, they may choose to revert to being "mere" acquaintances, with no more plans for joint activity. On the other hand, their choice may be to do more together, with either of them taking the initiative. This latter is their "accommodation" process, and is of a temporary nature.

3. *Testing* takes place as new friends spend more time together. They want to find out what the "currency of exchange" is going to be. Such testing may include making promises to see if they are going to be kept. There may be a certain amount of "conning," or even "seducing," to learn how the other will react. Forms of transaction are developed and tested. The types of words and phrases we can and cannot use with each other become known. Levels of tolerance for some of our idiosyncrasies are communicated. What can we laugh about together, and, perhaps, what can we cry about together?

4. *Preliminary contracting* accompanies the deepening of the relationship, with one party or the other making a move which will bring the relationship to a higher level of contact or even of intimacy. This may include suggestions to continue doing certain things or attempts to find other ways of getting together. It may also involve requests for a different type of "currency" to be exchanged, including the loan of money or property. New risks are being taken.

5. *Leveling the contract* takes place when both parties are satisfied with the amount of energy and time they are putting into and receiving from the relationship. Philips and Metzger suggest that this is often a temporary position. It is a plateau of comfort; when it is no longer comfortable, one party will press to move on or back off. One of the findings of the Philips and Metzger study is that where there is considerable stability in a community, with families living there over several generations with a minimum of mobility and change, there may be an accompanying stability in relationships. Leveling may remain on a plateau for longer periods of time, sometimes for years. This can be seen in small farming towns and in ethnic neighborhoods in larger cities. Persons know each other "well." Friends know the limits of the sarcasm and joking which are acceptable; there is a repetitiveness and regularity in their conversation which is comfortable and meaningful. A good deal of common experience is shared and, perhaps, ritualized.

If the plateau has been maintained, however, the relationship lacks real intimacy.

6. *Intimacy* will come after a level contract has been achieved and there is desire for more. This, of course, is the deepest stage and requires for most persons a feeling of security and stability in the relationship. For that reason, premature disclosures accompanying "pseudo-intimacy" in a friendship will often betray the relationship. Real intimacy is the goal—and the fruit—of a depth relationship.

Interesting parallels to this description are found in the "process toward friendship" detailed by Muriel James and Louis Savary.[13] They emphasize a stage preceding "acquaintanceship." This earlier step is one in which there is awareness of the "*matrix*," or setting, in which we become aware of each other. We usually know where we met or first saw each other and were beginning to be attracted to each other. From "matrix" we move to "*acquaintanceship*," in which we know each other's name and some basic facts. If we met each other on the street, in the presence of already established friends, we would likely tell the others, after passing and greeting with a few words, "That is Myron X, an acquaintance of mine from work." We then move to "*we-ness*," a stage in which there is recognition of shared experience, activity, meaning, or interest. Again, running into each other on the street while in company of other friends, we'd introduce each other with such additional information as "we sing together on Wednesday nights," or "we're in the same pottery class." This stage moves on to "*casual friends*," persons we are glad to see and for whom there is some affection but to whom there are limited commitments. Our meeting on the street, in the company of other friends, will involve some time taken for introductions all around, confirmation of plans we've made to get together, sharing of an incident or joke with the others, and perhaps some physical contact. We'll part with reaffirmation of our intent to see each other soon. We may phone the other a short time later to share information about the persons met on this occasion, or to pick up on incomplete comments during the meeting.

The next stage is "*close friends*." We now have very real expectations of each other. We know in what ways we care about each other, and are specific and intentional about our time commitments to each other. It is at the level of "close friends," (the "intimacy" level) that we are able to move to the ultimate stage, the "*third self.*"

Beyond Two Selves

What is the "third self?" James and Savary call it a "meta-person," or a "meta-self." "Meta," in this sense, is both *after* and *beyond*. "Two people, like two notes, come together in such a way that, without losing their individualities, they form a new unity."[14] This idea is demonstrated through the notion of a "Friendship Mathematics," which pictures three different viewpoints on friendship.

In Viewpoint 1, 1/2 person + 1/2 person = 1 person. In this perspective, hallowed by centuries of time, each person is really only partially complete and will only find wholeness when the "other half" is located. They can then form the whole for which they were intended. This viewpoint, passed on to us through art forms, music, poetry, and legends, still prevails in this century, although a new perspective has become popular in recent decades.

In Viewpoint 2, 1 person + 1 person = 1 person + 1 person. This perspective, somewhat the product of twentieth century psychology and literature, recognizes that each person is already a whole person; when two such persons come together, their friendship is not a melting together into a totally merged unity. Rather, we have two separate and independent entities maintaining their separateness while enjoying what they can share. This is characterized in the now famous statement by Fritz Perls which has become attributed to a variety of sources, and is often called the "Gestalt Prayer":

I do my thing, and you do your thing.
I am not in this world to live up to your expectations and you are not in this
    world to live up to mine.
You are you and I am I,
And if by chance we find each other, its beautiful.
If not, it can't be helped.[15]

If this seems a bit "cold," it should be noted that it was part of a conviction that real intimacy with another is approached only from a stance of complete independence. This may have some similarities to the notion of "negotiating from strength" which dominates many approaches to international politics.

In Viewpoint 3, 1 person + 1 person = 1 person + 1 person + *1 third self.* This perspective, preferred by James and Savary, recognizes that, when two persons share deeply with each other, something beyond each of them is created (similar to viewpoint 1). It recognizes, with viewpoint 2, that a healthy friendship needs to bring together two fully developed persons, each of whom has independence and is a complete self. The dimension added in Viewpoint 3 is the creation of an entity beyond the two, a "self" that is neither of the two parties but a shared reality which now exists because of the fullness of their experience together. It is their history, their nuances of meaning, not shared with anyone else. Each of these persons may have close friendships with others, but their "third selves" with others will not be the same. Just as each individual person is unique, so each "third self" is unique. It "transcends" each of the persons; yet, each is inextricably a part of it. One of the parties in the friendship may die, but the third self may remain alive and active. This may explain some of the experiences of the presence of a loved one sometimes described by persons after that person's death. Likewise, if a relationship is not nurtured, it may die, and a "third self" may no longer have life, although the two persons who created it are still alive. The peak of a friendship experience is the sharing in the "meta-self," which is created by two healthy persons as they open themselves as fully as they can to each other.[16]

"Just Friends"

It is not uncommon to hear someone say, "oh, we're just friends." *Just friends*. What does that mean? The odds are that the relationship being discussed is with a person of the opposite sex, but is not a "romantic" one, or does not involve sexual intercourse. The person may go on to say, "of course we *are* close, and we mean a great deal to each other, but . . ."

Sorting out friendship and romance can be complicated. Some would insist that *any* love experience, including friendship, has some kind of sexual quality about it. Others would argue that one of the strengths of friendship is that it is not complicated by the passions that accompany romantic attraction. Keen, for instance, contends that "Precisely because friendships are formed when two people are drawn to each other by a mutual liking, and not by a mad, passionate, biologically driven need, they are usually more orderly and enduring than romance."[17] Keen wants to distinguish friendship from other forms of commitment and love expression. Thus, he further claims for friendship a status of "sanctuary," different from and apart from our private experiences with family, and the public realms of the corporation and political life. Friendship also frees us, according to Keen, from the "sweet burden of sexuality" and the "ambiguities of sexual love." Although the erotic and the sexual may be confused in friendship, especially (but not necessarily restricted to) when it involves persons of opposite sex, Keen would prefer the friends' opportunity to steer clear of the sexual attraction:

> Wouldn't it be marvelous if our best friend could be our most passionate lover? But longtime experience testifies that it seldom works. The demands of genital sexuality and friendship overlap, but do not always mix well. Nowadays, in the dark ages of friendship, husbands and wives, or

lovers, often claim they are each other's best friends. But I suspect this signals more a decline in the fortunes of friendship than an advance in the fortunes of marriage. The bonds of familiar and sexual love have their own special flavor—a warm, intimate, mixed fragrance of biology and choice. The deepest appeal of friendship is that it sets us free from the necessities imposed upon us by biology and politics. What is created within friendship is a relationship whose sole purpose is to be enjoyed. It is probably because it is rare and precious to know ourselves as useless and wonderful that we are willing to sacrifice genital pleasure to enjoy the dignities of friendship.[18]

What about the claim of husbands and wives, or lovers, that they are each other's best friends? In his essay on friendship, Andrew Greeley asserts that the basic model of friendship is indeed marriage, and that a satisfying sexual relationship is impossible without friendship. Greeley, of course, cannot be totally separated from his Roman Catholic tradition which locates the fundamental, primary love unit for human beings in the family and the marriage which secures it. These two writers are emphasizing different aspects of their concern for friendship. Keen is not saying that marriage partners or lovers with a sexual relationship cannot be friends, nor is Greeley saying that there is no friendship without sexual intercourse. In their efforts to identify and encourage the basic qualities of friendship, they make clear that the essence of the friend relationship is self-revelation, transparency, sharing of feelings and deepest identity.

Who, then, are "just friends?" Persons who might otherwise be candidates for romance and sexual alliance, but have ruled that out of their relationship? In an age when we seem to be programmed to orient all our feelings toward the glitter of romance and to identify most of our bodily tingles with an eventual fulfillment in intercourse, how can we succeed at being "just friends?" It's not easy, but no love relationship is; certainly the commitment to a lover or a mate is fraught with multiple complication and frustrations.

For many years I, a male, have had a good friend, a female. Early in our growing friendship we recognized that we liked each other in many ways, including the sexual pull each of us felt. We are both married. By recognizing our feelings and finding any number of playful ways to enjoy them, we eliminated any pressure to follow through on them. Sex is not "left out" of our relationship; we feel it, but it has relatively little bodily expression (we *do* enjoy a hug when we get together) and no genital expression. We are very much "alive" when we are together, and we share in ways that close friends do. Somehow, it doesn't seem adequate to say we are "just" friends; perhaps we are close-just-friends!

Male-Female Differences

A growing number of males have noticed that a special kind of friendship appears to be shared by many women, in ways that the social conditioning of men denies to them. The observed depth and freedom of support and sharing is precious. It is celebrated in the song by Margie Adam, "Sweet Friend":

Sweet friend of mine, it took so long to find you
All the growing pains behind you, right up till now
Sweet friend of mine, it took so long to see you
All the things you did to free you, right up till now
The sun's gonna shine, and the music will flow
Sweet, sweet friend of mine!

Sweet friend of mine, we are together changing
Living lives of rearranging, right from the heart
Sweet friend of mine, we are together growing
Standing side by side and knowing, right from the heart
The sun's gonna shine, and the music will flow—
　　Sweet, sweet friend of mine

Letting others define us kept us apart
Now that we're together, let us begin
Demanding the things that give us the wings
　　To fly . . . to fly . . . to fly

Sweet friend of mine, we are together growing
Standing side by side and knowing, right from the heart
The sun's gonna shine, and the music will flow
Sweet, sweet friend . . . sweet sister
Sweet, sweet friend of mine.[19]

Apparent differences in male and female approaches to friendship have been observed in social psychology research. These studies reveal a tendency for friendships between women to emphasize *emotional sharing,* whereas men seek to look to friendships with other males for the *sharing of activities.* In her extensive discussion of intimate friendships, Sharon Brehm considers one researcher's designation of "face-to-face" relationships for women and "side-by-side" for men as especially good descriptions. "Face-to-face" recognizes that women tend to utilize a friendship for the expression of deep feelings. "Side-by-side" describes men's tendencies to nurture friendships with other males through doing things together. They *do* talk—friends will normally talk a lot—but their talk tends not to explore and express personal feelings. The photographs in Brehm's book say it well: in one, two women are seated facing each other over coffee cups, in intense conversation; in the other, two men are standing next to one another, mutually caught up in an exciting moment at an athletic event.[20]

Men, it seems, are much more likely to turn to a person of the opposite sex for sharing of emotional concerns. (This is especially true of heterosexual men.) Women are more likely to do such sharing with each other, although many will seek male friends for such sharing. Men are likely to focus whatever emotional expression they muster with one romantic partner. Women, on the other hand, seem to be more conditioned to share significant feelings with one or more friends, of the same or opposite sex, and do not depend as much on a romantic partner for that sharing.[21] One may conclude that these differences have a number of important implications for the meaning of friendship within a committed relationship. Marriages, for instance, that close off individual friendships of the marriage partners in favor of "couple friendships" may severely limit important resources to each of the partners and thus to the relationship. When a relationship ends—through death, divorce, or other termination—friendship patterns and how they have or have not been maintained become very important. As Brehm puts it, "if we do not make the effort to maintain our friendships during good times, we may find ourselves without friends during those bad times when our need for them is greatest."[22] In addition, she notes, separate friendships outside the marriage are often found to be enriching to the marriage relationship, giving it "a better chance of lasting."

We have a lot to learn about friendship. Most of us have to do a certain amount of "letting go" to be a friend, to have a friend. Greeley's assessment is sobering: "There may have been a time when trust and friendship were optional for the human condition; in the modern world they are becoming essential." Why does he say so? The survival of society is at stake.

Friendship between black and white can hardly be expected to be the same as friendship between husband and wife or two close friends who share many values in common, though one must say that if friendship is not more widespread between husbands and wives we are not likely to have children who are capable of any kind of trust in dealing with those who are different from them. But if the relationship between people of different human groupings is not likely to be intimate, it still must involve some trust, some invitation, some promise, some gift-giving, some delight, perhaps even some faint touches of ecstasy. There is no other way . . . to conquer terror, and terror is the root of hatred.

To put the matter more bluntly, in the modern world friendship is not optional.

And so, whether we like it or not, all of us have to learn to love one another.[23]

The longing for friendship is universal. James Kavanaugh has caught that longing in his poetic plea; the friend he seeks is one:

Who far beyond the feebleness of any vow or tie
Will touch the secret place where I am really I,
To know the pain of lips that plead and eyes that weep,
Who will not run away when you find me in the street
Alone and lying mangled by my quota of defeats
But will stop and stay—to tell me of another day
When I was beautiful.[24]

Shared Experiences and Insights

Perhaps it would seem I'm really hung up on spending a great amount of time in my friendships. That's not necessarily true. As I look over the list of people who are friends . . . the difference is that when "we choose" to be together our energies are focused on being together—whether that's a five-minute sharing in the office or an entire evening partying or working on a project together. The choosing together and the energy together are the important aspects.

A Friend Is:

Someone who can wipe my nose without making either of us feel embarrassed.

Someone who can enjoy coffee with me even though my sink is full of dirty dishes.

Someone whom I can see after an extended absence, and we can take up right where we left off.

Someone who can allow me to go off by myself without feeling rejected.

Someone who can plan a whole dinner party so that the menu contains no wheat, cheese, or chocolate—because I'm allergic to them.

Someone who thinks most of my jokes are hilarious, but refuses to laugh at the one which, to her, is not funny.

Someone who stays all night at my house because I'm so depressed that I'm afraid to be alone tonight.

Someone who refuses to let me go ahead with a selfish action without warning me that I may be very sorry afterward.

We never wonder if we can trust each other. It is no longer necessary to preface a confidence with "Don't say anything about this . . ." Trust is a given between us. And we seem to laugh or cry more easily with each other as time goes on. Sometimes we face each other, but sometimes we face outward together, absorbed in something else—a sunset, an idea, a concert—and it is better because we share it. We have even learned sometimes just to be quiet together, sensing those times when pain is too deep for words, but a hug or a hand held quietly is what is needed most. You never oppress me with possessiveness or make me feel you are trying to fit me into a mold that exists in your head. And I try to give you the same freedom. We do not own each other.

There are four qualities I look for in friendship: mutuality, growthfulness, freedom, and uniqueness. By mutuality I simply mean that both I and the other desire to have the friendship. This may seem obvious at first, but when I reflect on how many people refer to me as their friend and I only consider an acquaintance, I soon realize that mutuality is an important dimension of what I look for in friendship. Growthfulness says that the people involved in the friendship will be better, more fully human people for their involvement. The third quality, freedom, has many nuances to it. Freedom, in this case, does not refer to a lack of commitment, but rather to a lack of expectation. This freedom not only involves myself and the other, but the relationship as well; I am free to give in whatever way we shape it. There are no predetermined patterns of what it will look like after a given period of time. In uniqueness, there is a recognition that both I and the other may be involved in other relationships including other friendships, but there is also a recognition that this one is special enough to devote our attention to its development.

4

Commitment in Living Together

Many of us think the best way for two persons to live together in a committed relationship is in marriage. Not everyone, however, wants to be married. Some who are married wish they were not. Some who are not wish they were. Others who are not married intend to stay that way, although they sometimes change their minds. Nonetheless, it is true that one of the dominant forms of human organization and experience is marriage. In much conventional thinking, marriage is what love leads to; it is the "norm" for loving relationships. It is not at all unusual to pick up a book about "love" and find that the author openly assumes that the best way to discuss love, its attributes and problems, is in the framework of marriage. It would seem that the way to really, *really* experience loving is to be married.

Being married is certainly *one* way to experience loving. It is not, however, the *only* way. After all, we are all born single; even if we marry, we spend from sixteen to thirty or more years single before we enter into marriage, and may well spend many more years in one or more states of being single after that. We could, in fact, think of marriage as being "un-single", rather than submitting without thinking to the common practice of labelling those who are single as "unmarried."

This chapter looks at ways in which persons commit themselves to living together as loving partners. We will first examine the growing practice of "living together" without marriage. This raises the "commitment" question that will then lead us to probe marriage as a context of loving relationships, with the problems and opportunities it offers. The taboo question of marriage for persons of the same sex is then opened for exploration. The chapter concludes with some comments on procreation and family contexts for loving.

What About "Living Together?"

Let's be blunt about what we are talking about. "Living together" isn't *just* living together. Roommates live together. Families live together. Members of religious orders live together. "Living together" is the increasingly accepted practice of two persons, usually of the opposite sex, living in the same location and sharing sex, without being married. Granted, there are some who decide to live together with an agreement not to sleep together, or have intercourse, but to otherwise share life in ways that used to be confined primarily to marriage. Those persons are often considered a little strange, but they are not really the issue. The issue is that there are now a significant number of persons around who appear to want to "act as though they are married," but are legally not. After all, what is marriage, if it is not the open sharing of a household and, especially, a bed? No, you say, it's more than that. We'll get to that "more than," shortly.

It seems obvious that much of the discomfort experienced by relatives, friends, or whoever is upset, when two persons start living together, is based in the fact that they are openly entering into an assumed regular sex life without having "paid their dues," or getting married. "Openly" is important; the assumptions which have been operative for generations are defied, or ignored. We might not have liked it, even though we knew it, when young people used their automobiles, a friend's apartment, a motel room, or many options in the great outdoors, as trysting places for sexual intercourse. They were hiding it, and it was thus possible for others to pretend it wasn't happening . . . unless, of course, they made a "mistake" and the woman became pregnant. Besides, there's a certain excitement and romance to all that. But now, they share the same furniture, meals, and bed, on a daily basis, and other people know about it. What happens to "sex is for marriage"? Or, was it the other way around?

This new reality which, incidentally, is hardly limited to the young, raises a number of important questions, only a few of which will be addressed here. The underlying emotional reaction strongly suggests that some of the suspicions held by certain critics of marriage are true: underneath, what marriage *really* means in our culture (as well as many others), is license to have sex! Whatever else we may say about marriage as a fulfilling part of human experience, our prevailing value systems have carefully taught us that we shouldn't "do it" before—or outside of—marriage. It appears that a significant shift in moral emphasis is emerging that needs to be examined very seriously: rather than demanding virginity before marriage, the emphasis is now placed on sexual fidelity within a committed relationship.[1] Perhaps it is sufficient at this point to recognize that the increasing acceptance of the open patterns of "living together" being done by adults of all ages suggests that there is a change in process, regarding the necessary correlation of being married and having sexual intercourse. What used to be an occasional and certainly deviant aspect of community life is now openly practiced, and is done so with decreasing hassle from others.

More important, perhaps, than establishing the appropriate context for regular sexual practice, is the significance of commitment, the "more than." When I talk with persons about the difference between "living together" and "being married," some will insist that there is not much difference—both, they say, require a commitment to each other and to the relationship. When pursuing the discussion, however, it is not unusual for the defenders of "living together" to say that one of its values is to learn about each other and about the self before taking a step that is such a big *commitment* as marriage. Researchers on this phenomenon often find that observation, as well. The "long-term" commitment involved in marriage is certainly different. In many situations, it involves the question of having children, and providing a home for their nurture. It may involve decisions about jobs and careers, property ownership, settling in a particular geographical location, investment of money into particular goals, and so forth. Some will argue, occasionally persuasively, that they are able to enter into those commitments *without* taking on the legal aspects of being married, and are thus freed from some of the negative constraints they perceive to have accumulated around that hallowed state. Perhaps. If so, they will make an important contribution to something that has happened all through human history—the development of new and different ways of organizing human life for the fuller benefit of its participants.

Clearly, there are differing levels of commitment. To what? To whom? For what purposes? With what expenditure of energy? At what level of tenacity, of "hanging in there?" If there are limits to the extent to which I am prepared to open myself to this other person, to move forward in life with this person, what is the basis of our living together? Are we agreed on the limits? If not, how healthy is it? If so, given our limits, how productive will the experience be? These—and other—questions need to be asked, and they can be answered only by the individuals involved. Guidance and some wisdom are available from the experience of others and from the past, but they may not be communicated very well, or received very well. The many faces of commitment certainly need to be considered in a relationship in which we are going to join life with another or others in sharing shelter, meals, material and emotional resources, physical expressions of affection, and plans for the future. When are we "mature enough" to make such commitments? Or, to enter into the process of making and remaking commitments based on promises? Certainly, that maturity is required for making and sustaining a marriage relationship.

Marriage and Family in Historical/Traditional Perspective

Although not necessarily the *norm* for loving, marriage is definitely one of the major contexts of loving relationship in the experience of most of us, as is the family which normally extends from it. Our social experience leads us to have expectations about marriage—what it is, what we're supposed to feel like, how we are to act—and we hold these expectations whether we intend to be married or not. Our expectations, indeed, may have a great deal to do with whether or not we look upon marriage as something positive and want it for our own lives.

Marriage in our society, we are often told, is in trouble. Divorce statistics are cited to support the claim that marriage is in serious difficulty. Such statistics suggest that contemporary marriage is *unstable*—indeed, there can be little question about that. *Marriage* statistics, however, also indicate that being married continues to be an extremely popular condition. Persons *do* want to live together, and vast numbers of us desire to live together in marriage, even a second or third time. Couples are still marrying, looking to that institution to provide for certain desires and needs in their lives. What is it that is so desirable and, at the same time, so difficult about marriage? An important factor in answering that question is an examination of some of the history of family and marriage in human experience.

The record of humanity confirms that human beings want to live together—few of us desire to live completely alone. There have been many reasons for that choice. Our ancestors found that they were better able to protect themselves from hungry animals or hostile neighbors in the company of others. Child-bearing and nurture promotes some ties between adults, as well as between parent and child. The securing of adequate food and shelter is a task more productively shared with another or others. Studies of human and cultural evolution suggest any number of reasons for the bonding of persons into families and tribes. The tribe/family provided protection, nurture, identity, and ways of relating to the world. The tribe was concerned with maintenance and continuation of the group; at various stages along the way, therefore, mating for reproduction was recognized not only as something that happened to individuals, and pairs, but was a matter of some considerable concern for the group. As culture developed, marriage became a way of uniting families, of strengthening economic and political ties.

The ancient Hebrews saw something special in the origins of marriage—in one of their versions of Creation, the original human being was deemed by the Creator to be lonely, and the only satisfactory companion was to be another human being (Gen. 2:18–24). Some theologians and biblical scholars suggest that companionship for God was behind the creation of humans in the first place—their creation "in the image of God" (Gen. 1:27) not only brought to a conclusion the various orders of creation, but brought into being creatures who held a special relationship with God. Thus, in this tradition, marriage is originated in the process of completing creation, assuring that the created order will be fruitful and multiply, and that there is a special unity in their companionship. The unfolding of the stories in scripture leads very quickly to families, to the merging of families, and the extension of families through lines of descendants. Now, many centuries later, we have come to think of marriage as the appropriate context for sexual relationships and as, primarily, a tie between individuals. Keen, however, puts the matter into proper perspective when he notes that:

> Although marriage may present the most satisfying form of sexual expression for a majority of people, it is not designed primarily for sexual pleasure or companionship, or indeed, even as a relationship between individuals. Traditionally, marriage has been understood not as a culmination of a romantic urge, but as a uniting of families.[2]

The importance of the family, both for the individual and for the society, has remained, in varying ways, throughout history. My great aunt, age 92 at the time, commented at the end of a family reunion: "We should do this more often so that we can remember who we are." Human beings look to family arrangements for identity—not for just a name, but for a deeper sense of where we came from and what life means to us. The home, for centuries, has been recognized in every society as the primary unit, the central entity in social organization. We have our origins there, learn about nurture there, gain our values in that setting, practice our social skills there, and develop role identities and skills there. This centrality of the family, and its marriage base, is recognized in tradition, in religious norms, in cultural symbol systems, and in law and custom. The actual *forms* taken by family, as well as marriage, have varied a great deal more than any individual or group, at a particular point in history (including the present), are usually able to recognize. At the same time, it is easy to be misled by changes in structures of family, expectations of marriage, and role/power relationships, and ignore the continuing *basic* influence of the institutional nature of marriage.

In the family unit, social responsibility was learned and practiced. The responsibility of the family to the community, or tribe, was paramount, and marriages were instrumental to that relationship. Power relationships were formed, continued, and strengthened through the family and its place in the larger unit. Thus, marriage was basic to the understanding and development of power—social, economic, and political. Both within the matrimonial bond and in the relationship of the family to the larger unit, roles and the forms of exercising power have been experienced.

Where is love in all this? It is safe to say that throughout most of the history of marriage and family, love was not a *primary* factor in the choice of marriage partners, nor in the expectations held for the relationship. At the same time, the record is clear that love has often been present in marriages, although not, perhaps, in the romantic form we have become accustomed to expect in the twentieth century. Evidence is abundant that even marriages put together by matchmakers, parents, or some other community system, often produced caring, respect, loyalty, and commitment. Unique forms of sharing, mutual support, and genuine affection were experienced and valued in many marriages, as we know from religious and spiritual writings, as well as secular literature. Marriage has been considered to be the safest, least complicated locus for the sexual relationship for long centuries of time; in many societies, of course, it is the only permissible context, according to custom, or law, or both. *Love* as the *basis of choice* for marriage partners remains, however, a relatively recent phenomenon.

It is generally recognized that *romantic* love, as it has come to influence our twentieth century thinking and expectations, had its "flowering," if not its origins, in the Middle Ages. As Murstein has pointed out, the passion known as "romance" has probably been around since quite ancient times; it simply was not allowed, until very recent times, to have any influence on marital choice:

> It is sometimes made to appear that love was invented by the courtly troubadours of the late eleventh century and became the basis of marriage in seventeenth-century novels. Actually, we can speculate that love, if by that term we mean a powerful emotional passion accompanied by idealization, has existed much longer. However, it seems not to have played a significant role in marital choice because it posed a distinct threat to the existing kinship bonds that defined one's place in society. Marriage, more

than today, was a consanguineal affair, not a matter to be trusted to foolish, impetuous youths. Parents reasoned that love, if not blind, was sufficiently myopic to ensure that their offspring, when left to themselves, would rarely pair off in accordance with their parents' wishes . . . we have seen that society was indeed based on kinship lines and that, accordingly, it was incumbent upon society—through its agents, the parents—to control this dangerous passion.[3]

Certainly, strong interpersonal attraction and commitment have been a part of marriage for some throughout history. At the same time, it seems that, with few exceptions, *romance* remained unrelated to marriage until the current century. The romance of the "courtly love" period was so based on a "furtive and hidden embrace," often in the lovers' imaginations, that it simply had no place between a wife and husband. The overwhelming mystery of the other, so necessary to romance, is broken down by the type of real intimacy within which two persons actually get to know one another in depth. Romance and permanence were seen in the idealistic literature as incompatible. Romantic liaisons, to the extent that they ever actually happened, were usually broken by separation, rejection, or death of one or both of the parties.[4]

For a host of reasons, romantic love has "come alive" in the twentieth century. Romantic love has become much more important to us and is assumed to be the basis of marriage throughout popular literature, music, and art. Advertising especially plays on this theme and undoubtedly has had a great deal of influence. Many of the movies I watched as a child assured me that I would someday be stunned by the beauty and attraction of a beautiful young woman; I would sweep her off her feet (that was the male's task) and, when we were able to catch our breath for a moment, I would put to her THE QUESTION, for which she was waiting nervously, and to which she would breathe, (barely audibly) "yes." Silly, you say? That tape, I suspect, is playing, or at least stored and ready to play, in the computer supplied to each of us who were raised in the mainstream North American culture. Variations on that theme exist throughout the Western world. Marriage happens when there is an attraction between two persons. The attraction is physical, aesthetic, mental, and emotional, all at the same time. Since the pressure is strongest to get married at the age when physical and emotional responses are especially pronounced, they tend to dominate the attraction.

Ask someone, "why do you want to marry him?" The odds are that the answer will be, "because I love him." Love is the one fundamental requirement for marriage. A popular song of many years ago, made famous by the young Frank Sinatra, proclaimed that "love and marriage . . . go together like a horse and carriage." "You can't have one," the song assured us, "without the other." A powerful sentiment . . . but is it true? Actually, a horse can do fine without a carriage; in fact, the horse will probably be happier if not restricted to the confines of a carriage. A carriage, on the other hand, built to be pulled by a horse, can't do much without one. It can look very attractive, and hopeful; without the horse it isn't going anywhere. Love doesn't *require* marriage. There are many ways to love another person, or be loved, without being married to that person. But marriage—does it have to have love, just as the carriage has to have the horse, if it is to do anything but sit there and be of little use? Most would say yes. Marriage must have love if it is to serve the purposes we have for it, if it is to be a *real* marriage. Thus, we expect marriage to be the "carriage" of love: to house it, to protect it, to nourish it, make it grow, give it direction and purpose. Sometimes it doesn't work that way. Perhaps we have overburdened the institution of marriage. Do we expect too much of it?

By now we are trying to combine most of the historical functions of marriage with some newer, contemporary expectations. We want identity, security, community recognition and acceptance, sex and, sometimes, procreation. We also want passion, romance, intimacy, personal fulfillment for each member, altered understandings of power relationships, autonomy and freedom. We want a haven from what we have learned to perceive as a hostile world, and we want a companion in that haven who can be trusted. At the same time, we want a base for relating to the world constructively and productively, being able to benefit from the opportunities "out there," as well as to cope with its dangers. Murstein sums up our situation well:

> While the concept of love as the primary determinant of marital choice is today accepted as obvious, this was not always the case. A few hundred years ago, love was considered to be independent of, if not antithetical to, marital choice. In the nineteenth century, most spouses were satisfied to be polite to each other and socially compatible, while frequently leading separate lives. Today, vis-a-vis each other, married persons are assuming the roles of lover, therapist, friend, sports partner, and colleague, to name a few. Will marriage survive such demanding expectations? Is marriage obsolete and doomed to inevitable decline, or will it surmount these challenges, as it has managed to do throughout the ages?[5]

If marriage is to be a *loving* relationship, one with stability and permanence, how can we be realistic in our approach to it? As a beginning, we need to recognize that it is, in addition to being a relationship between two or more persons, a social institution.

Marriage as a Social Institution

A realistic look at marriage, its meaning and its purposes, requires a recognition of marriage as an institution. By "institution," I don't mean to suggest that marriage is a hospital, prison, or school, although it may seem at times to be any one or all three of those. The word "institution," in the sense of "social institution," refers to a form of human organization, developed through experience to fulfill certain needs and functions. It has a way of dividing labor, performing roles, ascribing identity, forming and perpetuating values, and taking care of the economic and political arrangements designated to it by the larger society. Marriage, among other things, *is* an institution. The significance of that fact may be taken as a background to understanding some of what seems to be happening to marriage as a loving relationship in our day.

One way to get a feel for what it means to see marriage as an institution is to note a part of the wedding ceremony that is still carried on in many public settings, especially in Christian churches. The groom and his attendants enter the room at the front and stand in waiting while the bride's attendants walk up the aisle. Then, the bride enters: usually on the arm of her father, she moves slowly to the front of the room to the strains of organ music, while people admire the beauty of her gown and the radiance of her countenance. On arriving at the front, she remains on the arm of her father, or at least near him, while the opening statements of the ceremony are made by the celebrant. Eventually, the question is asked, "Who gives this woman to be married to this man?" The father replies, "Her mother and I do," or in the older tradition, "I do." He then takes her arm, delivers it over to the groom, and steps back to sit by his wife as the ceremony proceeds. The transaction has been completed. A young female, the property of one male, has now been turned over to her new master, and she now becomes his property.

"Wait a minute," you object, "we don't think like that anymore! Just look at the rest of the ceremony. The vows are fairly egalitarian, and besides, it is just a ritual." It's true, many of us don't think like that any more. But, did anyone ask, "Who gives this man to be married to this woman?" You probably haven't heard that question unless you've been to one of those highly irregular "contemporary" weddings. True, it *is* a ritual. Although most of us don't consciously think of women as property of men any more (although there is considerable evidence that such a notion is anything but dead), rituals *do* mean something. The rituals by which we symbolize the beginning of marriage continue to project a form of the marriage institution that was a definite, widespread reality not too many years ago, and continues to have a very real influence on marriage in our time.

Marriage is a *political* institution. As such, it defines the accepted power relationships between males and females, and between parents and children. The family which is produced by the marriage is related to a larger community, and the nature of that relationship is a part of the political order. The forms in which marriage may be political now are not nearly so clear as in the "old days." Changes are occurring, and most are necessary changes. This does not mean, however, that there are no longer power issues in marriage and the family. A very humorous and deeply insightful treatment of changes in roles, and alterations of power, is found in Rick Masten's poem, "Coming and Going:"

> i have noticed
> that men
> somewhere around forty
> tend to come in from the field
> with a sigh
> and removing their coat in the hall
> call into the kitchen
>
>> you were right
>> grace
>> it ain't out there
>> just like you've always said
>
> and she
> with the children gone at last
> breathless
> puts her hat on her head
>> the hell it ain't
>
> coming and going
> they pass
> in the doorway![6]

Marriage remains a political institution, and the shaping of the power relationships is one of the crucial aspects of clarifying the loving nature of this context.

Marriage is an *economic* institution. Traditionally, women have had almost total dependence on the marriage relationship for a socially respectable economic security. For men, marriage and family have defined the structure within which a major portion of economic productivity was defined, and heavy social and legal customs were developed around those definitions. Economic roles have been given shape within marriage and the family. Clearly, the form of economic structure and roles in marriage is changing somewhat and is often muddled. What happens when a family has two "breadwinners" who are also husband and wife, as well as mother and father? What happens when a family which has become dependent on the economic productivity of two "breadwinners" is, for one reason or another, reduced to *one* "breadwinner"? How are power relationships related to economic productivity? How does "love" enter into these questions?

Marriage is a *social* institution. Boys and girls prepare for marriage by learning accepted behaviors toward the opposite sex, all the way from public manners to sexual expectations. Traditionally, marriage has been the accepted arena (although, obviously, not the only one in practice) for sexual relationships. In most societies, the replenishing of the social unit through reproduction is assigned to a particular family structure based in marriage. Marriage has defined appropriate relationships to others in the community, especially for women and children. Marriage and its family product provide specific personal identity, value orientation, and religious training. Many of the societal expectations of marriage and a particular form of family as the basic social unit are undergoing change. There is no question, however, that this remains a primary function of marriage, highly operative, no matter how clear or unclear it is to us.

Marriage cannot escape being a *legal* institution. All the former aspects are brought together in the legal arena, since the larger community has much at stake in how well marriage performs the functions of human organization. Laws, both civil and religious, are written to structure it, protect it, relate it to property, children, and other institutional forms, begin it, and end it. We are thus grossly naive when we say that "marriage is *just* a piece of paper," as a result of the legal forms with which we are familiar. That particular piece of paper represents a lot of reality, influencing us in a myriad of ways.

Marriage is an institution, with political, economic, social, and legal forms and expectations. We have already noted that, until recently in Western society and right up to the present in many parts of the world, the security and success of marriage as an institution was protected by the selection of marriage partners by those who "knew best"—the parents, aided by other elders. Given what marriage was expected to do for the family, the community, and the two persons, it was much too important to be left to the whims of two young, inexperienced persons. Furthermore, the relationship between the two persons was well defined by these various institutional forms, and there was not much reason or need for choice by the marrying partners. Now, *enter love*. In addition to all those other things, we got the idea in fairly recent times that *love* should be a basis for choice of a marriage partner, not just something that might develop within the relationship. Not only should marriage be a political, economic, social, and legal relationship but should also, first and foremost, be a loving relationship! When we came up with that one, we may very well have overburdened the institution of marriage, making it very difficult, if not impossible, for it to fulfill all expectations.

As mentioned in the chapter on friendship, it has been assumed throughout a major portion of human history that one's close friendship needs would be met through a choice relationship with a person usually of the same sex. That friendship might, and often did, include much affection, the form of which was dictated by the customs of the community at the time. Marriage provided a structure for raising children, for safe and relatively uncomplicated sexual relationships, and for the orderly transmission of property and name. If it also developed into friendship and love, that was nice—but not necessary. Lack of love was no reason to dissolve a marriage, because it was not that essential to begin with. Certainly, romantic love as an ingredient in marriage has become much more important to us.

Perhaps you have seen the play or movie version of *Fiddler on the Roof.* You have undoubtedly heard some of its music. Tevye, the husband and father, watches traditions fall around him but attempts to maintain some firm grounding in the midst of it all. Yet, he too begins to question when he asks his wife, "Do you love me?" She is startled and answers with the expected assurances that she cooks his meals, cleans his clothes, and beds with him, implying that these activities surely answer the question. He is not satisfied, saying, "But, do you *love* me?" Therein is our problem. We want marriage to be a *loving* relationship, according to what we have been conditioned to expect love to mean.

A further complication of marriage as a loving way to live together is highlighted by Erich Fromm. It is his claim that love has "disintegrated" in Western culture. As part of this claim, he argues that the market orientation in our economic system has pushed individuals to approach marriage as a "haven" against a hostile world.[7] The world is seen as hostile because it seems to be destructive to identity, to meaningful personal productivity, and to anything but competitive relationships. Thus it has become easy to see marriage as a team relationship, an idea that has its roots in the nineteenth century. The couple see themselves as "two against the world." With this as their functioning mode, their alliance may be mistaken for intimacy and love, and the two persons settle into a pattern of politeness and making each other feel better. Such an alliance may inhibit relating from the center of one to the center of the other. After being involved in any number of complex interactions during the work day, there is little incentive for engaging in further complexities within the haven of one's home. Real "dialogue" between persons is essential to authentic love, making it possible for lovers to grow together. M. C. Dillon has shown that such striving is a "means of negotiating values and projects which may, initially, be in conflict." In such communication, it is important to explore "truth and reality perception."[8] In an alliance of "two against the world," however, such depth of interaction is not likely to happen.

The desire for marriage to provide all that it has been expected to provide as well as a deep, sharing, and romantic friendship, frankly, is a lot to expect. It is no wonder that many youth in our era sense that something is out of balance. Marriage is seen as an awesome set of responsibilities and commitments that they are not sure they can handle. Can *any* of us handle it? Many of us are responding by attempting to *restructure the institution,* not really knowing that is what we are doing. Such a process takes time in the ongoing human drama, and it is bound to be uncomfortable, to say the least, while we are working it out. We are in the midst of that kind of process in our society, as are many others in the world.

Having surveyed the institutional nature of marriage, let's now look at a specific aspect of a social institution which seems to impinge heavily on our being able to live together in loving ways. The concept of "role" is a complicated one, but it has to do with specific tasks and functions that we take on as part of a particular form of relationship—as well as attitudes toward those tasks and functions. We may be "wife," "mother," "husband," "father," "daughter," "teacher," and so on. With each role, whether it be family related, job related, or community designated, there are a number of expectations. This is where things become especially complicated. Marriage partners have roles. There are things they expect to do, ways they expect to behave, and feelings they expect to have, based on their perceptions of their roles. They also have expectations of the role of the other person(s). Parents, likewise, expect certain things of their children, not because they are Kathy, or Brian, but because they are children, *their* children.

Roles are convenient ways to organize our thinking, and they allow a certain amount of predictability and security in our lives. They can also burden us and others with expectations that are impossible, or very difficult, to fulfill. Our marriage and family roles are made even more complex by the fact that we derive our role expectations from sources about which we are often unaware. For example, persons who enter marriage with a firm decision, after much rational discussion, to "divide the dirty work" may still find that the husband is really expecting the wife to wash dishes, do the laundry, and keep the bathroom clean. What may be even more frustrating for the wife is that she may find that *she* expects that of herself as well! Why? It is likely that each of them grew up observing that their mothers did such work and that their fathers expected it. Such observations are more likely to form our basic expectations of roles than are our rational, intellectual decisions about these matters.

Roles are necessary to our functioning in social systems, and a home is one kind of social system. If we are to organize our behavior such that our intentions for loving and caring are to be actualized, we have to look carefully at the source of our concept of role, and what shape it takes. It is not at all unusual for persons who have lived together for some time, perhaps even years, to discover that they relate to each other differently once they become married, in spite of believing that things would not be different at all. What happened? The answer may be more simple than it seems. They weren't married before. Now they are. The "tapes" that were recorded in their childhood and stored in the computers in their heads had not been turned on, or at least not very loudly, while they were living without the designation of being married. Once they take that turn, however, the machine is turned on— the tape begins to spin, so to speak—and the other person is now seen in a role that was not there before. Likewise, one sees oneself in a role that did not exist before. Not rational, you say? Of course not! It is real, nonetheless, perhaps even more influential on our behavior than our rational decisions. This kind of change, without understanding what is going on, can be very stressful to a relationship, and undoubtedly contributes to such increasingly familiar situations as the one described next.

Two persons who have been very happily living together for six months or more decide that they are really compatible and want to get married. They are divorced six months later. They complain that a perfectly good loving friendship was destroyed by becoming married. They were not prepared for the change, for the roles that existed in their own unconscious, and for the roles that were pressed on them by the outside world. Furthermore, without some work on their part, it is likely that they will later enter another situation with similar results.

As a number of marriage and family counselors have learned, we tend to model our behavior in marriage and with the family from our "family of origin." Whether or not we liked that original experience does not matter, nor do our vows we may have made never to do what our parents did. Roles are important. They are "where we live." Roles may structure our capacity to love others, or they may get in the way. If we are going to change the structures, we need to be prepared for the fact that it is hard work and requires patience as well as conscious observation and evaluation of our progress.

One of the best examples of the complexity of changing roles is found in the "two-career marriage." Patricia Ferris McGinn has provided some extremely helpful perspectives on this phenomenon. Having named the primary roles passed on to modern marriages as "wife-and-mother" and "husband and leader," she makes this observation:

> The deep imprinting most of us have about what is required to make a family is very difficult to grow out of, and I think it is often a silent, powerful and unacknowledged enemy of the two-career partnership. When we have been raised in patriarchal families—even if we have rebelled against them—it is difficult and confusing to construct a communal life when there is no wife-and-mother at home, and no husband-and-leader for the family.[9]

What are the functions of these two roles? First, the "wife-and-mother":

> First, she was in charge of preserving the marriage by making her husband happy. This would ensure the social and financial stability of the family. Second, she was responsible for making the home a place in which everyone in the family could feel well cared for. Third, she concentrated on nurturing her young physically and emotionally. Fourth, she specialized in the relationships in the family. And last, her job was to be a steady, loving center, the one who was always there, the heart of the home, the "fixed foot," as John Donne called his wife. For her, "outside interests" were just that, outside. Nothing took priority over the needs of her family.[10]

The "husband-and-leader" functions:

> First, he was the chief breadwinner of the family: the whole family depended on his career for survival and social position. He had to be ultimately responsible for everyone else in the family, and they were all his dependents. Second, he was the chief leader of the family. No serious decision could be made unless he made it or at least ratified it. Third, the family was organized in a way he was comfortable with, and his needs were taken seriously and attended to. Last, he was often the final word on matters of discipline and finance.[11]

The successful dual-career family, McGinn believes, "is the one that finds some way to fulfill most of these functions within the family." One difficulty in doing so is the fact that many of us have given up the "functionaries who specialized" in these tasks. Therefore, the expectation that one specific person will perform each one of these roles must be given up. Both persons are, in fact, each aspect of each role. This requires the marriage partners to "relate to each other as equals in spite of our hierarchical upbringing," making it possible that "we will be much more successful at standing there, eyeball to eyeball, and working out a system of cooperative team effort between friends and partners.[12] This will only happen where efforts are made to organize time and tasks carefully, the relationship is protected from jobs, children and other adults, communication is kept open and practiced, and time is protected for an enjoyable sex life. Decisions about having children and sharing of child care are crucial; equality in parenting is a must. McGinn concludes with this observation:

> No one prepared my husband and me for our two-career family, no one showed us how to do it, and that has meant frustration and conflict for us. But there is another side to all this—it is interesting to work out solutions to these new situations, and it is exciting to think of implanting new patterns of family living into the heritage of our own descendants. It is a very special kind of generativity for this time in our culture.[13]

New patterns of family living, closely related to changing patterns of marriage and role expectations in marriage, are emerging. New and/or different, they have their roots in traditions that have been meaningful for human beings who have chosen to live together, to share life in a structure that allows both security and growth. The "structure" is built on promises and commitment.

Promises and Commitment

One of the best sources of understanding the depth and meaning of something is the language used in rituals from the past. Ritual language emerges from the experience of the participants. Its meaning, although not timeless in its particular form of expression, is the product of experiences, and reflection on those experiences, over generations of time. Some very interesting phrases appear in the oldest wedding ceremonies in the English language. A look at just one of these will offer us some valuable insights.

Early in the ceremony, the celebrant instructs the couple being married to remember that "no other human ties are more *tender,* no vows more *sacred,* than these which you are about to assume." These two words, tender and sacred, reveal something to us about the nature of the relationship.

The ties are "tender" in at least two respects. There are deep feelings involved: tenderness, caring, affection and preciousness. There is a softness about these feelings, and the word "tender" describes it well. There is another sense in which the word is descriptive: this tie is especially *vulnerable*. It is easily bruised, even easily broken. It needs to be guarded and protected. That protection can come from each of the parties, and it may be aided by the larger body of those who care about the two. This tie is tender, and there is a great power in the *shared vulnerability* when it is thus recognized. The ceremony's vows are, in part, a recognition of that tenderness and a commitment to both maintain and protect it. The presence of the witnesses, family, church, etc., is also a vow to recognize and aid in protecting the tenderness of the relationship.

The vows are "sacred." Even if the vows are made outside any religious connotation (to which the word "sacred" is most often tied in our understanding), the very fact of making vows to one another, of making and keeping promises, recognizes that there is something that *transcends* the two persons individually. That which transcends may be the relationship itself, or it may be something which is beyond the relationship. Many will call it God. Some will speak of it in other terms, perhaps in a quite amorphous fashion. There is, nonetheless, a sense of the transcendent in their coming together, a feeling of something beyond themselves which is at the center of their tie to each other.

Law has an important role in the experience of making tender promises which recognize a transcendent dimension. Dillon states it well:

> The marriage ceremony sanctions the vows in the double sense of making them lawful and bringing them under law. The will of the individual is transformed by church and state into a moral and legal responsibility— with the primary intent of insuring the permanence of the relationship. Whatever their personal motives may be, individuals who choose to marry are asking the civil and religious community to acknowledge and enforce their promises, their future responsibility to abide by their present intent. In this act, they surrender some of their autonomy.[14]

Two persons who desire to make their bond a permanent one receive the assistance of others in making their desires and intention "lawful"—that is, the structure within which they agree to shape future decisions and actions. They also act to enter into that larger community of sisters and brothers who have made similar decisions and commitments before them, and to take their experiences and wisdom seriously—coming "under law."

We've used the term "commitment" a number of times. In Chapter 8, we give attention to commitment along with trust and intimacy, all of which are essential to the marriage relationship. In *The Committed Marriage,* Elizabeth Achtemeier identifies some important aspects of commitment for marriage.[15] Writing as a Biblical scholar and strong interpreter of the Christian faith, Achtemeier lists her understandings of commitment that are essential to "Christian marriage." It seems to me that her perspectives apply to *any* marriage that is, indeed, a *loving* relationship, and that what makes these items of commitment "Christian," or anything else, is the set of faith resources one brings to interpret and support the understandings.

First, "total commitment" is required. This is an *unreserved dedication of one's whole self to the relationship*. One's faith perspectives become important here, because there will certainly be a connection between one's world view, or life values, and one's willingness or ability to dedicate the self, without reservation, to anything! The second of Achtemeier's points is "accepting commitment," something which is repeated in many ways in our treatment of loving relationships. This, she says, involves *learning to love and value the other for the imperfect person he or she is*. Her third point is crucial and, again, is basic to our entire discussion: an accepting commitment is an act of "grace." Love is a gift, is given freely, and must be received as that kind of gift. We *cannot earn or deserve the other's love* when it is given as an act of grace. As a partner in one of our case studies (chapter 1) put it, "Respect, as I experience it from him, is something I can't give to myself." Closely related to this gift is the freedom which flows from such commitment:

> It is the mystery of love in marriage that commitment leads to freedom— freedom to move out from a sure base of security and acceptance, freedom to plumb all my creativity, freedom to be my authentic self much more than if I did not have such security . . . When we commit ourselves, when we lose ourselves in a total and accepting dedication to the other, then we most surely find our freedom to be ourselves, then we most fully discover that we can live and love.[16]

Such commitment is, as others have pointed out about erotic love in its best sense, an *exclusive* commitment to the other. The exclusivity is not only sexual; relating from center to center requires devotion to the primariness of the other, while at the same time experiencing contact, through that primary and exclusive relationship, with all that one values. Achtemeier takes note of an observation which I also consider to be significant in Carl Rogers' study of communal experiments with group relationships. He found an "underestimation of the need of each person for a reasonably secure, continuing one-to-one relationship. This need seems to run very deep and may be considered too lightly."[17] This commitment is, additionally, a *continuing* one, never made once and for all, but always in the process of re-formation as life takes shape. It is, therefore, a *changing* commitment, maturing and deepening with the unfolding of life experience.

It should be obvious by now that the kind of commitment being described by Achtemeier—one which has total dedication, is accepting, is healthily exclusive, is continuing and open to change—requires *maturity.*

> Those who are not whole persons in their own right, who are still dependent for their security and satisfactions on their parents, or who are seeking only the gratification of their own psychological or sexual needs, or who are looking for someone to take care of them emotionally and physically, obviously cannot even initially commit themselves to the self-expenditure of work and caring which Christian marriage requires. Those who desire to rule over or manipulate another person in order to bolster their own self-esteem or to foster their own sense of power and worth cannot commit themselves to the self-sacrifice and sharing that Christian marriage demands . . . There must be a basic health of personality before marriage is even contemplated.[18]

Such maturity allows for growth in the relationship as the inevitable change and modifications develop throughout life. She recommends an *anticipating* commitment, one which expects surprises and new experiences. Achtemeier's words are: "a commitment which anticipates that God has much yet to do with us." Finally, as we have recognized before in this exploration of relationships that are loving, this kind of marriage commitment bears a risk—the *risk of total vulnerability.*

All this points to marriage as an especially *committed* relationship. In a day when it is popular to speak of "having a relationship," often modified and expanded by the adjective "meaningful," we also find that many of us are increasingly approaching the possibility of marriage with caution and anxiety. We want it to be something of high quality, and we want it to last. Over a decade ago, Carl Rogers commented on the higher expectations which seem to be emerging for marriage, and their meaning in the future for permanence:

> It is becoming increasingly clear that a . . . relationship will have *permanence* only to the degree to which it satisfies the emotional, psychological, intellectual and physical needs of the partners. This means that the *permanent* marriage of the future will be even better than marriage in the present, because the ideals and goals for that marriage will be of a higher order. The partners will be demanding more of the relationship than they do today.[19]

What Rogers foresees is a very demanding relationship. It is certainly the kind of bonding with another that is desired by many persons. New ways of structuring marriages, with open, clear, reshaped expectations of roles will probably be necessary.

Love and marriage . . . do they "go together like a horse and carriage?" If so, the "carriage" may need some redesigning in order to permit the "horse" the maximum freedom of movement and direction, and to minimize the bumpy rides while rolling on to new and deeper adventures. Carriage designers—and redesigners—need a better understanding of the basic structures before they can proceed with their work in a successful fashion. And the "horses" will need better training to attain the discipline required for the most satisfactory functioning while hitched to the "carriage," as well as seeing the unlimited opportunities lying ahead on the unfenced roads.

Marriage for Straights Only?

Our discussion of marriage as a loving relationship has concentrated, primarily, on a mature level of commitment made by two adults to each other for their mutual growth and fulfillment. The aspects of commitment identified above by Achtemeier basically assume a relationship of two caring adults. Is it absolutely essential that these two persons be of opposite sex?

It is time—perhaps past time—to open up the discussion of marriage between persons who are homosexual. This is a book on loving relationships, and the chapter on "Sex and Sexuality" gives some attention to relationships with the same sex. Obviously, we are approaching a matter which easily generates a great deal of emotion and irrationality. This is a complex issue, requiring much attention and careful thought—more than can be done in a few pages. It is, however, important to pose the question: can marriage be a live option for gay or lesbian persons who are committed to each other?

For a beginning, it is probably well to review the values which appear to be primary in regard to marriage and family in our day. The marriage state offers:

1. A safe, recognized "place" for procreation, for nurture and protection of children;
2. A public affirmation of a fully committed relationship with another adult;
3. A symbol to self and others of an important commitment, a statement about self;
4. An ongoing experience of caring, loyalty, and fidelity within a framework of shared vulnerability;
5. A context of developing and experiencing intimacy—emotional, sexual, psychological—through dialogue;
6. Support and protection of the larger community;
7. A secure base from which one functions with others;

8. Opportunities for companionship, planning for the future, participating in the unfolding "future" with a trusted ally;
9. Time for growth, personal and together;
10. A "place" where love for self, others, and the transcendent can be nurtured, shaped, practiced, and extended.

The placement of number 1 on the list is intentional. Over long periods of time, and in most cultures, it has been a top priority in marriage. It is also a reason often given why marriages between persons who are homosexual are "impossible" or "shouldn't be allowed." There are two rather obvious problems with such a response. First, there is no requirement that couples who are *heterosexual* have children. Admittedly, there have been times in human history when such was absolutely expected, and, even in this century, it has been an operating norm. In some cultures, marriage is entered into only when persons have experimented with sex rather freely in their adolescence and are ready to have children. In such instances, marriage is strictly tied to reproduction. In Western culture, an increasing number of persons are deciding *not* to have children; others are deciding to have children, but not marriage. Clearly, the relation between marriage and having children is not a 1:1 equation.

Furthermore, when we look at the rest of the items on the list, we are aware that vast numbers of persons value the marriage relationship as a form in which to experience some very special opportunities of human life, apart from having children. In our society, a primary human symbol for a committed relationship, with permanent intentions and promise for mutual fulfillment, is marriage. The human commitment so symbolized *does not per se* require that the parties be of the opposite sex. In fact, when it comes to the kind of commitment made to each other, and through each other to the larger society, implied in the list above, (except for the first item) the biological sex of the individual partners is irrelevant. These observations are summed up by Daniel Maguire:

> Marriage is the highest form of interpersonal commitment and friendship achievable between sexually attracted persons. Nothing in that definition requires that the sexually attracted persons who are conjoined in committed, conjugal friendship must be heterosexual. Neither is the capacity for having children required. Reproductive fertility is not of the essence of genuine marriage.[20]

A second reason why marriage/family as a locus for nurture of children does not necessarily prohibit marriages between persons who are gay or lesbian can be seen when we examine the reality of family life in our society: it is extremely mixed, with many "single" parents, with "blended" families (two persons, each having children from a previous marriage, marrying and blending their families together), and with a constant need for adults who will adopt parentless children. This discussion cannot satisfy anyone who wishes to argue that persons who are homosexual are constitutionally (by their nature) bad parents and inevitably harmful to the "normal" development of children. There is too much evidence to the contrary for a rational inquirer into this matter to accept that argument. The fact is that many who are homosexual, for a variety of reasons, become parents. If they are married to their parent partner, the marriage may or may not continue. As is the case with married persons who are primarily heterosexual, whether or not they remain married to each other does not necessarily determine the loving effectiveness of their parental relationships. Single-parent or blended family arrangements continue to provide opportunities for constructive and healthy parent-child relationships, and there is no inherent reason why this is not true for persons who are gay or lesbian, as well as those who are straight. The conduct of adult sex life with children in the household is a sensitive matter requiring mature, sensible responsibility by those adults, whatever their sexual orientation. Adults who are caring, sensitive, and affectionate with their partners, as well as with others, are positive role models for children. It should also be clear that *some* who are homosexual, like *some* who are heterosexual, make good adoptive parents.

A society that is dominantly homophobic, as is ours, faces many problems in dealing with this issue. Our culture as a whole is being confronted with the necessity to take seriously the civil rights of all citizens, to be more open to the great varieties of sexual makeup of individuals, and to combat the harmful effects of socializing children into rigid sex roles. How we respond to this ferment will be very important for the health of our society as well as the health of individuals. The historic religious teachings of Christianity and Judaism often confuse our attempts to think through what is really important. Major religious bodies today are, in fact, involved in careful re-examination of their interpretations of scripture and tradition that have led to contemporary understandings and attitudes toward homosexuality. A good example is illustrated in Maguire's analysis of Roman Catholic thinking:

> The Second Vatican Council produced a major statement on the dignity and value of married life. The council Fathers were, of course, speaking of marriage between heterosexual persons. In fact, however, aside from the "good of offspring," which they stress is not essential for a genuine marriage, the goods and value they attach to marriage are not exclusively heterosexual in kind. The needs that marriage fulfills are human needs.

The values that marriage enhances are integral to humanity as such and not to humanity as heterosexual. In fact, the *indispensable* goods of marriage are those that do not relate intrinsically to heterosexuality. The *dispensable* good—offspring—is the only good that does relate to heterosexuality.[21]

For the purpose of our discussion of marriage as a loving relationship, the important point is to be aware of what marriage represents in our society, its value institutions, and to the individuals who live in it. To the extent that it is primarily a symbol of a committed relationship of persons who love each other and wish to have both the community recognition and support for that relationship; and to the extent that it is understood as a context within which two caring adults may deepen their caring and through it reach out to others; it is destructive for a society to prohibit persons from having that experience on grounds that are irrelevant. If, however, marriage is only marriage when it is the locus of procreation—for breeding, nurturing, and socializing children for the society—we have some major reversals to work out in the trends of the last century toward the dominance of the love relationship of two adults. If, in fact, it is to be some blending of these two functions, we are dealing with something much more complex than our traditional views allow, and we shall not long be able to continue to ignore—even deny—the ambiguities in our perceptions and attitudes.[22] In the meantime, our struggle for understanding will require that we hear each other's perceptions, fears, insights, and affirmations with care and respect.

Procreation and Family

I approach the topic of family relationships as loving relationships with some caution. Our understanding of the family as the fundamental, central unit of society—and as the basic structure for formation of human contacts—has produced centuries of wisdom, customs, and rituals before which any interpreter (or *re*interpreter) must stand in awe. I have not set aside a chapter on parent-child, child-parent, or sibling relationships as a context of loving relationships, but have, instead, chosen to relate material throughout the book to such relationships. Nonetheless, a few comments at this point are decidedly in order.

Our family relationships are, to a certain extent, "given," rather than "chosen." Many parental partners have, of course, chosen to be married to each other. Few, however, could know enough of how the other would be as "mother" or "father," or *co-parent*, to have consciously chosen *that* relationship. Many parent partners choose to conceive a child, but we exercise little choice of many significant results of that conception—the child's sex, appearance, degree of "normalcy," behavior, or response to the environment we try to create for it. Needless to say, the very conception of many children is not, in fact, chosen at the time. Children certainly do not choose their parents, nor, if they have any, their siblings. Many of us will admit to being happy that we ended up with the particular brothers or sisters bequeathed upon us by life, just as others sometimes insist that if they could have chosen, they certainly would have made other choices! To a considerable degree, our family ties are *given*.

Love affirms that what is given is a *gift*.

We have greater opportunity now than at any other time in history to choose to procreate. With care and intentionality we can avoid conception. With amazing assistance from medicine and technology, we can often conceive even though it earlier appeared that we could not. We can choose to terminate what we have conceived. We *do* exercise many choices. Yet—our procreation is in many of its most important aspects beyond our choosing and control. It is a gift.

We choose to reorganize our families. Some of us do not choose to marry or live with our parental partner. Many of us are choosing to no longer live with, or remain married to, our parental partners. Children have little choice over their parents' decisions. Remarriage partners are normally aware when their new commitment includes children already on the scene; yet, we are finding that distressingly few step-parents could adequately predict and prepare for how they feel toward and relate to their step-children, let alone to their marriage—but not parental—partner. Some of us experience great joy and satisfaction in the adoption of children. A common form of reassurance to an adopted child has been its parents' affirmation that "you are very special because we *chose* you." That, of course, is a beautiful, basically true assertion—yet adoptive parents have no more predictability over the future of their adopted child than they would their "own," and exercise none of the genetic contribution. Very little real choice is exercised in such family relationships. They are gifts.

How do we receive such gifts? What do we do with them? Although the family tie is a special human context, members of the family are, before all else, distinctive, unique, individual human beings. Whatever "loving" means, it means no more and no less in this context, *although the special, obvious commitments we make in the family relationship* give us the opportunity to experience, express and practice that loving in crucial ways. There is no question that I *feel* something unique in holding my new-born, or five-year-old, or twenty-five year old, child— that I do not feel the same way with others. At the same time, that experience makes me sensitive to other children in ways that I would not have otherwise experienced. It is a gift to be shared.

Likewise, whatever family structure we find ourselves in, we learn in special ways what loving does—and often, does not—mean. *Living with* another or others is a constant opportunity and testing-ground for loving relationships. It is a gift that can be placed on a shelf, never opening it up to find out what is there. It can be opened and discarded because it doesn't appear to be what we thought we wanted. It can be allowed to be what it is, with gratitude for its presence and nurture given to its potentials. Whatever be the form of living together that we "choose"—and re-choose—its gifts are essential to our own life and growth, and to that of others.

Shared Experiences and Insights

Looking back, I feel that my marriage was overwhelmed by the basic condition for neurotic love, according to Fromm, that '. . . lies in the fact that one or both of the lovers have remained attached to the figure of a parent . . .' This was reinforced by the family systems of our individual families of origin and our extreme proximity to both in business and social life. My family system played tapes that said the family deals with everything. You do not discuss problems with anyone outside of that circle. Yet the judgmental attitude embodied within that system made it the last place you would want to discuss problems. Hence, my mother's amazement at our impending divorce. 'Why had I not said anything?' And her proposed solution to curing the problem was to sit us both down with all the family and get us 'straightened out.' In the name of love and duty, both families struggle to retain their children through a dependence upon the family.

I have been married more than twenty-four years. I have been reflecting on the roles, attitudes, values and expectations of marriage at the time I married.

It was fairly simple. The husband was to get up each morning, put on his Superman suit and go to work. He was to conquer all challenges there. He was to provide what his family needed and wanted. He was to keep the Superman suit on all the time. He took it off, of course, just before he went to bed and felt he wasn't very super in bed regardless of how he was performing in the rest of his life. He may have thought it important to act as if he were super but he was probably not sure of it.

The wife was to get up each morning and put on her Wonderwoman suit. (Notice, Superman is made of steel and bullets bounce off him naturally, but Wonderwoman has to be agile enough to deflect the bullets with the bracelets.) Her domain was the house and children. Women did not work outside the home unless they needed to for economic survival and if she did she was to be a secretary, teacher, or nurse. Wonderwoman was expected to do wonders with the resources given her and to make sacrifices on behalf of Superman's work (help him get through college, entertain the boss and out-of-town guests, etc.) She was to be passive-dependent-aggressive-caring, etc., which is how she got her name of Wonderwoman. Of course, she took off her costume before she got into bed, too. She was not very sure how wonderful she was then, either.

Superman and Wonderwoman had many expectations surrounding them and they bought into most of them. One of the unfortunate things for both of them is they wanted role identification before they wanted identity (to paraphrase Marshall McLuhan). So he was whatever his role was and she was whatever her role was. It probably did not occur to either of them for a long time that they could have "identities as persons."

One of the expectations for marriage was that each loved the other. The only time this expectation could be sidestepped was if ". . . the girl got pregnant . . ." then marriage was expected regardless of love. Wonderwoman had been taught that love and sex go together. Superman hadn't been taught it quite that way so there was always some confusion as to what love was really about. But they did hope it meant they could talk with each other (communicate), like each other (spend time together), make love together beautifully, and be happy. Sex was, we were told, to be practiced only within the confines of the husband/wife relationship and even then you are to be somewhat fearful because of possible pregnancy. There were no birth control pills. Abortions were not available. Sexual expressions between husband and wife were regulated by law and adultery was the only sure grounds for divorce. But love and sex were to go together. And you were to love one another. That was expected.

Another expectation was that the couple would be strong. That is why they were given the names they carried. They were to be invincible. They soon settled on appearing invincible. They understood they were not to need help and certainly not to ask for help if they needed it. They were to take care of their needs themselves . . .

There was to be sacrifice. That was expected. And both did make sacrifices. But the woman was expected to make a few more for the sake of the marriage. Wonderwoman may not have finished college but worked so Superman could. Superman may have quit college before receiving his degree so he could take care of Wonderwoman . . .

Superman and Wonderwoman were expected to have children. And the children were expected to be "super" and "wonderful." If they could not have children they were expected to make every effort to have them. Infertility was a matter of grief. If a couple chose to not have children that was a matter of scorn. Everyone was expected to have children. But you were expected, also, to not have too many children . . .

You were expected to be successful. Superman was expected to be "upwardly mobile" in his job/salary. Wonderwoman had the same expectations but they were more acceptably expressed socially. If you could not be successful, the expectations would settle for "industrious," but successful was better.

One morning Superman and Wonderwoman got out of bed and one of them didn't put on the costume. It doesn't matter which one. Superman had not really been impervious to all the bullets shot his way . . . some had penetrated a little. Wonderwoman had not been able to move her wrist bracelets quickly enough every time either. They were both wounded. But only one of them (the one that did not put on the suit) knew that.

Expectations began to change and the one still wearing the suit had difficulty understanding the one not wearing the suit. The terms of the marriage contract were changing and negotiations were necessary. "He must be sick," she thought of Superman. "She doesn't understand me," he thought of Wonderwoman.

I still want a relationship based on sharing, both triumphs and agonies of defeat. I would expect a mutual nurturance that would promote the growth of both partners. I look for a mutual respect that would allow personal differences to complement rather than conflict with each other. I would seek a knowledge of each other that would promote individual understanding of each member's strengths and weaknesses. I would want some humor present. Not the kind that occurs at the expense of the other, but a humor that can help each to better tolerate their humanness. I expect to share some interests with my partner, but also realize that both have individual interests and needs that may best be shared with other friends. I would also seek an open awareness of our sexual needs and differences, that they might be expressed without fear. Most of all, I would continue to search out the ability to admit problems and work together to resolve them through dialogue and discussion.

5

Loving In and Through Community

"Community" can be a confusing word. A trip to a dictionary reveals that the first definitions focus on geographical locations. Persons talking about "community" at church or temple seem to be speaking of a feeling, an atmosphere. Newspaper or magazine articles, as well as television reports and interviews, frequently refer to such terms as "the intelligence community," "the Black community," or "the NATO community." Those of us who work in colleges and universities speak confidently of "the academic community." When you or I allude to "my community," we are, most likely, referring to the town, or portion of a city, in which we live, and the boundaries are somewhat vague.

Likewise, the meaning is anything but immediately apparent when I suggest that we consider the community as a context of loving relationships. Our task at this point is to look beyond strictly one-on-one relationships or family ties. We are thinking now about ways in which human beings relate to each other outside these more intimate contexts. It is not easy to look seriously at social structures and systems. The loving person, however, must be concerned with what goes on between persons in those structures and systems, as well as what systems do to enhance or inhibit the life and growth of persons. We are "social" beings. Community is not something we can choose to do without. How will it be "loving?"

Social Structures and Systems

My use of the terms, "social structures or systems," takes into account that we human beings use a variety of ways to organize our lives to meet our manifold needs. We sometimes meet our needs by consciously organizing a method for doing something we want done. We value mass education as basic to a democracy, and we thus create public schools. To support and operate them, we create Boards of Education, tax systems, teacher certification processes, and so on. Sometimes we appear simply to allow a system of doing things to take shape, without consciously directing its development, such as the complex "system" (or "nonsystem," as some have called it) of delivering health care in the United States.

We have police departments for our protection and security, and a city council to establish city-wide regulations and policies governing police and many other services. We have a Chamber of Commerce to promote business interests and a Better Business Bureau to watchdog those who would promote their own interests unfairly or illegally. We have an Urban League and National Association for the Advancement of Colored People, voluntary organizations through which persons may work to improve opportunities for minority persons. We have commissions on civil rights at various levels of government to guarantee rights and opportunities through conciliation and legal means. We elect representatives to legislative bodies for the establishment of laws, and we pay lobbyists to promote special interests with those bodies. A small amount from federal taxes goes to support the United Nations and its many agencies doing cultural, social, educational, health, development, and economic work throughout the world. We voluntarily assist in providing resources to human interests and need through "Bread for the World," "Amnesty International," International Red Cross, International Olympic Committee, religious organizations for relief and development, and literally thousands of other such organizations.

The list is endless. With billions of human beings inhabiting the earth, there seem to be limitless ways to organize efforts to meet needs, interests, and desires and to achieve goals. Those structures or organizations *may contribute to* our active caring for each other. Conversely, they *may inhibit* our active caring. The important question, then, is whether the social structures and systems aid us, or get in our way, as we try to live out our attempts to be "loving" persons.

Loving persons know that they are not only tied to those in their immediate household, their friends, and their romantic partners. Søren Kierkegaard put it in the language of "neighbor": "If there are only two men, the other man is the neighbor; if there are millions, each one of these is the neighbor . . ."[1] The "neighbor" resides in our neighborhood . . . or, in the farthest reaches of the planet. (Actually, we are increasingly aware that the neighbor includes other planets as well. As Sam Keen puts it, the fully matured lover is a cosmic lover.)

But, wait a minute, you say. How can I love everyone everywhere? Aren't there practical limits to my knowing others, and feeling for another? Of course there are. The community context of caring, however, rests on at least three important assumptions. First, loving and liking are not necessarily the same. We don't always *like* the ones we love. *Caring* about what happens to another human being doesn't require *liking* that person as a *personality.* This leads to the second point, closely related to the first: caring for or about others does not require *shared* affection. Not only do I not have to like those I love, there is no necessary reciprocity in our relationship that requires our "feeling good" about each other. In some portions of the Christian scriptures, as well as the texts of the Hellenistic Jews, the word "mercy" is often used rather than "love," in reference to the desired relations with one's "neighbor." This suggests a recognition that an important form of loving is to "show mercy."[2] Furthermore, a third assumption asserts that our active concern for another or others does not require that we "know" that person. I may never meet you, but my involvement in our shared community may well include my being sure that there are adequate schools for your children whether I have school-age children or not. Even though I normally take safe drinking water for granted in my locale, I'll want to be sure that it becomes available to you if you don't have it, whether we ever see each other or not. I am concerned that you have clean air to breathe, although you may be reading this long after my own body no longer needs air to breathe.

My government may tell me that you are my enemy. Our doctor may tell me that you are emotionally unstable and dangerous. My culture may tell me that your culture is radically different from mine and that we can't possibly share values. My socialization may tell me that your sexuality is perverse and my "way of life" is threatened by your preferences and behavior. Your language may be very different from mine and I may conclude that we can never really talk with each other. Yet, I may choose to love you. I may decide to include you in my community of love.

Community is a context of active loving relationships to the extent that we actively provide others the opportunity to grow, to learn, to experience productivity as persons, to be in environments where love can be given and received. Our active loving will also include eliminating barriers to such opportunities as they exist in our various organizations and systems.

It can be very difficult to "get at" the problems of active loving within complex social structures. This is illustrated by George Webber, one of the organizers of the East Harlem Protestant Parish in New York:

> Don Benedict, the first full-time clergyman of the East Harlem Protestant Parish, was standing on the corner of 104th Street and Second Avenue in East Harlem one afternoon when a coal truck raced through a red light and in the process knocked an old man down in the gutter. The instinctive response was to pick the man up and rush him to the hospital, but the requirements of our society demand that an ambulance be called and that one express his instinctive desire to be a Good Samaritan by calling for help and making the man comfortable until the government provides the means of conveyance to proper medical care. Don did this and then sat by the man for an hour and thirty-seven minutes awaiting the arrival of the city ambulance. In thinking about the episode afterwards, we recognized how the obvious desire to be a good Samaritan in our society has been made so much more complicated. The only way to get better ambulance service is to put pressure on the local political boss and ultimately on city hall. But you have no pressure to exert unless you and those who feel as you do have been actively engaged in the political enterprise.[3]

Some of our oldest and most consistent religious and secular values assert that deeds of love are deeds of service to the neighbor. Within that assertion is also the understanding that the doer is *in* the deed, the lover is present in the action. The loving person identifies both with the action taken and with the person who is served by the action. Thus, the relationship is established, or deepened (again, whether the persons "know each other" or not). *Taking* such loving action, and identifying with the recipient of the action in some meaningful way, seems increasingly complicated, if not impossible, in our world. It is tempting to despair, to lose hope that one's loving actually reaches beyond a very close range.

In the day's mail, I receive an appeal from Amnesty International. I may write a check for a few dollars and return it in the envelope which they have enclosed. In reading their letter, I've been "touched" by their documentation of fellow human beings who are being tortured and whose families suffer intensely because these persons had the audacity to disagree in some way with their governments. The dollars sent in the mail help the organization do its work—they have, however, expanded my loving in a relatively small way. Next, however, AI writes and asks me to be a part of a group that writes letters to a particular government, protesting their abusive treatment of a particular individual. Furthermore, they ask me to write that person and her or his family members to assure them that others know of their plight, are standing with them, and are trying to get something done about it. By now, I am more identified with my actions, with the object of my deeds, and the process of loving is more real. There is a political, social, cultural system at work of which I am not directly a part and which, it seems, I cannot influence. Upon accepting the reality that it *is* a part of my community, however, I can begin to participate in activity designed to counteract a system that *inhibits* the life, growth, and productivity of fellow human beings. I have chosen to involve myself in a complicated, but very real, loving relationship. Like many relationships, it may bring pain and frustration, when I learn that our efforts have not succeeded, and the person has been executed, or has succumbed to torture and disease in the prison. Or, the relationship may bring elation and joy when word comes that the regime has relented and allowed the prisoner to return to family and friends. To further confuse things, I have begun to sense (and the persons on the scene often remind us) that the torturers, the jailers, the military and political leaders, are not "animals," but are, in one way and another, human beings like me. They, too, are a part of my community, and I am driven to try to understand how love can also reach to them.

Closer to home, in some ways, is a demonstration of a way in which "loving" has been mobilized in the town in which I live. I don't recall hearing anyone describe this situation as a process of loving—but it is. A number of years ago, several concerned citizens were aroused by the fact that women who were raped in our town faced serious problems in receiving help. If they reported it to the police, they faced the probability of being treated with anything but sensitivity by those whose job it was to enforce the law. It was not unusual for them to face accusing comments and questions about how they got into such a predicament. If they reported to the emergency room at the local hospital for medical treatment, they might be treated with scorn and insensitivity by personnel there. As they continued to suffer the agony of their experience, they had no idea to whom to turn for some kind of emotional support.

In order to help correct this situation, a local group organized the Rape Victim Support Service, as has happened in many locales. They provided training for law enforcement and health care personnel, helping them to be better sensitized to the trauma of the rape victim. They sponsored an educational program in the community to gain more interest in and support for improving the safety of women out at night. They encouraged better lighting in problem areas, emergency telephone installation, and carried on a whistle selling campaign (especially among university students) to provide more self-protection and to publicize the problem. Things are clearly different now. A rape victim can expect, more often than not, to be treated with sympathy and understanding by police and medical personnel. A support service is available for dealing with the continuing emotional injury. A new community-wide awareness of the issue has changed the climate. It has *not* eliminated the commission of rapes. It *has* markedly improved some of the conditions for those who are victims of such violence. This is very real loving action in the community context. Such activity alone does not get at the roots of violence in the society and in individuals which result in rape—the horrendous violation of one person by another, the abusive attack on and wounding of spirit in another human being. The community has not yet been sufficiently self-critical of the many ways it supports views of women as the property of men, or "asking for" violent treatment. A "loving" community will definitely support victims; it will also devote its energies to reducing the incidences of need for such support.

Barriers to Community

We have seen that it is difficult to perceive "community" as a context of loving relationships, and it is complicated to find ways to be loving in and through community. Why is this the case? Is it just because "those people out there" are never going to change, as many of my students assert when I pose this problem to them? (The inference always seems to be that *we* are willing to be and do what is needed, but it is those *other* folks who will always keep it from happening!) Several answers have been given to this very old question over the centuries. Contemporary answers are usually not new—they are simply framed in current language. One insight which I find quite helpful is that of Erich Fromm. As an insider in our economic-social-political system, Fromm points out that the "principle underlying capitalistic society and the principle underlying love are incompatible."[4] He is here reminding us that the underlying principle of capitalism is competition, with value centered in marketability. A thing, or even a person, has value based on what it, he, or she can claim in the marketplace. The underlying principle of love is cooperation, with value centered in the essence of the person. When we enter a "competitive world," we are prepared to "eliminate the competition." Don't be a "bleeding heart"; if those persons can't "make it" out there in the "real world," they don't deserve to succeed, and they'll have to move over to make room for those who have better resources to compete. It's tough, and sometimes people get hurt, but that's just the *way it is*. Oh—and the best way to prepare for this real world is through the competition of athletics. Do everything you can to win, but also learn to lose like a "real man!" (Is that line being modified now that we have girls playing in the Little

Leagues?) And what is the language of competition? The weekend sports page headlines tell it: "a *crushes* b"; "d *clobbers* f"; "x *gangs up* on y." When we go to the game, we are implored by cheerleaders to chant, "hit 'em again, hit 'em again, harder, *harder!*" All about us, people are leaping around, especially in front of television cameras, proclaiming, "We're Number One!" No one is happily shouting, "We're number Two," or "We're Number Twelve."

When so much of life's meaning is wrapped up in being "number one," it can be disconcerting to learn that the United States, in spite of our constant self-assurances, is *not* Number One—in such things as certain health statistics ("but we do have the best system in the world!"), in quality automobile production ("but they have cheaper labor!"), in Olympic Gold Medals ("but they have full-time athletes!") or in adult literacy ("but our people have more freedom!"). We might be able to afford a few of those slippages, but we cannot afford to be anything but Number One in "national security," in the production and ownership of instruments of multiple overkill! ("Hit 'em again, harder, harder!")

If competition is found to be deeply pervasive in our society, so is the value of marketability. How much does your work, or status, claim in the marketplace? Recent surveys of public opinion regarding status related to vocations is instructive. Although Supreme Court Justices rank higher in the list than do corporation presidents who have incomes considerably higher than the Justices, one will have to look very far down on the list to find the library clerks, typists, or assembly line workers on whom they are so dependent for their "success." Market value is displayed in other ways: those who "legitimately" cannot work, according to the Ronald Reagan worldview, are "deserving" of some small assistance from the rest of us. Those who for one reason or another have chosen not to work, or can't find jobs, simply have no real value. The persons whose value is especially distorted are those who are "able" to work, and do, but only find work which pays less than enough for a dignified existence for themselves and their dependents. They meet the basic requirement of the system—they *work*—but their productivity in the marketplace is not sufficient for humanness according to the measurements of the larger society. They have no voice, no influence. Through some strength of background and support of persons meaningful to them, they may maintain sufficient personal pride to sustain a useful life. The larger system, however, is not helping them to do that.

We are not devoid of *cooperation* in our experience. Just as we learn to compete in school and athletic experiences, we learn some element of "teamwork" which requires cooperation. In many instances, that is shortcircuited by the competitive goal, but the experience of cooperation is nonetheless meaningful and instructive for many. In a cooperative situation, the goal is to achieve something that is of benefit to all—and each—of the participants. Ways are found for each member to contribute within her/his capabilities, and to "profit" from the experience in ways that are relevant to that person's situation and needs. Many of the voluntary group associations to which most of us belong are actually based on and encourage cooperation. In these settings, the value of persons is related to what they are able to contribute to the goal for which they are cooperating. "Market price" is not the basis of value; at the same time, productivity in terms of the group goal may still be an active measure. *Relationships based on love, although they encourage productivity, nonetheless value the person primarily as one who is a unique human being, regardless of the quality of the contribution perceived to be gained from the person.*

It must be said that the economic system in the United States is, in fact, "mixed." Although we are capitalists in name, we have intentionally modified our capitalism in many ways, and these ways take into account the value of cooperation as well as concern for individuals which the system, in its "pure" form, cannot be expected to worry about. Further, we also need to be aware that Fromm's observation is meant to recognize the *complexity* of loving within economic and political systems. His analysis does not claim that loving is impossible within capitalism. It is helpful, however, to be aware that the basic principles of an unmodified capitalist philosophy are incompatible with those of other-centered love. This insight helps us to understand the dilemma which is often experienced and articulated as we consider what it means to turn our community experience into a context of loving relationships.

All economic and social systems have some elements that run counter to love. This is recognized in biblical warnings about "this world"; the advice of St. Paul to be "in but not of this world" is but one such recognition. In various of his writings, Fromm has emphasized ways in which persons can resist the power of the systems in which they live, in order to function more in tune with the power of love. We are, I take it, urged to find the ways to live *in* a competitive, market-oriented, person-reducing society, but acting as members of a community of love. Fromm is convinced that individual human beings have a "social, loving nature"; he is concerned, with us, that this nature not become separated from our "social existence," but rather become united with it. He is also certain that the translation of our social, loving nature into the larger social realm necessitates "important and radical changes in our social structure."

Social and Structural Change

Changes in structures are also envisioned by the 1980 recipient of the Nobel Peace Prize, Adolfo Perez Esquivel. Perez Esquivel is a Roman Catholic educator from Argentina, devoted to nonviolent change in Latin America. His acceptance speech for the award included affirmations of hope for a new order:

> When we look at the world our people live in, we see what is an affront to God. For millions of children, young people, adults, and elderly persons live under the sign and mark of underdevelopment.
>
> The institutionalized violence, the poverty and the oppression generate a dual reality—the result of the maintenance of political and economic systems that create injustice and sanctify a social order that benefits only a few . . .
>
> Despite so much suffering and pain, I live in hope because I feel Latin America has risen to its feet. Its liberation can be delayed but never dented.
>
> We live in hope because we believe, like St. Paul, that love never dies. Human beings in the historical process have created enclaves of love by their active practice of solidarity throughout the world, and with a view to the full-orbited liberation of peoples and all humanity.
>
> Because of our faith in Christ and humankind, we must apply our humble efforts to the construction of a more just and humane world. And I want to declare emphatically: *Such a world is possible.*
>
> To create this new society, we must present outstretched and friendly hands, without hatred and rancor, even as we show great determination and never waver in the defense of truth and justice. Because we know that we cannot sow seeds with clenched fists. To sow we must open our hands.[5]

Perez Esquivel's words, as well as his work for truth and justice are expressions of community forms of neighbor love. They also support Fromm's insight: love of another and love of all humanity are intertwined. This interaction is inescapable:

> Any true love for another person has a particular quality: for I love in that person not only the person but humanity itself, or as a Christian or Jewish believer would say: God. In the same way, if I love my country, this love is at the same time a love for man and mankind; and if it is not that, it is an attachment based on one's incapacity for independence and, in the last analysis, another manifestation of idolatry.[6]

The boundaries of our consideration are pushed out by this suggestion that unless our caring about our country is a reflection of our caring about what happens to persons throughout the world, it is a fixation on a lesser concern, or "idolatry." This, of course, is in tune with the biblical understanding that any concentration of dedication or commitment to a power lesser than the most ultimate power is, indeed, idolatry.

Nothing is subtracted from the quality of a particular other, or one's devotion to that other, by asserting that *in* the other one loves all that is. My love for you is not diminished, nor is it somehow expanded into meaninglessness, by my insistence that I am in touch with the rest of creation through you. Here is expressed a very old and valued human awareness—in you I love all, and, if I do not love all, my professed love for you is hollow. This apparent paradox is fundamental to the community context of love.

How is love known and felt for all of life, through the actual experience of bonding with another person, extended out to the community in a meaningful way? How does Perez Esquivel's "more just and humane world" come into reality? We humans have struggled with those questions for centuries. Throughout history, human beings have developed a faith, a vision, an expectation of a world order which encourages, supports and facilitates the life and growth of each of its members. As tempting as it may be to write off such visions as foolish dreams, it is especially clear to the modern mind that social systems and specific institutions are created and directed by human beings and are thus amenable to direction and control by human decisions. Contemporary technology is a demonstration of the enormous human capacity to construct and manage both ideas and things that are desired. The *social* norm for love is justice. Perez Esquivel appeals for "defense of truth and justice" because those are the ways in which loving is done in the larger community context. Movements for social change have, in this century, brought voting rights for persons otherwise disenfranchised; they have produced the end to child labor in industrial countries, as well as the replacement of "robber barons" by collective bargaining and consumer advocacy; they have started wars, modified wars, and ended wars; they have created a new direction for the relationship of women and men in society. Human social structures and institutions have been used to enhance life and growth; others have been restructured to remove barriers to life and growth. Loving does take place in community context, and much more can be learned about how it is done.

Communion of Consciousness

One of the most important ideas developed by Rollo May in his monumental *Love and Will* is that of the "communion of conscious-

ness." He points out that we can and do develop a consciousness of
another person or group in our contact with the world around us. We
can, in fact, direct our energies toward a willful growth in our awareness of another or others, including a sensitivity to feelings and needs.
Likewise, we can develop a consciousness *in* the other of our own
existence, feelings, and needs. This exchange process is a "communion" of consciousness. His example is James Baldwin's appeal for
black people and white people to, "like lovers, insist on, or create, the
consciousness of the others . . ."[7] Persons who grow in awareness of
others and create awareness of themselves in others, enter into a relationship in which they *affect* each other. "Affect," as May reminds us,
means both to influence and to have feeling. There is thus a "we-
relation" which some have said is the basis of community.[8] The communion of consciousness creates not only a sense of mutual awareness,
but also produces a new reality in which each party has an investment,
a commitment. The experience of community is an experience of procreation. Joining in community, in a communion of consciousness, is
an act of procreation. New creation not otherwise possible may now
emerge. The act of procreation may produce a child. It may result in a
piece of music, or a book. A social movement may emerge. Whatever
the product, the act always involves, as Keen recognized, more than a
single ego.[9]

No one has more eloquently and meaningfully stated the case for
viewing all levels of community as contexts for human loving than did
Martin Luther King Jr. Throughout his work, this winner of the Nobel
Peace Prize spoke of the goal of his efforts as being "the Beloved
Community." He was speaking of the bond between all human beings
that had existed since the beginning of time and is the basic reality of
all existence. All of life, he was convinced, is interrelated. The rich are
impoverished by the agony of the poor; we cannot avoid being "our
brother's keeper," because we are "our brother's brother," or sister. All
are affected indirectly by what happens to one person directly.

The basis of human community for King is agape love. This Greek
term, taken over into Christian biblical interpretation and theology,
refers to the love that human beings have for one another solely because
of the overpowering love in which they are held by God. King insisted
that such love is the reality operating in the universe. To the extent that
persons do *not* relate to each other in love, they are going *against* their
own basic nature and reality. Community is fractured and broken, not
because we can't achieve community, but because we refuse to act in
the ways that are basic to our being, preventing us from having what is
already there.

In his "I Have a Dream" speech, delivered at the Lincoln Memorial
in Washington, DC, King warned of a "rude awakening" if the nation

"returned to business as usual" after the message of the March on Washington. The nation attempted to return to business as usual, and there was, indeed, a rude awakening. King was not threatening violence. In the great tradition of the biblical prophets, he tried to tell the people what their behavior was leading to, what would inevitably happen unless they changed their ways. King remained, throughout his short span of leadership, totally committed to nonviolence. This commitment was based in part on his conviction that human community is restored only by working toward it in the same way in which that community lives . . . in love. To act otherwise is only to fracture and destroy community.

In his last book, King's concluding chapter is called "The World House." The world, he says, is a big house in which a large family has come into an inheritance of much wealth and resources. The only requirement for the family to continue living in the magnificent house they have inherited, and to benefit from the wealth and resources, is that they must find a way for all of them to live together in the house, in peace. Such a "house" (or community) will provide structures for growth, fulfillment of life, productivity, nurture, and protection for those who need it. The occupants of this "house" will find solutions to such major problems as poverty and racism. King spoke—and acted— as a person deeply immersed in Christian traditions. He was motivated by a basic recognition underlined by a New Testament scholar, Victor Furnish: "love is *only* authentic where it awakens the individual to the fact of his responsibilities within the whole complex web of interpersonal and interinstitutional relationships within which he is called to be obedient."[10] This led King to assert:

> The problems we now face must take us beyond slogans for their solution. In the final analysis, the right-wing slogans on "government control" and "creeping socialism" are as meaningless and adolescent as the Chinese Red Guard slogans against "bourgeois revisionism." An intelligent approach to the problems of poverty and racism will cause us to see that the words of the Psalmist—"The earth is the Lord's and the fullness thereof"—are still a judgment upon our use and abuse of the wealth and resources with which we have been endowed.[11]

In King's view, the gaining, or regaining, of human community requires a "revolution of values." This revolution will go beyond traditional capitalism *or* communism and discover the partial truths and weaknesses in both these systems. This revolution will "look uneasily on the glaring contrast of poverty and wealth."[12] It will say to the world order that war simply is not just and cannot be permitted to bring the destruction of humanity: "A nation that continues year after year to spend more money on military defense than on programs of social uplift is approaching spiritual death."[13] This revolution requires that loyalties become worldwide rather than sectional. Although an unconditional love for all persons is often misunderstood and misinterpreted, it must nonetheless be the basis for expanding concern for neighbor beyond tribe, class, race or nation; the survival of humankind makes this absolutely necessary.

Like Mahatma Gandhi, King was convinced that the re-creation of community could not be brought about with the use of violence. The very nature of what is being sought is both a goal and a process toward a goal. "Peace" is a way of being, not simply an absence of warfare. The millions of Americans who viewed the Oscar-winning film, "Gandhi," were moved by one man's determination to build community on the most positive elements within the human spirit, knowing that an appeal to anything else only destroys community. Sufficient numbers of Americans have likewise been moved by King's life—and tragic death—to encourage the United States Congress to declare King's birthday a national holiday. It is a strange irony that this nation experienced a unique combination of events within one week in 1983: the enshrinement of one totally committed to nonviolence as a national hero; "covert" military operations by US backed forces in Nicaragua and El Salvador; over 200 American Marines die in a truck-bombing of their headquarters in Beirut, Lebanon; President Reagan announces that American forces have invaded the tiny island of Grenada to "restore law and order, democracy," and protect US citizens perceived to be in some danger because of a recent coup.

Martin Luther King Jr., was concerned about our survival. Several years after his murder, others remain equally or even more concerned. King echoed a dream that has been shared by persons in all cultures throughout history that the entire human community will some day live together in love. Such love is not without friction and conflict, just as love between two persons is not without antagonism. This dream pictures a "world house" in which persons who don't know each other, or particularly like each other, nonetheless care about each other and know that their destinies are inextricably tied up with each other. Turning that dream into reality is love-in-community.

Love In Society—Idealism and Realism

Are King's dream, Gandhi's vision, and the longings that you and I feel for a world in which love is the norm, simply the daydreams of irrelevant idealists? Are such hopes and expectations mere illusions?

Five decades ago, Reinhold Niebuhr spoke to such questions in words that remain surprisingly contemporary:

> We live in an age in which personal moral idealism is easily accused of hypocrisy and frequently deserves it. It is an age in which honesty is possible only when it skirts the edges of cynicism. All this is rather tragic. For what the individual conscience feels . . . is not a luxury but a necessity of the soul. Yet there is beauty in our tragedy. We are, at least, rid of some of our illusions. We can no longer buy the highest satisfactions of the individual life at the expense of social injustice. We cannot build our individual ladders to heaven and leave the total human enterprise unredeemed of its excesses and corruptions.
>
> In the task of that redemption the most effective agents will be men who have substituted some new illusions for the abandoned ones. The most important of these illusions is that the collective life of mankind can achieve perfect justice. It is a very valuable illusion for the moment; for justice cannot be approximated if the hope of its perfect realization does not generate a sublime madness in the soul. Nothing but such madness will do battle with malignant power and "spiritual wickedness in high places." The illusion is dangerous because it encourages terrible fanaticisms. It must therefore be brought under the control of reason. One can only hope that reason will not destroy it before its work is done.[14]

A "sublime madness in the soul"—an "illusion"—is that what it means to see the community as a context of loving relationships? Niebuhr is both helpful and troublesome when he makes this distinction: "A rational ethic aims at justice, and a religious ethic makes love the ideal."[15] His description of the "rational ethic" is actually very close to the biblical injunction to love the neighbor as oneself. He suggests that the "religious ethic," particularly the Christian approach, is different in that the needs of the neighbor are paramount, "without a careful computation of relative needs." Critics argue, persuasively, that Niebuhr has concretized a split between love and justice, with love relegated to the private and justice to the public sphere. Certainly, Niebuhr considers the "religious" ethic, as he described it, to have more ethical purity than the "rational," but to be impossible to live out in many social and political circumstances. We are coming to understand, however, that justice does belong in the private realm, through respect and mutuality, and that love is projected into our public life through "right relationships."

Many persons have decided to view all other persons from a transcendent perspective, in the "agape" sense which motivated King, or from Gandhi's perspective that God resides in each person, in every creature. Such perceptions of reality lead to a greater concern for the well-being of others than for oneself. When I was an undergraduate, my professor in a "World Politics" course was a Quaker, a man committed to nonviolence. I remember clearly the day when one of my classmates objected to some of his statements with, "but you are being so idealistic! Don't you think that you have to be realistic?" His reply was, "you see, my ideals *are* my reality." This position, very real to those who hold it, is closer to what Niebuhr called "religious." Although I tend to hold that position myself, I am also convinced that the "lover" can approach community, at any level, from Niebuhr's "rational" position as well. Here, a primary concern is for justice, for equality, for the opportunity, as I've said before, to live, to grow, and to be productive as a unique being.

Practicing love in the community—whether a neighborhood, or the planet—involves the enhancement of, or the removal of barriers to, such life, and growth, and productivity of the precious unique others who share (and will, in the future, share) this planet.

Shared Experiences and Insights

One student summed up the matter in this way: "My solution, for now, is to know that the world I have now is not loving, but try to be and act as if I were the person I would be if the world were whole."

6

Loving Relationships with Nature

Are we humans divorced from our environment?

Have we become uprooted from nature?

What kind of a planet are we going to leave to the generations that follow us?

What does it mean to be "in tune with" nature?

These and similar questions bother many who view the human ties to nature as having been weakened and torn.[1] Changes in our *external* environment seem to take place at a rapid rate. It seems, however, that our *internal* capacity to understand the meaning of such changes and their impact on our total environment moves slowly and without sufficient energy and creativity.

Are we human beings a part of our environment, needing to learn to live with nature, relate lovingly with nature, and cooperate in mutual survival with nature? Or are we somehow *apart from* our environment, struggling to control it for whatever can be extracted from it?

Human Beings: Apart From or A-Part-of Nature?

Our religious concepts and value systems contain at least four general categories of human response to nature. The *first* is one that can be characterized by *fear*. The powers of nature are awesome, constantly posing a threat to human life and health. The world around us is inhabited by spirits that enter into elements and animals in order to unleash their power and show their unhappiness with us. The best we can do is to work out ways to strike bargains with these spirits, to satisfy their desires in relation to us in order that they not be more harmful to us. The concept of nature as something to be feared has dominated many human groups in history and is still alive and well in recognizable forms today.

A *second* approach is characterized in the creation story of Hebrew scriptures and accepted by Christian tradition. In this narrative, God is understood to be the source of all of creation, having made the elements, the animals, plant life, and all that we call nature. The culminating stage of this creative process was to create human beings, who according to the story, were given *dominion* over the other aspects of creation. Throughout much of our history, this dominion has been understood as a stewardship to be carried out in response to the Creator's love. Humans are namers and caretakers of the natural world within which they live.

With the advent of industrialization and technology, however, another understanding of "dominion" became more active, producing a *third* approach. Nature was seen as something to be dominated, used, and even exploited to meet the desires and demands of human beings. Nonhuman reality is open to conquest, and the challenge is to control and manipulate beings and force for human benefit (or, at least, the benefit of *some* humans, even though others are harmed in the process). This approach, most familiar to Americans of European descent, is gaining increasing critical attention from contemporary organized religious bodies. They are making a serious attempt to recapture the Biblical understanding of *stewardship* and *caretaking* and to counteract the misuse of the dominion concept. Resistance and opposition to the rhetoric and policies of James Watt, US Secretary of the Interior from 1981 to 1983, was mounted by religious groups concerned with reshaping the understanding of human stewardship of their companions in the created world. Many are trying to learn the cooperation and attunement that are inherent in this perspective.

A *fourth* perspective is found among a variety of groups, including some Native Americans. From their perspective, nature is something of which human beings are merely a part. The task of living human life is one of learning to *cooperate with nature,* to tune oneself and the community life of the group as fully as possible with nature. There is respect, even reverence, for other forms of life. This view is poignantly represented in a public service spot that occasionally appears on television. A Native American is seen sitting on a horse, looking out over a polluted environment, and a tear rolls down his cheek.

Members of the Findhorn Community in Scotland have responded to some unusual experiences with gardening in that particular location by giving themselves to a depth experiment with human/nature relationships. As one member of the Community put it, "we have not only to cooperate with the nature kingdoms, but we have to allow them to become one with us. Through this marriage, we are more truly human."[2] In their intense community experience, they have found that their meditations brought them into touch with spiritual realities that speak to them through their garden, as in this message:

> One who has been an inspiration of love to you, one who bore the embodiment of the Christ, said that he who would be the greatest of all must be the servant of all. In that statement lies full understanding. Man was never given dominion over the earth to express it in a one-sided and isolated state of consciousness. Man's dominion arises from the fact that his soul is an interweaving synthesis of vision and expression. Man represents a more complex and potentially more advanced form, with a wider range of creative possibilities open to his consciousness, than other kingdoms of life within nature.[3]

Although humans have this wide range of creative possibilities, the Findhorn participants believe that we have not yet reached an adequate attunement to our evolution, to our place within the created order.

Human Nurture By Nature

The ability of the other-than-human to touch something deep within us was brought out dramatically in some of the concentration camp experiences recounted by Viktor Frankl. This Austrian psychotherapist, who survived some of the most horrible of Nazi death camps in World War II, reflected on particular incidents in those experiences which had clear messages for him:

> As the inner life of the prisoner tended to become more intense he also experienced the beauty of art and nature as never before. Under their influence he sometimes even forgot his own frightful circumstances. If someone had seen our faces on the journey from Auschwitz to a Bavarian camp as we beheld the mountains of Salzburg with their summits glowing in the sunset, through the little barred windows of the prison carriage, he would never have believed that those were the faces of men who had given up all hope of life and liberty. Despite that factor—or maybe because of it—we were carried away by nature's beauty, which we had missed for so long.
> In camp, too, a man might draw the attention of a comrade working next to him to a nice view of the setting sun shining through the tall trees of the Bavarian woods (as in the famous water color by Durer), the same woods in which we had built an enormous, hidden munitions plant. One evening,

when we were already resting on the floor of our hut, dead tired, soup bowls in hand, a fellow prisoner rushed in and asked us to run out to the assembly grounds and see the wonderful sunset. Standing outside we saw sinister clouds glowing in the west and the whole sky alive with clouds of every-changing shapes and colors, from a steel-blue to blood red. The desolate gray mud huts provided a sharp contrast, while the puddles on the muddy ground reflected the glowing sky. Then, after minutes of moving silence, one prisoner said to another, "How beautiful the world *could* be!"[4]

Not many of us are likely to have been in such circumstances as Frankl. You may, however, have been in situations of adversity in which the beauty or wonder of nature allowed you to rise above the circumstances. That interaction is a part of a loving relationship.

Loren Eiseley is a naturalist, a paleontologist, and anthropologist whose scientific skills are transmitted through his engaging writing skills. He allows his readers to enter into the magnificent mystery of life in its many forms, in a journey that is both exciting and revealing. One of his most moving stories is told under the heading of "The Bird and the Machine." He had traveled into high country with some colleagues to search for bones. They were also assigned to bring back some live birds for a zoo. Eiseley entered an abandoned cabin at night and managed to capture a young male sparrow hawk. With his beak, the hawk injured his captor's hand, and in the process allowed his mate to escape through a hole in the cabin roof. The hawk was placed in a box until a cage could be built. The next morning, greeted by a clear, deep blue sky and a "wind as cool as a mountain spring," Eiseley noted that "it was a fine day to be alive." He looked around for the hawk's little mate, but could see it nowhere. He decided to have another look at his capture from the night before. The rest is best encountered through his words:

Secretively I looked again all around the camp and up and down and opened the box. I got him right out in my hand with his wings folded properly and I was careful not to startle him. He lay limp in my grasp and I could feel his heart pound under the feathers but he only looked beyond me and up.

I saw him look that last look away beyond me into a sky so full of light that I could not follow his gaze. The little breeze flowed over me again, and nearby a mountain aspen shook all its tiny leaves. I suppose I must have had an idea then of what I was going to do, but I never let it come up into consciousness. I just reached over and laid the hawk on the grass.

He lay there a long minute without hope, unmoving, his eyes still fixed on that blue vault above him. It must have been that he was already so far away in heart that he never felt the release from my hand. He never even stood. He just lay with his breast against the grass.

In the next second after that long minute he was gone. Like a flicker of light, he had vanished with my eyes full on him, but without actually seeing even a premonitory wing beat. He was gone straight into that towering emptiness of light and crystal that my eyes could scarcely bear to penetrate. For another long moment there was silence. I could not see him. The light was too intense. Then from far up somewhere a cry came ringing down.

I was young then and had seen little of the world, but when I heard that cry my heart turned over. It was not the cry of the hawk I had captured; for, by shifting my position against the sun, I was now seeing further up. Straight out of the sun's eye where she must have been soaring restlessly above us for untold hours, hurtled his mate. And from far up, ringing from peak to peak of the summits over us, came a cry of such unutterable and ecstatic joy that it sounds down across the years and tingles among the cups of my quiet breakfast table.

I saw them both now. He was rising fast to meet her. They met in a great soaring gyre that turned to a whirling circle and a dance of wings. Once more, just once, their two voices, joined in a harsh wild medley of question and response, struck and echoed against the pinnacles of the valley. Then they were gone forever somewhere into those upper regions beyond the eyes of men.[5]

Many years later, Eiseley reported that he was never able to imprison a bird. Further, he reflected on what human beings had been able to do with machines, and on the growing claim that there seems to be nothing in human "construction, constituents, or behavior" that science cannot duplicate and synthesize. His further reflection on what humans can do with machines led him to insist: "on the other hand the machine does not bleed, ache, hang for others in the empty sky in a torment of hope to learn the fate of another machine, nor does it cry out with joy nor dance in the air with the fierce passion of a bird."[6]

In his openness to the natural world around him, Eiseley garnered many insights about life and reality that deeply enriched him and others who have listened to, or read of, his experiences. A flock of tiny sparrows who observed a raven consuming one of their young nestlings nurtured him with a judgment about life. His description of the moment of quietness after the "murderer" raven completed its tragic meal moves to a display by the birds of a "judgment of life against death." Led by the single voice of a song sparrow, the others joined in, hesitantly at first, "Till suddenly they took heart and sang from many throats joyously together as birds are known to sing. They sang because life is sweet and sunlight beautiful."[7] Even though they sang under the shadow of the death-dealing raven, they sang of life, an affirmation against death.

Such judgments about life are gifts to humans from other parts of the created order around us. The messages come in uncounted ways, and open new vistas of life to those who receive them with love. Humans also share that love in nurture and caring for their shared environment.

Nature Nurture By Humans: Taking Care

Many of us are animal lovers in one way or another. When I ask persons to write about a loving relationship which they have observed, some will write about a person and an animal. There is no question that many of us have pets we love. What about other animals?

Peter Singer is a British philosopher who has given special attention to the welfare of animals and emphasizes the *rights* of other-than-human animals. His case is built on a notion of equality:

> The argument for extending the principle of equality beyond our own species is simple, so simple that it amounts to no more than a clear understanding of the nature of the principle of equal consideration of interests. We have seen that this principle implies that our concerns for others ought not to depend on what they are like, or what abilities they possess (although precisely what this concern requires us to do may vary according to the characteristics of those affected by what we do). It is on this basis that we are able to say that the fact that some people are not members of our race does not entitle us to exploit them, and similarly the fact that some people are less intelligent than others does not mean that their interests may be disregarded. But the principle also implies that the fact that beings are not members of our species does not entitle us to exploit them, and similarly the fact that other animals are less intelligent than we are does not mean that their interests may be disregarded.[8]

Singer's "principle of equal consideration of interests" might well be one way of providing a practical definition of a loving relationship. Singer is not alone in arguing for animal rights. Based on somewhat different philosophical presuppositions from those of Singer, Tom Regan argues that non-human animals, as all of nature, have moral rights because they, like humans, have inherent value.[9] Christopher Stone has argued that legal standing should be given as well to trees, rivers, and mountains, "so that we can better preserve our ecology and our bonds with nature."[10] The lack of legal rights, however, does not relieve human beings of accountability for our companions in nature. Stone points out that our current legal system criminalizes certain behaviors, such as dog beating, which in fact "implements care for dogs." In doing so, a right is not granted to dogs; rather, a liability is created for the dog beater.[11] Clearly, this is a recognition that our value system already takes seriously human accountability for other-than-human existence. Since we assume that human beings are alone in being capable of moral action, we can also expect that humans will take others into account in our moral choices. We can choose to care about what happens to a lake, or a snow leopard. Protection can be offered—even demanded.

In descriptions of human abuse of environment, many have chosen suitably graphic language—the "rape" of the earth, for example. If "rape" is an appropriate term for what we do, and I tend to think it is, I've seen a number of rape scenes, as I'm sure you have. One particular such scene was in Rocky Mountain National Park. I stopped at the high point on the beautiful drive that has been built through that park, at a spot where we can get out and look at "tundra." At a high place like that, the soil is very sensitive, and the extremely small plants and flowers which grow there can easily be damaged. Walkways are provided, and signs plead with visitors to stay on the walkways. Those pleas, of course, go unheeded, as many guests ignore the signs and walk over the flowers that take seven years to grow, either oblivious to what they are doing, or not caring. It was there that I saw the rape—actually, it was the aftermath of rape and murder. As I started back to my car, I saw a young man standing at the hood of his car, placing clumps of tundra and flowers he had dug up into small plastic bags! Did he really believe that the life in those bags could survive his drive several thousand feet down through the atmosphere? I tried to speak to him, but my anger and frustration got in the way—I didn't get across very well. I looked around for help, but the rapist-murderer got away because, as is often the case, a security officer could not be located.

Why, you may be saying, are you making such an issue of a few flowers and blades of grass, when there are so many more significant problems in the world? How can such activity be verbally equated with the violation of life and personality of another human being? Of course they are different. The issue arises from the recognition that our attitude toward the environment, toward nature around us, toward other-than-human beings, reveals a great deal about our attitude toward ourselves and other humans. Our willingness to exploit, dominate, and even destroy may be a demonstration of our willingness to do the same toward other human beings. The "neighbor" is not just the "human" one. Furthermore, it is becoming more and more clear to us that our willingness to exploit and damage the environment is a self-destructive act. We must take care that our concern is not simply that of "speciesism," as Tom Regan and others have pointed out.[12] If our concern with our environment is only to protect our own interests as particular human beings, we miss the point. Our love of self and our love of all that exists are, assuredly, inextricably interrelated. Love lives most fully in relationship.

A Love Affair With A Tree: Dialogue With Nature and Self

I have a love affair with a beautiful white pine tree. When we moved into a previous home, our yard had several trees that had been broken off, reportedly by neighborhood children. (It seems we had moved into a middle-class, suburban, high-crime area, when it comes to trees.) There was one exception—a pretty little white pine tree that stood in the side backyard, near the garage and not far from the street. I often looked at the tree as I drove in the driveway, "grounding" myself once again on my return home. As we began to replace the trees that had been broken, or nurture them along, we rejoiced in the healthiness of the pine. Then it happened. Early one morning, I came out of the house and was stunned to see that, during the night, about five feet of the crown of that tree had been broken off by some kind of marauder. What had been a promising, gorgeous ten-foot pine tree was now a five-foot bush. I grieved and mourned, and I painted the stump of the crown. Then I watered and fed the tree.

Over time, an amazing thing happened. A side branch bent toward the center and thrust into the air. What looked to be a bush became, once again, a tree. Now it is a glorious sight, over twenty feet tall. I could stand beside it, close my eyes, smell it and listen to the wind in its branches, and imagine that I was on a mountainside in Colorado. Or, on occasion, I might simply pause by the tree in gratitude for the message of life it offered. I hear again the words of the young woman lying near death in a concentration camp hospital, being treated by Viktor Frankl. She looked out the window, saw a tree, and heard it speak to her: the tree said, "I am here—I am here—I am life, eternal life."[13]

Does it make sense to speak of a "dialogue" with a tree, or with birds, or a mountain? Part of the meaning of dialogue is to listen to the other, letting the other speak in and on its own terms, from its own experience, in its own language. Real dialogue with a love partner requires learning the language of the other as well as possible. It calls for catching on to ways of hearing the interpretations of the other's experience. In many relationships, this requires an investment of time, and often produces surprises. For Jane Goodall, for instance, it has meant entering a third decade of living with and observation of chimpanzees, learning things that would never have been suspected in the first or even second decade. Such is also the case, of course, in our human relationships.

We have begun to understand, perhaps more clearly than ever before, that it is in trying to *live with* others around us, as productively as possible, that we increase our knowledge and understanding, as well as the possibility for survival of all. We are taken by surprise when it is suggested that we speech-centered creatures must learn to communicate with what is speechless around us. George Steiner insists that we must do just that:

> So far as we know, the world of the ecosystems out there is mute, it is speechless. Will we learn in time to modulate between that in us which is speech-centered, which makes us alive, which is discourse and that which cannot answer back, which cannot cry out against us articulately. For unless we find a communication, both parties are presumably doomed.[14]

One who takes much time to be in and with the natural world knows very well that the "speechless" have a number of ways of speaking. Our problem is that we make little or no effort to listen, to learn to communicate. Children, of course, do not necessarily require language for deep and intense communication. The "speechless other" may, indeed have enormous impact and become so much a part of the child's experience that it remains throughout life. Karl Menninger tells of his mother's great love for the Pennsylvania hills of her childhood, a love which she described in her autobiography:

> Many of my thoughts were associated with those lovely hills and they were very dear to me. It was harder for me to say goodbye to the hills than to any of my living friends, and today their memory is the brightest thing I hold from the Pennsylvania years. I well remember how, on the last after-noon in the old home, I went out back of the bake oven and sat under a big old apple tree that commanded a view of the hills, and to each I said goodbye out loud. Than I cried awhile to myself and said, "I want God to bless all of you because I love you. I know I shall miss you terribly, I hate so much to leave you and maybe I will never see you again." It took only a few short weeks for me to learn how truly I *did* miss them, and many a time I have been very homesick to see my hills again. But I never have.[15]

Perhaps you have had a love affair with a tree, or a flower, a mountain, a beach, or a butterfly. Perhaps it, too, brought you a message. It may have taught you, as "my" pine tree taught me, that by opening our senses to more than the structure in which we are encased, we are also getting in touch with something basic in our personhood. Letting ourselves "tune into" the world around us may well help us to tune in more to the world within us. Love lives in both. Its power comes even more alive when we open to that relationship and let it grow.

Shared Experiences and Insights

"Snow"

Snow turns trees into lace handkerchiefs and palaces.
It puts diamonds everywhere.
It silences every sound.
Walk in it late at night
and it seems like day
because all the world glows.
Soft as a womb.
Life sleeps,
smiling.

I grew up on a farm, and so my love for nature is experienced on several different levels. I fall head over heels as I witness the coming of each season. I must admit that my heaviest "crushes" are always in Spring and Fall, when I am shown what yellow, green, red and brown are *really* supposed to look like. I name my feelings at these times "crushes" because they are so close to what I experience when I first become interested in someone. My "beloved" suddenly represents all in life that is beautiful: I see sparkling waters in his blue eyes just as I see the strength of Samson in the tulip bowing in the wind.

"Through Nature's Eyes"

Have you ever felt blue, blue as the sky after a spring storm's passage?
Have you ever felt green, green as the thick waves of grass on a windy day?
Have you ever felt white, white as the freshly painted picket fence in the sweltering heat?
Have you ever felt black, black as the mud-clad roads to be walked through barefoot?
Have you ever felt yellow, yellow as the dandelions, huddled together reaching for the sun?
Have you ever felt red, red as a cardinal, perched above the earth, seeing it as we cannot?
Have you ever felt purple, purple as a grape with only a pit to make you think?
Have you ever felt orange, orange as a pumpkin on the cold dark floor of fall?
Have you ever felt like a rainbow? If so, you have loved.

I didn't discover the field until I was a little older. Leaving the dark wooded tractor path and entering the bright sun-lit field was like entering a whole different world. Sometimes I would sit in the field and stare at the black opening into the woods, imagining that it was a tunnel leading from one world to another. When the field was planted in oats I could run through the waist-high grain. When it wasn't planted it bloomed with weeds and wildflowers. Queen Anne's lace and clover dominated the growth there. Off to the side of the field, just behind the woods next to the pines was a young wooded area. The trees here were not over my head yet (though they are now!). It was here that I found the ant hills—huge ant hills! I used to stomp all over the hills, not to be vindictive, but because the ants would scramble so frantically that the entire hill seemed to glitter. I used to stand there daydreaming for a long time, watching the hills glitter until the shine wore off and the ants slowed down again.

I don't know why I quit stomping those ant hills. No one ever said that I shouldn't do it because it was mean. I do remember feeling bad. These were my first deep feelings. I took a jar and filled it with sugar. I must have read somewhere that ants liked sugar. I took the jar out to the mounds and sprinkled it like snow all over the mounds. This was my way of telling them I was sorry for messing up their home.

Those woods were my place; though I didn't own them, I claimed them with my feelings. I fled to them when I needed to cry and I stomped through them when I was angry. In the woods the wind became music and leaves were the voice of the trees and they sang to me . . . the first thing I do when I go home is walk down that short tractor path to touch base with where I grew up.

7

The Struggle with Self

My emphasis thus far has been on the "contexts" of loving relationships, the most common arenas within which we experience and practice loving. In friendships, in committed living arrangements including marriage and family, in community, and in our natural environment, we relate with others and have the opportunity to do so in productive, caring ways.

This approach to relationships also takes account of problems to be overcome and issues to be faced, as we learn and practice the art of being a lover. Turning to some of those issues, I begin with perhaps the most fundamental—the struggle with the self.

Self-Love and Self-Centeredness

In chapter two, we saw the necessary interconnection between love of self, other, and the Transcendent. The love of self was affirmed as basic to the ability to love others. It was further asserted that love of self and selfishness are *not* the same, that the love of self is actually the opposite of selfishness. When I love myself, I have no need to grasp, to cling, to insist on possessing. Those are needs that dominate the person who is insecure, who lacks assurance of self-worth. Likewise, self-love is not egotism. When I love myself and am comfortable with myself, I have no need to trumpet my value to others.

Affirmation in our childhood experience is crucial. If we don't get enough affection and security, we try to hoard what we *can* get, grasping whatever we can, to ourselves.[1]

Unfortunately, one cannot hoard and give at the same time. The one who is free to give is the one who loves the self enough not to be grasping for more. Self-centeredness is necessary when there are holes that demand filling. Self-love provides assurance that those "holes" are not devastating, that there are sufficient internal resources for dealing with them, and that the process of reaching out to others with the gift of self also has an indirect way of taking care of some of those holes.

Liking, we have noted, is not the same as loving. Liking is a response of attraction to certain qualities, behaviors, or appearances. I may or may not like some of the ways I act, some of my habitual responses, or the way I look. I may have done some things that go against some basic preferences or values I hold, and I don't like me for that. Loving, on the other hand, is an active process of acceptance, caring, supporting. While I may be aware that I don't like what I am doing, I know that I am capable of doing, or being, something else, and can engage my energies in the direction of growth, giving support to change.

It would not take long to fill a lengthy book shelf with prescriptions for self-love. Insights from two who have written on the subject are worth noting at this point. John Powell, a Jesuit teacher and writer, has produced several small volumes on the experience and meaning of love. He draws on a range of biblical, psychological, and theological understanding in interpreting common human experience. He posits the need for self-love in order to love others, with the deceptively simple suggestion that one's love of others makes one loveable. That is, one will experience love from others in the act of giving love—it is inherent in the nature of love that doing love makes it easier for others to love the lover. Therefore, he asserts, even the person who has been limited in the nurture of self can love *a little*—in so doing, one opens up the opportunity to be loved, and in receiving what others will share, the capacity for loving is increased. He goes so far as to advise that one "forget the self." This puts the focus on the other, on giving love rather than concentrating on receiving it. In this sense, he is making a similar point to that of Fromm, who diagnoses our most common problem as that of trying to be loved or become loveable, rather than to learn how to love, to give love. Powell recognizes that the capability of growth and loving is found only in the person who has experienced being loved. "It is a frightening but true reality of life," he insists, "that, by loving me or refusing to love me, others hold the potential of my maturity in their hands."[2] At the same time, concentration on self, attempting to relieve one's needs through others, increases one's isolation. Fortunately, he recognizes that it is not easy to "stop being concerned with ourselves and to begin to be concerned with others."[3] He assumes that *all* of us have *some* capacity to love, and he urges that we build on whatever is our experience of being loved.

Morton Kelsey has been more specific in recognizing that we need to learn to love ourselves, in order to reach to others, and he offers some suggestions for that learning. Writing from a theological and pastoral stance, he begins his suggestions with the perspective of religious faith:

1. "We need to make a conscious decision to see ourselves through the eyes of the divine lover."[4] One is aided in doing this by the process of keeping a regular journal, with opportunity for reflection and building on earlier awarenesses. The goal is to see myself as I really am.

2. It is necessary to recognize that everyone has a hard time loving the self. It is not an easy thing to do, and we are anything but alone.

3. We must see and accept ourselves as we are, without judgment and condemnation.[5]

4. "It is just as morally wrong to dislike, despise, and devalue ourselves as it is to have these attitudes toward others."[6] Kelsey notes that it may be even worse, because these attitudes constitute a denial of God's love for one self. Even though it should also be argued that those attitudes toward others might also reflect a denial of God's love for others, a serious moral issue, we can agree that morality does not permit the devaluing of self any more than others.

5. A major step in opening up oneself to love is learning to accept forgiveness from others. This is complicated. Kelsey asserts that it is much more difficult to be forgiven than to forgive. As complex as the experience may be, we do find that our capacity for self-love is increased as we allow ourselves to accept the forgiveness freely given by others.

6. An honesty with self is required in ways that we often overlook. Much of what we sometimes consider to be "evil" within us, therefore unloveable is actually earthy, a part of our being "of the earth." What we find ugly within us may not be something that has to be rooted out, but is a very necessary part of our humanity which requires understanding and redirection to more productive ends. An honest search within can reveal our capacities for intense evil as well as incalculable goods—capacities shared with all other human beings. Honest examination and acceptance of these extremely diverse aspects of our being provide us a step toward taking responsibility—the ability to respond to what we find in ourselves.[7]

This recognition that love of self requires acceptance of dimensions within the self usually overlooked and often feared is shared by many. One who has interpreted it in an especially helpful way is Rollo May, as he discusses the meaning of the power of the "Daimonic" as a part of our development of love and will.

The "Daimonic" and Self-Understanding

In our struggle with self-love, we are often aware that we sometimes feel, think, and act in undesirable ways. We may sense that there are very destructive forces within us. We have probably learned from experience, however, that those same forces, if properly directed and channeled, can be productive or positively growthful, even loving aspects of our personality and behavior. In an attempt to illuminate this struggle in our understanding, Rollo May draws on the potentially confusing concept of the *daimonic*. I like his use of it, even though the potential for misunderstanding is strong from the beginning. You may already have responded by asking yourself, "how can anything be loving that is demonic?" It is important to take seriously May's spelling of this term. More than a matter of personal preference, it is a recognition of something that has happened to a concept in our language.

By the use of the spelling, "*dai*monic," May is focusing on a return to meanings of this term in ancient Greek literature. When we see the word, but think "*de*monic," we are identifying it with a totally negative and dangerous force, often located in something external to one's own central being, but capable of invading the unsuspecting person and creating havoc. May defines the daimonic as "any natural function which has the power to take over the whole person. . . . the urge in every being to affirm itself, assert itself, perpetuate and increase itself."[8] "The daimonic can be either creative or destructive," he tells us, "and is normally both." The ancient Greek word, *daimon,* was unambiguous in including a positive meaning as well as negative, both divine and diabolical. All of life, then, is a flux between assertion of self which permits creativity, and excessive aggression, which is expressed in hostility and cruelty.[9] Our ability to assert ourselves is necessary for creativity, for reaching out to others in active love. Aggressiveness cares little about what happens to the òther in a confused expectation that something will be gained for oneself.

This is a natural function, something that happens individually in each person. But it is rooted in nature itself, from which all persons emerge. He is describing for us a "unique pattern of sensibilities and powers which constitutes the individual as a self in relation to his world."[10] Have you thought of yourself as a "pattern of sensibilities and powers?" Each one of us is, of course, and by allowing ourselves to think this way, we learn a good deal about ourselves.

We cannot escape the early Christian interest in "dualism." That is, reality is seen as divided into the two extremes of good and evil. In religious terms, what is "good" is represented by God, and "evil" is represented or controlled by Satan, or the devil. These two are constantly at war. It is not unusual to hear someone say, after doing some terrible, or at least mischievous, act, "I didn't mean to do it; the Devil made me do it." The strong inference is that something entered into the person from outside—an evil power took over, and produced the unacceptable behavior. This dualism, although still very much alive in the twentieth century, is not the whole story in Christian thought.

Also expressed through these twenty centuries is the idea that every human being is a *unity,* encompassing a wide array of possibilities. Peck absorbs this stream of thought in a very clear and forthright statement:

> Within each and every one of us there are two selves, one sick and one healthy—the life urge and the death urge, if you will. Each of us represents the whole human race; within each of us is the instinct for godhood and the hope for mankind, and within each of us is the original sin of laziness, the ever-present force of entropy pushing us back to childhood, to the womb and to the swamps from which we have evolved.[11]

May is sympathetic to Rainer Maria Rilke's observation, on withdrawing from psychotherapy after learning of its goals, "if my devils are to leave me, I am afraid my angels will take flight as well."[12] He would like to recover the recognition that we integrate the extreme differing parts of our personality, the warring elements of our urges, by accepting what is truly us and taking responsibility for our being.

What does this have to do with love? In our longing for union with another, our desire to participate in a relationship with some one or thing beyond the self, a self-assertion is required:

> One must have something to give and be able to give it. The danger, of course, is that he will overassert himself—which is the source of the experience shown in the notion of being taken over by a demon. But this negative side is not to be escaped by giving up self-assertion. For if one is unable to assert oneself, one is unable to participate in a genuine relationship. A dynamic dialectical relationship—I am tempted to call it a balance, but it is not a balance—is a continuous give-and-take in which one asserts himself, finds an answer in the other, then possibly asserts too far, senses a "no" in the other, backs up but does not give up, shifts the participation to a new form, and finds the way that is adequate for the wholeness of the other. This is the constructive use of the daimonic. It is an assertion of one's own individuality in relation to another person. It always skates on the edge of exploitation of the partner; but without it, there is no vital relationship.
> In its right proportion, the daimonic is the urge to reach out toward others, to increase life by way of sex, to create, to civilize; it is the joy and rapture, or the simple security of knowing that we matter, that we can affect others, can form them, can exert power which is demonstrably significant. It is a way of making certain that we are valued.

When the daimonic takes over completely, the unity of the self and the relationship is broken down; a fact confessed by the person when he or she says, "I had no control, I acted as if in a dream, I did not know it was I." The daimonic is the elementary power by which one is saved from the horror of not being one's self on one hand, and the horror, on the other hand, of feeling no connection and no vital drive toward the other person.[13]

I find especially helpful his brief comparison of the words "diabolic" and "symbolic." The diabolic, related to the "Devil," is that which "tears apart." The "symbolic," on the other hand, draws together and provides integration. What are you aware of in your own nature that, if allowed full rein, would tear apart or be destructive (your diabolic nature)? What "symbols" do you have in your experience, as a part of your regular functioning, for bringing together different urges in your life, thus producing constructive, growthful, perhaps even *joyous* experiences? Without knowing both of these, your capacity to love—both yourself and others, is more limited than it needs to be. Keen emphasizes how this process is involved in self-love:

To love the self is not to come upon an unchangeable image or essence, but to welcome all the diversity of experience into consciousness. To love myself is to proclaim that I will live in a democratic rather than a dictatorial relationship to the plurality within. I will allow all my subpersonalities, contradictory impulses, alien wills, strange desires, forbidden needs to live together within the commonwealth of my consciousness. . . . Loving myself, I respect the mystery that I am. I open myself to *be* more than I can ever *know* . . . The practice of self-love involves a discipline of paying attention to the intricate interweavings of one's physical, mental, and emotional states.[14]

The integration and channeling of powers within us requires the ability to name one's daimons. By examples from mythology, from the Bible, and from psychotherapy, May has demonstrated a longstanding human familiarity with the need to "name the devils" and thus gain control. One of his examples is that of Jacob, who wrestled throughout the night—apparently in a dream—with a man who is interpreted variously as an angel, a representative of God, and as the deity itself (Genesis 32:24-31). A significant part of that story is that Jacob confronted God "face to face" through that experience, and identified the confrontation in that way. Incidentally, Jacob was "maimed in the thigh"—or, more precisely, he suffered a dislocated hip. One does not escape a confrontation of this sort without some kind of scar, some significant change in mind, spirit, and/or body. Especially important is the fact that Jacob "hung on" through the struggle. He even sought the name of the deity. In Hebrew tradition one enters into such confrontation and naming with God at great risk to the self. The experience was so profound that Jacob himself takes on a new name—he is now "Israel," a name which means that he had striven with God, and with men, and had prevailed.[15]

A story of similar significance is found in the New Testament, and is referred to as the "Gerasene" or "Gadarene demoniac." The most similar accounts are in Mark (15:1–20) and Luke (8:26–39). A man who would now be termed mentally ill was living in the caves and tombs outside the city, considered dangerous to himself and others. Jesus confronted him without fear and challenged his identity. In answer to the question of his name, the man replied that "My name is Legion, for we are many." An English translation of this account says that he is controlled by a number of "demons," thus the name of Legion. After the confrontation and the naming, the demons flee the man, and when others come later, they find him talking quietly with Jesus, "clothed and in his right mind." Obviously, there is much to ponder in this story, all the way from exorcism to the damage done to the local agricultural economy (the devils are transferred into a nearby herd of pigs, who run into the river and are drowned!). However one chooses to interpret the many features of it, the central message of the story is that the person was only able to gain control over himself when the intense warring within was confronted—and named.[16] In other discussion, May refers to the importance of the "naming" process in psychotherapy, in the assisting of a person to become whole.

To refuse to recognize tendencies within us, to resist naming them for what they are, and to be unwilling to see what function such behavior serves for us is to assure that they will exercise unlimited power over us. It is only in "owning" the feeling, the urge, the behavior, that we bring it from an unconscious or impersonal level to a conscious and personal level, and begin to have some real freedom in giving direction to it. As Kelsey has put it, "I have come to trust only those people who are aware of their inner rage, of the inner murderers within them capable of murdering me. Only those who know their capacity to destroy can keep it in hand and deter it."[17] He goes on to insist that loving and knowing the self, "even the destructive and idiotic parts," are prerequisites to loving others.

In a class discussion on this topic, one student commented that one of her "daimons" was cigarette smoking. She insisted that she knew it is not good for her, that it was destructive, expensive, and silly—but that she did it anyway. I suggested that she might not be going far enough with May's insight. We might come closer to the "daimon" if we explored what the smoking represented to her, what function it performed for her. She thought a bit and said, "It's something 'naughty' that I can do. It lets me rebel." Now, we were getting somewhere. She went ahead to say she knew that she needed to do some things that aren't accepted by others, to rebel against certain conventions. Of course! That is an essential part of gaining identity. Her need *not* to accept others' expectations of her, or some of the expectations she might have for herself, is a strong and potentially positive force. What she does with that, and how she integrates it with other needs and values, may produce results that range from positive to destructive. The urge to rebel, to not accept rules or norms just because they are there, is a necessary element in anyone's creative growth. How one chooses to act on that may very well depend on the maturity that comes from recognizing the *daimon* and naming it for what it is—in this case, rebellion against the power of others' expectations.

The power of the need to rebel and what can be done with it is revealed in another account. A man recently released from a life sentence in prison was asked about changes in his life. How did he see himself differently from the person he was while committing the crimes that led to his incarceration? He replied that he now recognized that he was extremely rebellious when younger and acted out that rebellion in many destructive ways. As he gained maturity, in prison, he saw that he had this strong tendency to rebel and that it could take many forms. Earlier, his incarceration had led him to believe that his rebellion was "bad" and that there was no hope for him. In his first two years of prison, he tried to commit suicide by placing himself in situations in which he could get killed. Once he was more prepared to see the human possibilities in himself, he could see that his energy for rebellion was an important way of asserting that he is, indeed, a person. He made the decision to rebel only in ways that would produce positive results for himself and for others. Thus, when particular rules were being used to prevent him and others from gaining things that were rightly theirs, he found appropriate ways to confront the unjust system. The key is his decision, which he said he made when he became more "mature." That decision resulted from the rebelliousness moving from the unconscious, impersonal level to the conscious, personal level where he could recognize it for what it was, and see how its undirected expression had been so destructive to him. New experiences and exposure to new values brought him to a new dimension, which May calls the "transpersonal." The forces within us, called "daimons" by May, are "rooted in the objective world." The more we understand ourselves (the "personal" dimension), the more we are in touch with "a universal structure of reality,"[18] that which is beyond us but can live within us and through us. What now has meaning to us is a part of universal meaning and value, and we are strengthened by channeling our energies toward meaningful, positive ends. Rather than deciding that "rebelling is bad; I want to be 'good,' not get into trouble, and won't rebel," the prisoner gained control over this "natural function," as May put it. He integrated it, not allowing it to control his life, and used its energy for productive self-expression.

Rebellion, of course, is only *one* example of any number of expressions of self-assertion going on within the growing being. Others might be anger, resentment, desire for recognition, jealousy, and pride. A little self-exploration will lead to the discovery and naming of your own "daimons" and the many ways in which they make you a more exciting, potentially more loveable and loving individual. The key in this process, as May's analysis shows so well, is to move from anonymity to autonomy.

From Anonymity to Autonomy

When we are totally conforming, or "anonymous," we allow our "daimonic" a completely free rein. We are at the "impersonal" level when we remain anonymous to ourselves and to others. We "individualize," begin truly to be ourselves, when we reach toward the "personal" level, integrating the powers functioning within us while preserving spontaneity.

After pondering May's discussion of these concepts, a very perceptive woman commented that her strongest period of anonymity came just before completing her undergraduate degree, and continued through some years of job seeking, marriage, and early motherhood. "A part of the herd, doing what the herd does," was her self-description. In earlier years, she had struggled for her identity, her uniqueness, and a belief in her own individuality. In giving herself over to the "prescribed path of society," she found herself conformed to external norms, but alienated from herself. Bouts of melancholy led her to question her purpose, her identity, her goals, and her responsibilities. In order to combat this melancholy (which she interpreted as an expression of daimonic within her), she chose to assert her independence and personal power. Involving herself in activities of personal awareness and growth, she gained hope and energy for future potentialities, something she hadn't known for years. She discovered and accepted her self, with all its "magnificence of destruction and creativity." She concurred with May in recognizing that conformity and anonymity tend to relieve us of a burden of responsibility for our own urges while, at the same time, ensuring that they will be satisfied. This action also ensures that the urges will remain unavailable for individual integration: "The price the person pays is to forfeit his or her chance to develop their own capacities in their own unique way. The punishment is that the person, the self, is never known, and that I very much did not want."

Autonomy is self-powered life. It does not mean that one is out of touch with others, or unaffected by transcendent meaning. It does mean that the self is open to examination and accepted, in all its complexity and multiple possibilities for expression. External and internal forces are integrated into a striving for wholeness. Such a self will not remain anonymous and quietly conform. It knows and says its name, and is response-able to who and what it is. The autonomous person is empowered by self-love.

What name would you give yourself? You can, of course, if you wish to. Each of us can even make a legal change of name, if we desire. On the other hand, you may remember the time when you *gave yourself* the name your parents had been calling you since birth. If so, you exercised the choice to accept who you already are, and to take control over that being. Whatever name we take, the act of giving oneself a name is an important act of self-love, a way of providing personal integration and positive self-assertion.

Loneliness, Aloneness, and Solitude

The struggle with the self, even when moving toward wholeness, or autonomy, is often a lonely one. To acknowledge and celebrate that I am unique is to also recognize that, in many respects, I am alone. Sometimes we feel our aloneness most intensely when we have given ourselves most fully to a relationship. If I let myself really love myself, and extend that love to others, I guarantee myself times of loneliness. Does that make sense?

In the growing literature about the human experience of loneliness, there is an awareness that, like most things, loneliness may be interpreted in a variety of ways. Some tell us that there's no problem with being alone, it's being lone*ly* that hurts. For our health, we need to be alone at times, with time to think, meditate, dream, or whatever we do with such moments. In our being alone, we are sometimes able to really concentrate on an idea, a feeling, a concept, a sensation, a memory. Fromm thus concludes that only the person who is able to be alone is able to love. Being lone-ly, on the other hand, is often interpreted as an experience of anxiety and thus is not productive. Loneliness can be a time of despair, of depression, of inability to focus and center on the self or others.

Psychologist Clark Moustakas has shown that it is important to make a distinction between loneliness and anxiety about loneliness. Such anxiety is a fear of being alone or lonely. When we are snared by that anxiety we cannot allow ourselves to experience being alone, go into the feelings and live through them. To Moustakas, health and the ability to love requires that we be open to and make good use of loneliness, being alone, and the practice of solitude.

In speaking of loneliness, I differentiate between *existential loneliness,* which is a reality of being human, of being aware, and of facing ultimate experiences of upheaval, tragedy, and change, the intrinsic loneliness of being born, of living at the extremes, of dying; and *the anxiety of loneliness,* which is not true loneliness but a defense that attempts to eliminate it by constantly seeking activity with others or by continually keeping busy to avoid facing the crucial questions of life and death. Existential loneliness, with many variations, expresses itself in two basic forms; the loneliness of solitude, which is a peaceful state of being alone with the ultimate mystery of life—people, nature, the universe—the harmony and wholeness of existence; and *the loneliness of a broken life,* a life suddenly shattered by betrayal, deceit, rejection, gross misunderstanding, pain, separation, illness, death, tragedy, and crisis that severely alter not only one's sense of self, but the world in which one lives, one's relationships, and work projects.[19]

Any such experience includes an encounter with the self. This may be a confrontation with disturbing emotional experiences, forcing one to come to terms with one's self. It may also be a "joyous experience of self-discovery," when one is able to connect with the self and at the same time feel connected with all of life. "Being lonely is a way back to oneself," Moustakas tells us. The "bouts of melancholy," referred to earlier, through which the woman struggled to encounter herself, are a good example. These bouts led her, she said, to question her purpose, her identity, her goals, and her responsibilities. Whom did she question? Her own self! She grew to care enough about herself to ask those questions, and to listen to the answers. In Moustakas' view, forcing the question, "Does the way I live really matter?" is a necessary part of the human struggle. This struggle will inevitably involve pain, frustration, and suffering, but will also lead to the achievement of individuality and identity.[20]

Being alone is contrasted with loneliness by Moustakas, as an "act of conscious control, volition, thought, and determination." It is a "necessary pause," while being lonely "is an ultimate condition." We are evolving through a continuity of experience in being alone, but we may experience more radical change in loneliness.

In our self-struggle, we may distinguish two different sides of human aloneness: loneliness is an expression of pain in being alone, whereas *solitude* expresses the "glory of being alone."[21] For many, solitude is something that is chosen, a time to be "with oneself," for reflection, for tuning in to nature, for utilization of imagination and imaging. It offers the opportunity for self-expansion, for contact with transcendent reality, for drawing on memory in order to construct the future. Many turn to solitude for the practice of prayer. One who turns to the self in love, in solitude and willingness to be both alone and lonely, will be more ready to return to others in love.

Having written convincingly of the importance of loneliness in personal growth and the capacity to love both the self and others, Moustakas concludes with a magnificent description of the relationship between loneliness and love:

> From the lonely struggle the person experiences a new determination, a resolve to confront life actively with the full presence of the self. Loneliness is an inevitable outcome of real love, but it is also a process through which new love becomes possible. In the alive person, the rhythms of loneliness and love deepen and enrich human existence. The lonely experience gives a person back to himself, affirms his identity, and enables him to take steps toward new life. The experience of love is the spark and energy of excitement and joy, it is what makes activity purposeful. A balance is essential. Exaggeration of either loneliness or love leads to self-denial and despair. Love has no meaning without loneliness; loneliness becomes real only as a response to love.[22]

We are thinking, here, of what Henri Nouwen calls a "solitude of heart." The individual is not focused on the meeting of "craving needs," but on a developing sensitivity within oneself that is able to allow others in. It is an expansion within, making one able to reach out—whether in physical terms to others bodily present, or in "spiritual" terms of including others within one's solitariness.[23]

Intentionality and Reaching Out

The struggle with self-love is wrapped up in problems with loving others. Nouwen contributes an important insight with his idea of "creating space for strangers." He draws on the biblical, Hebrew, and Middle Eastern tradition of offering hospitality to strangers, in which it is obligatory "to offer an open and hospitable space where strangers can cast off their strangeness and become our fellow human beings."[24] The first such space is *within oneself.* We don't find it easy to accept our own strangeness, the many "strangers" we find lurking within our own personality. We feel hostile toward some of those very real aspects of ourselves, and we don't immediately warm up to the idea of making space for those parts of us we don't like or don't understand, perhaps fear, and prefer to avoid. Hospitality insists on welcoming in the stranger (or welcoming the stranger within!), combatting the hostility by becoming acquainted and offering openness to what the unknown person can bring. Reaching out, then, starts with reaching in, opening up the space within.

You may recall Peck's definition of love: "The will to extend one's self for the purpose of nurturing one's own or another's spiritual growth." Nurturing one's own spiritual growth is an essential, basic part of loving. It is a willful act, requiring an extension of the self to do it. Laziness is a temptation, and also an assurance that one will not really love. The struggle is to be engaged, accepting the suffering and the joy, the pain and the ecstasy.

I want to turn again to Rollo May for a term used in his rejoining of love and will. "Intentionality" is the word he uses to describe the "structure which gives meaning to experience."[25] This is not the same as "intentions," but is rather what underlies them, our capacity to have intentions. Every act which we do consciously is tending toward something—it involves commitment to some end. Furthermore, it *means* something. Not only do we intend that a particular action will take place, but we also expect to express some meaning through that act. As a therapist, May sees therapy bringing together wish, will, and decision, and intentionality is present in all three. *Wish* is the level of awareness—we want something, and we experience any number of reactions to that awareness, even though we may do so quite passively. Wish, though, is telling us something very important about what is meaningful to us, what is of value, what we might be prepared to stand on. What is at the level of awareness, if we are to grow, can be brought into the level of self-consciousness, where *will* is active. Self-consciousness means I am the one having these wishes. They are not just happening, floating around in my imagination—I am doing something in the act of dreaming, or daydreaming, or imagining . . . my recognition that *I* am doing it calls me to make a judgment about it. There is a move toward objectivity here, as I accept the world of my wishes and apply my own perspectives to these wishes, considering how they may or may not become actualities. Since this is a higher level of consciousness, I begin to think of what I shall *do with* what is alive in my awareness. I may want to share it, interpret it, incorporate it into some other expression—or set it aside until a later time. The third level, *decision and responsibility,* responds to the previous dimensions, making decisions which create "a pattern of acting and living which is empowered and enriched by wishes, asserted by will, and is responsive to and responsible for the significant other-persons who are important to one's self in the realizing of the long-term goals."[26]

A young woman may be struck, as she walks on a beautiful spring day, with the beauty of new flowers bursting forth in gardens which she passes. She is aware of their beauty, as well as her wish that she could be surrounded by them all the time. She remembers playing in flowers as a child, and wishes she could again pick some for her mother. As the agent of this wish, it becomes more and more clear to her that flowers are a significant part of her world as well as the world she has known with her mother and others who are important to her. She makes a decision to buy some flowers for herself, and have some sent to her mother. There is a structure of meaning in this activity which is not at all limited to the aesthetic experience of seeing the flower gardens. Once she takes it into herself, and reflects on it, she is in-formed by relationship with others in her world. Furthermore, the action of sharing the flowers becomes a part of something much more than just sharing a momentary aesthetic pleasure, or saying "happy birthday." It becomes an expression of a total relationship and is affected by symbols and meanings that are a part of that relationship, as well as expectations and hopes for how it might be in the future. That is what intentionality is about. We act freely in response to various levels of consciousness. We respond to meanings and create new meanings. Our reaching in—and reaching out—are ways of responding to a world within us and outside us at the same time, and the act of reaching expresses meaning as well as giving shape to new meanings. We *extend* the self for a purpose—it means something for us to nurture the self and another.

Meaning is related to choices in a very special way. Viktor Frankl found, in his concentration camp experience, that it is precisely his *choice* regarding the meaning of experience that makes life possible under the most horrible of conditions. In the circumstances of the extermination/labor camp, Frankl learned that when all else was taken away—family, friends, the work of his life, the hair off his body, all the normal indices of dignity—he could still exercise some choice over the meaning of his suffering. The Nazis could take most of the things valued in life from him, but he did not have to surrender to anyone how he chose to interpret what was happening to him. Frankl found that those who survived the experience, while others gave in and died, seemed to be those who hung on to that choice. Everything can be taken from a person, he writes, "but one thing: the last of the human freedoms—to choose one's attitude in any given set of circumstances, to choose one's own way."[27] There was framework for the meaning, something central to each person's life. May's "intentionality" is a similar idea. What we do is a response to what life *means* to us. That meaning is constantly growing, reshaping, refocusing, as we reflect inwardly on the interaction of our experience with the world outside of us.

Knowing oneself. Accepting oneself. Respecting one's decisions and choices. Integrating the self and enhancing the ways in which the self can be trusted. All these and more are, as we have seen, involved in the struggle to love the self and reach out to others. It isn't easy. If we look seriously into ourselves, or even listen occasionally to our feelings, we find within ourselves the "element of self-aggrandizement and distortion" that May assures us will always accompany our finding our own convictions and acting on them.[28] The growth in our relationships with others begins when we start coming to terms with "who we are," with particular powers that make up our own personality and being. If we are realistic about ourselves, we are more likely to be realistic about others and allow them the same freedom. We shall have more difficulty labeling others as bad or evil when we have seen more clearly the paradoxes within ourselves that sometimes lean toward the destructive. Likewise, we are more able to celebrate with others their joy and self-worth when we have celebrated our own.

Shared Experiences and Insights

The evils of the world do not frighten me near as much as my own possibility for evil.

I accept the daimonic as . . . the pattern of being which constitutes my center. I experience the daimon as inner guidance. The more I recognize the daimonic the more personal meaning I can form out of what was previously a threatening impersonal chaos. If I repress the daimonic, I find these powers constantly returning to overcome me; whereas, if I allow them to stay, I have to struggle to a new level of consciousness to integrate them.

Assertion and dedication are necessary for the struggle, and although I may achieve genuine self-realization I am maimed in the process. Another can see the whole story in the eyes of the person who has struggled and prevailed. And, for me, this is where humility occurs; for anyone who has really struggled for self-realization, humility is inherent in the results of that struggle.

In my own experience, the concept of the "daimonic" is now very obvious to me. I am a recovering alcoholic and drug addict. In May's view, I would say my addiction is the symbolic sense of my daimons. Until I was forced to confront them, I was pulling away from society, and pulling myself apart. I consider my daimons to be a sense of insecurity, dependence, and a need to conform. I felt so unsure of myself I developed a dependence on those around me for acceptance. I needed to do what others were doing in order to face reality. I started out in junior high occasionally drinking with the other kids. In high school, the majority of the school was into drug usage. I enjoyed this because when I was loaded I didn't have to face reality, anything dramatic or traumatic. I was able to repress my self-doubt, fears, low self-esteem, and little self-acceptance. There is no question that I was spiritually bankrupt. As I got older and continued with the drugs and alcohol, I became more and more emotionally bankrupt. Along the way, my daimonic erupted in a destructive manner known as the disease of alcoholism and drug addiction. I went for what seemed to be a long time, admitting I had a problem but never accepting it. Finally, I was forced to confront my disease due to destructed physical condition. I had become so self-destructive that I was facing my own death.

I believe that God has a purpose for me here on earth and has spared my mortal life. I don't know what that purpose is but I want to grow spiritually. I believe it is the foundation for my emotional being. The realization that God loves me helps me to love myself. I want to continue to grow. . . .

I guess you could say I'm trying to direct my daimons in a spiritual way. I am confronting my insecurities, dependencies, low self-esteem, and self acceptance. I am learning how to love myself, as I am.

8

Power and Dignity in Loving Relationships

Let's eavesdrop on some snatches of conversation:

"I *know* I don't own your body, but it really upsets me when you keep talking to a guy who is looking you over like he was!"

"Mom! Where you been? It's about time you got home! I want something to eat!"

"Yes, I remember asking 'when are you going to grow up?'—but this isn't exactly the change I expected."

"No, it doesn't mean I don't like you, or that our friendship doesn't mean anything any more, but I just want to go to the movies with these others tonight, without being with you at the same time."

"Who's your letter from?"

"But, Dad, I thought you'd be happy to see me making my own decisions for a change . . ."

"I just want a 'girls night out.' I *know* that you and I haven't been anywhere together this week, because of your Lion's Club meeting *and* your bowling team, but I just want to be with my friends tonight."

"What are other people going to think, seeing you out at lunch with her, when you're married to me?"

"Why can't those people see that *we* only want what's *best* for *them*?"

Perhaps you heard your own voice in some of these phrases. They reveal to us that it is not easy to allow freedom, either to oneself or to others, nor to resist possessiveness. They also suggest to us that it is hard to deal with being controlled by another, or several others. We don't like being manipulated by their ideas of what our roles or behaviors should be; we resent their implying that we have certain duties to them. It is a challenge to cope with freedom in a responsible way in a relationship, in order that the intimacy and sharing of the relationship are nurtured.

Possessiveness and Protection

Possessiveness and freedom can be real problems in loving relationships. Each of us wants to be an individual, to exercise freedom and not be controlled by someone else. At the same time, the very act of entering into (or being born into) a relationship with another or others creates limitations on freedom. We usually ask for those limitations. As a child, we want and expect certain things from others to fulfill our basic needs. As we grow older, we find attributes in others that are attractive to us, and we want to benefit from those attributes. In addition, we may also find that it is more comfortable to have someone else meeting some of our needs than to meet them for ourselves.

Each of us needs, or wants, some *protection* at various times in our lives. (It is often difficult to distinguish between "need" and "want," isn't it?) We need a "place" to come in out of the cold, a source of comfort, a feeling of security, and some support. That feels warm, and good. We do *not* want to feel *possessed*. Usually, that does *not* feel good.

I have discovered that what some persons call "possessiveness" in a relationship, others call "protection." I'm assuming, however, that these terms do actually describe very different aspects of relationships. The line between them can, at points, be quite narrow. Placed on a continuum, however, these terms can help us to differentiate between two extremes in our experience.

How do you feel when you think that someone is possessing you, or is behaving possessively toward you? I have asked this question in classes or discussion groups a number of times, and some of the words that emerged most often are:

"stifled"
"controlled"
"suffocated"
"powerless"
"not taken seriously"
"angry"
"dominated"
"hemmed in"
"frustrated"

These terms clearly indicate a destructive direction in the relationship. As one person wrote about such an experience, "it felt smothering, and insulting, and strangely impersonal. My response was first to feel guilty and acquiesce, and then to be outraged, rebellious, and finally leave the relationship." Another put it this way:

> It's really hard to explain to someone what it feels like to be interrogated on your whereabouts, who you were with, and trying to be changed to fit someone else's nice little mold. I've been giving it a lot of thought, and last Friday night the possessiveness and jealousy came out in my boyfriend for no reason, again. I said *no more* and we split up. I was able to recognize what he was doing and I didn't want to go through it any more. I need to grow and he was stifling that growth. I can't say I feel wonderful and good because I miss him very much. However, I can't belong to anyone but myself.

You've probably heard someone say, "I can't live without you," or her, or him. How does that sound to you? If that actually were the case, you wouldn't dare to die, or move away, or make any major changes, would you? It's a very controlling statement and, usually, not even true. We do, however, say such things to persons we care about, and that reveals our own inclinations to possessiveness.

Possessiveness is not only something others do to us . . . we do it to others. I have also asked classes and other groups to say the words describing how they feel when they are possessive *toward* someone else. These words came out:

"powerful"
"controlling"
"empty"
"protective"
"threatened"
"defensive"
"insecure"
"guilty"

One person volunteered that this approach in a relationship grows from fear that there is "not enough love to go around" and "I will be left out." Another said, "it is because I am afraid they will find someone else more attractive and fun to be around." The fact that the word "protective" came as some reflected on their approach to others indicates how complicated this issue can be.

How do you feel when you feel "protected"? This question usually prompts such responses as, "someone cares about me," "I feel warm and secure," "supported," "taken care of," "worried over," and "loved." One young woman told of having lunch one day with her lover and a professor with whom he worked. She became upset and flustered when the professor, whom she had just met, began asking her a lot of questions. She was greatly helped when she felt a caring hand from the lover squeeze her under the table, "assuring me that he was there to defend me if need be." That simple gesture was deeply appreciated: "Protection does not have to be a physical thing—more often than not, it is letting a person know that you are standing by them and with them, that you understand them. At this particular point, he was also saying that he loved me."

I suggested earlier that possessiveness and protection are at opposite ends of a continuum, that the first is more destructive to a relationship and the latter more constructive. One person has put it, "Possession is something one does for oneself; protection is something one does for the other." There is no doubt that it is easy for one of these qualities of experience to "shade" over into the other. A particularly thoughtful student distinguished between the terms this way:

> Protectiveness has connotations of caring and concern, a lifting up rather than the closing in of possessiveness. The most distinctive aspect of protectiveness seems to be a recognition of the other and thus a wish to help, care for, keep the other from unnecessary external dangers.

You may prefer to use different terms as you think about your own experience. Basically, we are concerned with the nature and quality of a relationship: whether it promotes dependency and limited individuality, or the kind of freedom which facilitates response/ability to choices and the capacity to enter into loving interdependence. The quality and nature of a relationship often determine whether possessiveness or protection are experienced. A particular behavior may be either, depending on the relationship. Take, for instance, the statement, "I will *not* let you walk alone down town at night," said by a father to his nineteen year old daughter. With no further discussion of alternatives, such a statement could easily draw the response, "when are you ever going to let me grow up!" Stated by a caring friend, accompanied by an offer to accompany her, or check on her by phone at her destination, the words are likely to be received as a welcome attempt at protection. A "protective" action which I take toward my five year old son could likely be experienced as illegitimate possessiveness by my 21 year old daughter. A concern expressed to that same daughter may be experienced by her as a sincere concern fitting into a warm pattern of parent-child relationship; a similar concern expressed to my spouse could well be taken as an inappropriate attempt to control.

Each of us has our own ways of responding to the experience I'm discussing. Some of us like the feeling of "specialness" that comes with another feeling possessive toward us. Others of us feel crowded and confined if *anyone* is trying to protect us from something, especially if we feel that it is the very risk-taking from which they are trying to protect us that is necessary for our growth. You can sort out those terms and the experiences they represent for yourself. The important issue is the *feeling* involved and the extent to which there is real freedom in the relationship for each person to grow and give to both self and other.

Freedom and Change

Ellen had known for a long time that she needed to do some things for herself. She enjoyed her family, and housekeeping and cooking had never been a burden to her, as they seemed to be for some of her friends. Still, she simply hadn't taken the time to follow up on the interests she developed in college and her early years of marriage; she seldom read novels, let alone tried to do any creative writing, even though it was her undergraduate major. Both her husband and her three children had encouraged her to "get out and do something for herself." So, she did. She enrolled in a Continuing Education course in writing, and it was exciting! One afternoon after her class, she and a friend had a drink together and read each other's short stories, sharing criticisms and supporting the strengths they found in each other's work. When Ellen finally noticed the time, she hurried off for home, gaining some consolation from her friend's reminder that her family wanted her to have this experience and would be understanding of her late return. As she walked in the house, she heard thirteen-year-old Jason's just-changed voice call out, "Mom! Where you been? It's about time you got here! I'm hungry." She hurried to the kitchen, and had just opened the refrigerator when her husband Bill hurried into the house with, "Oh my God, isn't dinner even started yet? I've got to be back to the office in forty-five minutes to finish the contract proposal!" Ten-year-old Michelle slipped into the kitchen and held her hand while Ellen tried to decide between lashing out with profanities or dissolving into tears. Just then Julie, their seventeen-year-old, called out for all to hear, "Today is my payday and I'm treating us all to pizza! I'll call the order while you get into the car. Dad, we can eat and drop you at the office no more than fifteen minutes late! That will still get you there before anybody else, if I know those guys you work with!" The wink and pat she gave her mother as she brushed by her on the way to the phone helped Ellen to pull together some of the feelings tugging at her:

> You are free to change, as long as things remain the same for me!
> Sure, I want *you* to grow, but *I* don't want to be uncomfortable in the process!
> Of course my schedule sometimes changes at the last minute, but I have to be able to depend on someone (you) for some stability . . .

These are fairly normal responses when one party to a relationship decides to make a change. Each of us wants the freedom to be, and become, who we are and need to be; it isn't always easy to decide to exercise that freedom. It is more comfortable, however, if we can depend on a rather certain predictability in the behavior and attitudes of other parties to the relationship.

Jason, the early adolescent, thought it was nice for Mom to do something that would make her a little less dull—but he was hungry. Soccer practice had increased his usually ravenous appetite and, besides, "we *always* eat at six!" And, dinner is "mom's job." Michelle saw the look on her mother's face and remembered how *she* felt when someone reminded her of something they thought she should have done. Bill had one thing on his mind, getting his project done at work, and he assumed that this concern held highest priority. Julie was growing out of her adolescence, and had recently reflected on how much change she had been going through and how disruptive some of her behavior had been for others around her.

A major ingredient in a loving relationship is growth, and growth inevitably means change. Change in one person in a relationship must have an impact on others. Being a part of a loving relationship requires willingness to have one's life disrupted by the changes chosen by other parties.

Freedom within a caring relationship is as difficult and complex as it is necessary. Freedom, between intimates, takes on the elements of a dance: it requires movement, space, rhythm and coordination. Thus, while one person, or one group, is involved in self-expression and growth in self-awareness, that action also takes place in the context of responding to another or others. I experience increased freedom as I come to know that the deepest feelings of others toward me are active admiration for *who* I am. The "who" I am is both fluctuating and steady; thus, the dance.[1]

A psychiatrist who has done much counseling with persons in committed and married relationships has offered some good suggestions for approaching this issue through the consideration of certain "rights." David Viscott emphasizes that we all have the right, and need the freedom, to grow. He is realistic in recognizing what this can mean for a relationship: "partners must allow each other the freedom to grow even if that freedom is a threat to the relationship. The freedom to grow *up* is also the freedom to grow apart."[2] Here we have the suggestion of a major reason why many of us are so resistant to real freedom. Exercising that freedom is scary! My agreement to your right to grow and freedom to pursue who you are opens to me the fear that you might do something that I don't like; you might take a direction that is quite different from what I had foreseen for you and us; I may find that my feelings are hurt; we may, in fact, grow apart. If I open myself to growth and change, I may get a new and different perspective on our relationship, one that requires some changes in the way we encounter each other. Or, it may mean that I'll have to accept some things about me, and about us, that are disappointing. Do we want that kind of growth and freedom? Unfortunately, there is no *real* growth or freedom that does not contain such risks. The risks, however, are not the whole story. There is also enrichment, excitement, and spontaneity when parties to a relationship are allowed to discover and develop new or undeveloped parts of themselves. Ari Kiev has stated the matter clearly:

> If your love is to remain alive, you must be active and flexible. The alternative is a forced and false sense of coherence which only leads to stagnation. Standing water—so goes an old proverb—breeds only disease. The pool of possibilities must, in any relationship, be periodically stirred to foster progression. You may not want to disturb the apparently smooth surface of your relationship in this way, but psychologically such a disturbance may provide exactly the regenerative impulse it needs.
>
> In good relationships, people accept one another's idiosyncrasies and work continuously on improving communication. Rather than avoiding change, they actually build a "change factor" into their relationships, allowing for individual growth and shifts in expectations as the patterns of relating evolve. Relationships evolve best when you are neither so exclusively self-interested that there isn't room for the needs of the other, nor so unaware of your own needs that you lose your identity in meeting the other's demands.[3]

The "rights" proposed by Viscott are closely interrelated. In addition to the "right to grow," he stresses the right to "become the person you were destined to become," and "the right to be free." Becoming the person we want to be, feel destined to become, is crucial to each of us, (as individuals, and as groups or nations), even when we are not at all clear just who or what that person, or group, will ultimately look like! Obstacles that prevent self-fulfillment, especially those demanded by a relationship, can eat away at an individual and the relationship. Structured obstacles, even repression, in political entities, eat away at the tie between individual and the group, or nation. Commitment to a relationship, whether an interpersonal one or a citizen-nation relationship, will not remain strong and productive where potential for self-fulfillment is stifled. Likewise, the leaders of a powerful nation who insist on imposing their view of reality on those of another society are violating very basic human rights of self-exploration, discovery and fulfillment; such is a denial of a loving relationship in the larger community context.

The right to be "free" prohibits any party to a relationship from being the "caretaker" or "guardian" of the other, except in the temporary circumstances of parent-child ties or the emergency of injury or disablement. The caretaker attitude that presumes to know what is best for the other and insists that the other be a certain way eliminates the exercise of free choice and self-expression. Most of us have times, of course, when we are frustrated by choices that face us, and we welcome the possibility that someone else might make the decisions for us. A relationship in which that is the dominant mode, however, is one that few of us would want—we certainly would not find it to be a loving one.

A loving relationship, we are saying, requires freedom. It has a high tolerance for change, for uncertainty, for the unpredictable, for exploration and discovery, even for occasional separation and solitude. More than mere tolerance, it may even thrive on these dynamics. Such a relationship values autonomy, accepts risk, and is willing to share vulnerability.

Autonomy and Shared Vulnerability

Permanence and commitment are matters of real interest and concern in contemporary literature on relationships. If freedom is a right, how far does it go? Viscott asserts that "in a free relationship both partners always keep an option to walk out if and whenever they choose to."[4] Ouch! That sounds uncaring, not at all like persons who are committed to each other and to their "third self!" On the other hand, this assertion is based on a profound insight. A shared vulnerability is produced when partners in a relationship understand and accept the *fact* of this option. Whether we say our commitment is forever or not, the reality of human experience is that we constantly face possibilities for leaving or breaking the commitment. The sharing of vulnerability allows respect for the feelings of the other. It promotes the assumption of accountability for consequences of our actions. The partners *choose* to be together within "a shared view of the world that allows each . . . to be free," in which each can trust the love of the other.[5]

Perhaps that makes a little more sense. Shared vulnerability can be the basis of deep respect and commitment to full responsibility for one's own behavior toward the other. The freedom which allows deep intimacy in a relationship is not possible without that shared vulnerability.

You may be helped, as I have been, in understanding the dynamics of such freedom and its risks, by thinking not only of what it means in interpersonal relations but also in a person's relationship with an institution. Several years ago, I learned of a dean of a graduate professional school in a major university who seemed to have a great deal of freedom in his work. Even though he was an important administrator, he was at the time involved in matters considered highly controversial by some in the public. I once asked one of his colleagues how this dean managed it. His reply was, "It's simple. He carries a signed resignation letter in his pocket at all times." *That* is freedom of the sort described by Viscott. What we need to add to the story is that he never did walk out on the relationship, nor did the institution ever sever it. He eventually retired as the dean with longest seniority among the university's administrators, as well as an impressively lengthy tenure on the faculty itself. He was deeply in love with that institution. He could have walked out any day—not without pain, disappointment, and a sense of loss—but as a whole person able to move on to other commitments. He didn't. He knew his own vulnerability and that of the institution, and in the sharing of it, their mutual freedoms fed their relationship rather than stifling it.

Another way in which Viscott pulls us up short is with his reminder that "you cannot control the affections of another person."[6] When we reach a certain level of commitment in a relationship, we certainly hope that we can count on the affection, or loyalty, or patriotism of the other party. It is easy for that "counting on" to edge over into something experienced as control. Controlling affections can't be done. What *can* be done is to allow feelings to be stated and understood, to have trust in the other's intentions, and to make allowances for each other's frailties. The impossibility of controlling fidelity, affection, and guilt is summed up: "You cannot be loved by someone who does not have the right not to love you."[7] Someone can love you, fully love you, only when they have the freedom *not* to love you. That is tough to accept, but any thoughtful parent or otherwise experienced lover knows the deep truth in the statement.

One way of describing what is required for freedom within a caring relationship is "personal autonomy." The idea of autonomy has been closely examined in recent years, with the seeming rise in the value of the individual in our modern era. An autonomous person is one who is self-governing and independent. Autonomy involves freedom from control by the will of others. It often implies that one is free not only in action but in definition, or interpretation, of experience. For autonomy to simply lead to aloofness, defying deep commitments, would be a perversion of growing in love. The "law of the self" frees one sufficiently from control of others to enter into new levels of interaction and interdependence as a lover. Milton Mayeroff describes this reality:

> Autonomy does not mean being detached and without strong ties; that would imply that attachments and strong ties necessarily tie me down and enslave me. Again, autonomy does not mean being self-enclosed and "free as a bird." On the contrary, I am autonomous because of my devotion to others and my dependence on them, when dependence is the *kind* that liberates both me and my others.[8]

We are warned by George Bach and Ronald Deutsch about some possible pitfalls in the contemporary notion that two totally independent individuals are required for a healthy relationship. They liken the situation to the building of a fire: "Conventional psychology sees two logs; the better the logs, the better the fire. So it aims to perfect the logs, on the assumption that the fire will take care of itself." To Bach and Deutsch, the approach is limited. They prefer to emphasize that "the crucial element is the fire between the logs, the dynamics between the pair."[9]

How do we bring about this combination of autonomy and dependence, which creates the real warmth of the fire *between* the logs? Being dependent on another doesn't sound altogether healthy or intimacy producing. Nor, however, do we see much likelihood of depth encounter between totally independent persons. A loving relationship is one which is *interdependent*.

Dependence, Independence, and Interdependence

The family reunion had been a special, precious time. My 92-year-old great aunt, small and frail, was ready to walk to a waiting car on the cold wintry night. Since the sidewalk from the house to the car was icy, I thought I would be helpful by holding her arm while she walked.

Quietly and patiently, but with sufficient firmness to penetrate my insensitivity, she freed her arm from my grip, and reached for my hand. Her words still ring in my ears: "I can keep my balance better if I can hold someone's hand, rather than have them hold on to me."

Of course! I was going to *hold her up; she* preferred to control *her own balance!* If I'm going to let her hold my hand, I'll not be in control. If that big man holds her, *she* feels out of balance, out of control of herself. A hand to hold assures the maintenance of that necessary balance in an unsteady situation. The only way I can really help her, in a way that protects her dignity, (and balance!) is to *not* be in control. Her safety, and my desire to help, require, *interdependence*.

John Crosby has provided a very helpful way to visualize some differences between the experiences of dependence, independence, and interdependence. Through the clever device of letter "frames," he demonstrates differences in stance and feeling between the three:

A FRAME	*H FRAME*	*M FRAME*
A	**H**	**M**
Dependence	*Independence*	*Interdependence*
If one lets go, the other falls	If one lets go, the other hardly feels a thing	If one lets go, the other feels a loss but recovers balance
No individual identity	Strong individual identity	Healthy individual identity
Self absorbed in the other	Self-sufficient	Self relates meaningfully to other
Strong Couple identity	No couple identity	Meaningful couple identity

In this chart, you can see that Crosby's intention is to modify the **A** and **H** frames into the **M**.[10] In the interdependence **M** frame, a healthy individual identity combines a commitment to the self with a commitment to the other, and contributes to a fulfilling relationship. The "meaningful couple" identity is something to which both parties contribute. Each person will stand on her or his own, but together they will also have a clear identity that is the product of their individual personalities in interaction. This identity has stability while remaining in flux.

Crosby's model is designed as a part of his discussion of love and marriage. Marriage is also the focus of the comments by Nancy Friday:

We all need a close, intimate relationship . . . To be held in someone's arms, to be able to say, "I'm scared, lonely, tell me everything will be all right. Comfort me and I'll do the same for you when you feel this way"— that is not asking to be guaranteed against all the vicissitudes of life. The woman or man who says this is merely asking for a resting place, a fueling station in which to gather strength to go on again. It is not submitting to a superior-inferior relationship. It is the pause that refreshes.

On the other hand, when "take care of me" means asking someone to permanently interpose herself/himself between us and reality, the wish is destructive to the self, and therefore to the marriage.[11]

This is not only an issue in the marriage relationship; the capacity to develop interdependence is fundamental to any loving relationship. Drawing on Abraham Maslow's theory of human motivation, Crosby distinguished between "illegitimate needs" (Maslow's "deficiency" needs) and "legitimate" or "being" needs. Legitimate needs are those which contribute to our sense of being, and they grow in a commitment that is based on "trust, honesty, freedom and caring." Maslow recognizes that we may have some weaknesses which we expect others, or another, to take care of for us, thus a deficiency need. In a relationship, this is recognized as an "illegitimate ego need," coming from dependence and "an unconscious desire to make another person responsible for 'who I am.' "[12] Certain aspects of our personality development, such as personal identity, a sense of being OK and a basic self-confidence, are not things that others can give us in a mature relationship. If we are lacking in those areas, we have a "deficiency need" which requires our own efforts and struggle. Others may support us and help us to see possibilities for our growth. They cannot, however, meet those needs for us, and a relationship with another cannot be a substitute for taking care of those needs. To live with another person because we need a place to live will fulfill, at least temporarily, a basic human need for shelter; the shelter, of course, should not be confused with intimacy. Likewise, a warm body in bed next to us is exactly that—a warm body, fulfilling some unmet needs for warmth. Again, that in itself is not intimacy, nor is it necessarily love.

On the other hand, we continue to have needs, all our lives, to grow beyond the basic stages of our development if we are to be happy and productive human beings. We have "growth" needs, and we can look to each other to be sensitive to and supportive of our ways of responding to these needs. A commitment to be supportive of each other's perceptions of, as well as fulfillment of, growth needs will be crucial to a loving relationship.

As noted earlier, the comments from Friday and the chart by Crosby were directed to the marriage relationship. The community dimension of relationships is replete with examples of groups attempting to keep others in a dependent status, with individuals and groups struggling for independence, and with the necessity for the emergence of interdependence in order to have a healthy environment for human life. White Americans remain resistant to understanding the slogans of "black power," "red power," and "brown power," as declarations of independence for self-definition of identity. If I use superior external force to subjugate you, then place an impersonal, artificial label ("Indian," "Negro," "Mexican") on you, while reducing you to dependent status, it is not possible for us to relate meaningfully. You may well choose to respond, in a move toward independence, by asserting your own name for yourself and your group, your own identity. The white majority may be confused when Cassius Clay becomes Muhammed Ali; the content of the name, however, is not as important as the *act* of moving out of the dependent role and taking the responsibility for naming oneself. Likewise, "grey power" is an insistence that the American "cult of youth" will not determine what it is like to be "old." "Women's liberation" declares the independence of females from a male stranglehold over their self-definition. "Men's liberation" will free men from macho images and self-definitions requiring control over others, allowing fuller humanity for everyone. Claims of independence (however uncomfortable for those who were previously in control of identity) are necessary steps toward an eventual relationship of interdependence, in which self-loving and self-confident persons are sufficiently secure in their own identity to share vulnerability with others. Only then can trust lead to a commitment that produces intimacy.

Trust, Commitment, Intimacy, and Jealousy

An interdependent relationship requires trust. Coming to terms with that fact is tricky, because our common ideas about trust sometimes mislead us. Often, when we hear the word, "trust" in a conversation, we can track down its meaning to be something like this: I am able to predict how you will behave; I feel certain that you will not do or say anything about which I will feel badly; what I have told you will not be repeated to anyone by you. Strength in love between persons (and/or groups) will be built with a somewhat different understanding of trust. As Mayeroff puts it, "Caring involves trusting the other to grow in its own time and in its own way. It appreciates the independent existence of the other, that the other is *other*."[13] Basically, he seems to be saying, I trust you to *be you*. The focus, then, is not on your pleasing me, but rather on your being true to yourself. If I really care about you, it will please me that you maintain your own integrity, even when that leads you to behavior that is counter to what I wanted from you. After focusing on trusting another to make mistakes and learn from them, Mayeroff gives us content for considerable meditation in saying, "We trust the child *now* to make those decisions for himself that are reasonably commensurate with his experience and his abilities."[14] "Reasonably commensurate with . . ." is very much like "being true to oneself." It is, perhaps, easier for us to tolerate a child's not meeting our expectations, because, after all. . . . The same basic activity, however, is involved in trust at all levels, whether child, adolescent or adult. What else could a person rely on, other than experience and abilities? What else, unless we really mean that I only trust you if you do what I am expecting from you?

I am more likely to trust you if I trust myself. I trust me to be and do what I am (and that is always in a process of growth, even though there is a central core that remains steady). I trust the general environment in which we function, to be and do what it *is*. Therefore I can open myself to you without fear that you will destroy me, because you simply do not have the power. Things may happen as part of our interaction which are hurtful to me, or to you. As long as we trust each other to be who we are, allowing for mistakes and errors in judgment, as well as expression of feelings, we can grow toward intimacy. Once more, I find Mayeroff putting it exceedingly well:

> The realization that "he trusts me" has its own way of activating the person cared for to justify such trust and to trust himself to grow. In working out ideas we show trust in following their lead and allowing organization to emerge from them. We also show trust in letting them "come home" to us so that we may understand what it is we are doing, and in ultimately exposing them to examination and criticism by others. *Trusting the other is to let go; it includes an element of risk and a leap into the unknown, both of which take courage.*
>
> We show lack of trust by trying to dominate and force the other into a mold, or by requiring guarantees as to the outcome, or even by "caring" too much. Insofar as schooling or religious instruction is primarily indoctrination without allowing the opportunity to question and reflect on what is taught, it is rooted in lack of trust in the other. The man who fears and avoids the unknown, who must always be sure how it will all turn out, cannot allow the other to grow in its own way. He becomes unresponsive to the needs of the other.[15]

Risk is what makes commitment possible. When we commit ourselves to someone or some thing, we don't really know how it will turn out. Viscott's words about keeping an option to walk out always elicit a response from some in my classes: "that's not commitment!" or, "how can there be any real trust if you always keep the 'back door' open?'' As thinking, knowing, feeling human beings, we always have the *option* to do something other than what we have promised. Commitment will involve the choice *not* to exercise such an option. A more positive way to put it is that commitment undergirds the choice to continue and strengthen a relationship when confronted with a choice not to do so.

Commitment which is productive of intimacy is one that chooses a relationship based on a balance of power. When I have committed myself to a relationship in which you have the freedom to be you, there is no way in which you can then be "mine." We cannot own each other. We *can* own our individual commitments to our mutual freedom and our interdependence in support of freedom and growth. I am not yours, and you are not mine; our relationship, however, *is* ours, and we can trust each other to be there to support each of our efforts to fulfill our uniqueness as well as to create our togetherness.

We *want,* even *need,* intimacy. Intimacy provides safety for relaxation, exposure, and unconditional giving.[16] It is reached by interdependence, by two or more persons who "own" themselves enough that they are able to release themselves to the protection of the other, or others.

But, if I am going to release myself to your care, be vulnerable to you, I want you to be the same way toward me. If I see any of that energy going some other direction, then I become jealous!

> As long as human beings need affection, there will be some jealousy. It probably cannot be completely eradicated. Even if you are relatively successful in working with your jealousy it will most likely recur in some form at some time. Don't be surprised when this happens. The jealous flash is a perfectly natural response. You'll feel it every time an important relationship appears to be threatened. Your jealousy is neither proof of love nor evidence of personal failure. It is merely a signal which tells you to attend to your relationship and to yourself.[17]

These comments from studies of jealousy by Gordon Clanton and Lynn Smith help us to understand that the *feeling* of jealousy is related to fear that we are out of control in a relationship. It may be dominated by a fear of loss; the loss may be of a primary place in another person's attentions, being left out of an activity, or perhaps the actual loss of the other person (or that person's affections). If the feeling of loss of control is involved, it may ultimately include a sense of loss of control over oneself.

Jealousy, then, is a warning signal. It is a warning to attend to the relationship, and it is probably a warning to attend to oneself. By growing toward autonomy and self-direction, one becomes more permanently secure. With less susceptibility to insecurity, a person is less likely to be jealous, and at the same time exhibits a personal strength that is attractive to a partner.[18]

As many observors of the human condition have pointed out, our search is constantly for a balance. We long for unity with another, and we need to be alone. There are fears related to either end of the continuum, which Keen calls "a continual dance between bonding and returning to our boundaries."[19] Many of those fears are, to some extent, alleviated by the development and maintenance of power and dignity in one's relationship with self and with others.

Power and Dignity

One of the more popular one-liners quoted in books about love in recent years is a poetic statement by Rainer Maria Rilke: "Love consists of this, that two solitudes protect and touch and greet each other."[20] "*Two solitudes.*" Without the rest of the sentence, this sounds like Crosby's **H**-frame. These solitudes, however, are reaching *to* each other in a way that becomes the **M**-frame. I am struck by some implications of the three actions taken by the solitudes toward each other, and shall consider them in reverse order.

Greet each other. A greeting is an acknowledgment, a recognition, an affirmation of existence and importance. A *real* greeting is usually by name: I do not feel nearly as greeted by a "hi," or "hello" in passing as I do by a "hello Bob." What's in a name? there are many historical answers to that, but we get at the issue more quickly by asking, what's in *no* name? Little or nothing. We greet another individual, one who is *someone,* who has a name brought to our interaction by the person. When you and I meet, you tell me your name; I don't give you a name that fits my convenience and increases my power.

Think of the many ways in which persons do not have names. We are concerned, rightly, in our contemporary age, with apparent depersonalization represented by the assigning of numbers. There are other forms of no-names, however, which represent identity only through others. Notice, for instance, what can be found on the society or women's page of many local newspapers. We see a photograph of a group of women standing or seated around a table, and the caption under the picture tells us they are planning some future event of significance. Then their names are given: "Mrs. Joseph Jones, Mrs. Thomas Thompson, Mrs. Fred Fredricks, Mrs. Robert Robertson." There are four or more well-dressed, intelligent-looking, seemingly competent human beings, all without real names. They are all Mrs. Somebody Else. We see images of persons in these photographs, but the only identity the newspaper shares with us is the name of another person who is, apparently, the real source of their identity. (The same papers won't even do that to children! A pictured child has a name first, then a role identity: "Mary Michaels, daughter of Mr. and Mrs. Mike Michaels.") An inquiry to such journalists as to the reason for this procedure will elicit the answer that it is just a formality, one of the niceties that ought to be maintained in an age of dying decorum. Nicety? How "nice" is it to have only someone else's identity? There is a sense in which it *is* "nice"—for those who thus maintain power in a vastly unequal relationship of men over women.

Television news, with its need to communicate something in a very brief interval, picks up on a headline approach and further encourages us to be acquainted only through imposed labels. A story will, usually, mention a name, but what gets across to us is the neat category into which the object is placed: "Cuban," "homosexual," "activist," or "Marine." Most of our social structures do not encourage, or even permit us to really greet each other from our solitudes.

We have to break through that, and we do. It is not unusual, while walking across a university campus at class-break time, with literally thousands of persons on the move in a relatively small space, to hear someone call out, loudly, "hey, Charlie," or "Teresa, how ya doing?" Many yards away, the recognized person will emerge from the mass, with a broad smile and a hand waving, perhaps with a shout of response, and the greeting is completed. A unique individual has been acknowledged, recognized, and included in someone else's life, if only for a moment. Two solitudes have greeted each other, and that is part of love.

Touch each other. You have probably been to a hospital room to see a friend or relative. You didn't know what to say; words came, but they seemed inadequate, if not inane. Finally, after feeling awkward while thinking about it, you reached out and touched the person. You could tell from their look and your feeling that it was the thing to do: two solitudes touching each other.

Having grown up in a family and environment that did not particularly encourage touching, it was a learning experience for me, as an adult, to discover the significance of touch in interpersonal communication. After a few years of work on that, I happened to be invited to speak in a church in which I had been involved years earlier. "Touching" was chosen as my theme and I hoped to explore it in several ways. I also decided to get the congregation involved in some physical touching, and asked them to reach to persons sitting beside them and hold hands during the pastoral prayer. Perhaps this doesn't sound very threatening—but, for many, it clearly was. As I was warming them up for this experience, I noticed that one elderly man was sitting alone, far off to the side, in his traditional pew; trying to be subtle, I suggested to the congregation that they look around, and be sure to include anyone who did not have anyone near them. It didn't work. No one moved to be within touching distance of the man sitting alone, and he remained quietly where he was. Finally, when it was time to begin the prayer, I stepped from the chancel and walked over to where I could hold out my hand to him. With a glow on his face that I shall forever have etched in my memory, he reached to me, and we held hands through the prayer. Two solitudes touched each other.

We can touch with a word, with eyes, with physical contact. When we touch we become vulnerable. The custom of shaking hands, we are sometimes told, originated in a time when it was important to demonstrate to another that one did not have a weapon in one's hand. An open, empty hand held out to another is a signal that no danger is intended; the party offering the hand takes a risk in that opening. Touching each other is potentially dangerous. It's also essential for intimacy.

Protect each other. Gaylin tells us that being cared for "refers to all aspects of that word: to be taken care of, to be concerned about, to be worried over, to be supervised, to be attended to—to be loved."[21] Persons who greet each other as unique and precious individuals can take care of each other without taking away any personhood. Helping with needs and guaranteeing some security can be done, even for disabled persons, in ways that allow those persons to hang on to personal strength and dignity.

While doing some research on the relationship of religion, life styles, and health, I was talking with a woman who is a member of a Roman Catholic order. She noted in our conversation that, although her order has many elderly members and they have their own infirmary, there are seldom patients there and they usually don't stay long. Whatever their age, they have roles to play in the community, and others who need them. She gave a revealing example: when an 80-year-old member is not able to carry her own food tray in the cafeteria, who carries it for her? A 40-year-old? No—another 80, or perhaps, 70-year-old. Among the many beautiful features of the play and movie, *On Golden Pond,* are the ways in which persons take care of, protect each other. Ethel protects Norman in his increasing frustration and occasional confusion; he protects her with his affection and the consistent dryness of his humor. The elder man and the young boy find increasing ways to protect each other as the depth of their relationship grows.

"Two solitudes"—persons who can stand on their own, with individual power and dignity—share their vulnerability with each other. They respect and guard the uniqueness of the other. They open up, risking some nakedness and potential harm, and thus expose tender places that can be touched. And they call each other by name—not just "dear," or "daddy," or "wife," or "doctor,"—as meaningful or affectionate as those titles might be. They are not merely roles to each other, but persons who bring their own identity to a relationship in which that identity can be discovered, explored, nurtured, and encouraged to grow. They protect, touch, and greet each other.

Groups and nations can act that way, too. It's not easy (anyone who has tried knows that it's not easy on an individual basis, either). Nations that are friendly have all sorts of ways, formal and informal, to protect each other. Besides the many economic and military forms of protection, peoples are encouraged through cultural exchanges and other travel to "touch each other." It becomes fashionable, at times, to acknowledge and affirm the unique cultural, culinary, and work product attributes of another nation. Sensitive and loving members of the society will insist on approaching, in a similar way, those peoples whose nations do not happen to be on the friendly list at the time.

This chapter offers many ways of looking at the flux and flow between possessiveness and protection, freedom and commitment, change and intimacy, dependency and independence, trust and jealousy. Its real concern is with power and dignity. Loving relationships encourage individual power over one's life and restrain power that would impose itself over a precious and unique individual. Such relationships build upon and promote more individual and shared dignity.

Shared Experiences and Insights

Curiously, jealousy seems understandable, even okay, to a moderate degree, for it alerts us to our own sense of self-worth and to the depth of attachments we have formed. Indeed, I cannot imagine a world without jealousy. But feeling jealous and actively trying to possess another are not the same; and it is when jealousy prompts repressive actions that it is destructive.

Protection is looking out for your friend because you love them. Possession is looking out for your friend because you need them.

How easy it was to be a child under the care of my parents. So few worries because they took care of everything. It is so easy to just want to run back. But they won't always be there will they?

Love means not always solving a problem for someone, but helping them to grow by making them do it by themselves sometimes.

I have been in many relationships in which I have been both the possessed and the possessor. It was a stifling, stagnating, suffocating feeling.
We were both so afraid to let our partners explore other relationships,
especially those with members of the opposite sex, that we cut off *all*
outside sources, excepting those, of course, of our own choosing . . . we
chose each other's friends. Actually, we did not even choose each other's
friends—we *allowed* them to see *our* friends.

A mother wrote a poem about protection of her child's power and
dignity:

> Please Mom, don't wake me yet.
> I want to finish my dream.
>> And so I gently
>> covered him again,
> knowing that dream completion
>> is rare for most,
>> Indeed impossible for some.
> And so he too must learn of this one day.
> But now I let him lure himself beyond reality.
>> I dare not rob his world
>> of one completed dream.

My first instinct when she told me her deepest fears . . . was to wrap
my arms around her and "protect" her from everything and everyone who
might be capable of hurting her or making her lose control and become
sick. I would be very careful not to expect or to ask for support from her
because, I surmised, she did not need additional pressure of any sort. I
would allow her more "space" in our relationship so she would not feel
the discomfort that comes from disclosure and shared vulnerability. I
would do all these things for her because I love her. I would make her an
invalid.

I realize now that what I instinctively thought of as "protection" was
really "possessiveness." In order to save her from hurt, I would deny her
wholeness and health. I would deny that she had not only survived for
more than twenty years without my "protection," she had succeeded. She
had built, stone upon stone, a life in which she felt in control and justifi-
ably proud. My instinct to possess her, to isolate her and insulate her from
harm, disappointed and saddened her.

Because I love and care about my friend, I would prefer that she not be
sick, that she not lose control, that nothing hurt her, that no one ever
discover her secret.

I can no more guarantee that those things will not happen than she would
want me to. As long as she is able to control her life, the most that I can
do, and the most that she needs me to do, is to celebrate her victories, kiss
her hurts, and pick her up if she should fall . . . respect is both the "why"
and "how" of my love for this friend.

9

Conflict in Loving Relationships

"Get off my case! I can't stand it any longer!"

"I just got through telling you *not* to do that."

"Why is it that we always do what *you* want to do, but don't seem to get around to doing what *I* want?"

"I hate this house!"

"But we spent Christmas with *your* relatives last year!"

"I wish you wouldn't be so childish about this!"

"I can't believe you just said what you did . . .!"

"When you get angry like that, and sound so hateful, I know you really don't love me. People who really love each other have no need to get angry."

"You sound just like your father!"

"I *hate you!*"

"It will do no good to talk about reasons why. You are grounded for the rest of the week, and that is that!"

Is there a place for conflict in loving relationships? Several years ago, a popular book was turned into a popular movie, from which the idea emerged: "Love means never having to say you're sorry." That sounds so nice—do you believe it? Perhaps it means that nothing ever happens in the relationship to be sorry about. It might also mean that there is such absolutely clear communication that the participants know their feelings without having to say them. Neither of these possibilities seems real in the human lives with which I am familiar, and I suspect you agree. It would seem more reasonable to suggest that "love means *knowing how* to say we're sorry." If so, the problem for loving relationships is not the avoidance or elimination of conflict, but the constructive and productive management of differences.

Roles of Conflict in Loving Relationships

Conflict is real. It happens if two or more persons set out to share life in any significant way. When two persons actually try to relate "from the center of their beings," allowing each other to be unique and expressing that uniqueness, they are bound to have differences. If we care about ourselves, we care about our feelings and about something that means a great deal to us—a value, an opinion, an experience, a prior commitment. At the same time, we care about another person, with whom there is a disagreement about a value, a clear difference of opinion, a sharply different perception of an experience (or a distinctly different set of experiences being shared), and differing priorities regarding a commitment. Thus we have at least a dual conflict: one within the self, and one with the other person(s). To complicate things, there are feelings about each level of the conflict, and those feelings leave us confused and defensive, as well as angry, withdrawn, or, perhaps, hostile. A range of emotions comes to the surface when we find ourselves in this situation, and we have very little preparation in our upbringing which will help us to cope with the heat created when these differences develop within and between us.[1]

Since we are alive, we are growing, changing creatures. In significant ways, each of us is not the same person today that we were yesterday. Because we are growing and changing, it is inevitable that we shall not always be in tune with those around us, especially those whom we love. The simple fact that we care about one another and are open to what is going on in the other makes us more sensitive to change, difference, and the distance that develops with change. It is tempting to overlook the reality that the wonderful, exciting experience of *harmony* between persons is possible only because of the contrasts that exist between them. Harmony, after all, is not undifferentiated unity. It is made up of contrasts which have somehow been brought together through skillful attention to the possibilities for blending; those possibilities are dependent on the strength of contrast.[2] When I listen to some of my favorite music, whether it be of two or more voices or instruments, I am aware that it is the clarity and strengths of their differences that contribute to the beauty of their harmony. Without care, attention, and practice, their individual sounds will not come together in a way that is pleasant for anyone to hear. The wonder of a symphony requires a strong collection of differences, each free to express itself in its own way, coming together only at the risk of considerable disharmony and a series of efforts marked by frustration and discouragement. A marked change in tempo, in volume, in complexity, may threaten the continued pleasure of musicians and listeners. If handled with discipline and care, however, such change may also heighten the excitement and deepen the intensity of the experience.

Negative feelings *do* come up between persons who care about each other. We probably have messages stored up inside us that lead us to think differently. Some of our training—especially some forms of religious training—encourage us to believe that there is no room in caring relationships for such feelings. I like John Powell's comment that "the 'friction' of negative emotions is not a bad sign at all, but rather a sign of health and vitality in a relationship."[3] If there are *no* negative feelings, there is a good chance that a minimum of feelings of any kind exists in the relationship. To be in conflict is to be aware of an internal struggle which is stimulated—or restimulated—by interaction with another who is significant to us. An essential element of the conflict—often unrecognized—is internal disunity, within the self, as well as disunity with another. Confrontation is necessary. "To fail to confront," Peck notes, "when confrontation is required for the nurture of spiritual growth represents a failure to love equally as much as does thoughtless criticism or condemnation and other forms of active deprivation of caring."[4] Moustakas puts it even more bluntly: "To restore this unity of self with others, an open battle is sometimes essential."[5] By "open battle," he is referring to the reality that one acts on another and there is reciprocation—that is, there is *life* between the two. We know that *we* are alive, that something between *us* matters, that *we* feel, that *we* encounter each other on significant levels.

Conflict in loving relationships is the experience of very real differences between persons who care. A disagreement, or argument, or explosion of anger may be about something that is only a symptom of the real conflict. These differences involve feelings, values, personal goals, perceptions. They can go as deep as a sense of identity, unspoken expectations, and the inevitable process of change that happens in each of us, as well as between us. They are often about *power* and its unequal distribution. The experience of conflict is an indication of distance in the relationship. The challenge is to *reduce the distance* and *increase the intimacy* sought in the relationship.

Goals of Conflict: Decreased Distance and Increased Intimacy

The "human predicament" involves us in trying to overcome a sense of isolation from self and from each other. As we make that effort, out of great need and desire for unity with others, we learn that those to whom we are attracted see some things differently or disagree with us in important ways. In the clash, there is heat, and we know there is distance. In our moments of conscious caring, we want to reduce that distance, and move toward the intimacy that pulled us in the first place. So, how do we respond? We probably hear a rather loud voice, from some incident in our childhood, reminding us, "If you can't say something *nice,* don't say anything." Being nice, however, when we don't *feel* nice, doesn't help much in decreasing distance, nor does it provide much of a foundation for intimacy.

We have a variety of options for responding to conflict. I'll suggest a few, and you may very well find yourself in one or more of these.

1. *Avoidance.* This response is very common. We may pretend the conflict isn't there. We may *know* it is there, but decide not to say anything about it, at least directly. We tell ourselves we'll forget it, from fear of bringing it up, or perhaps from the feeling that it's not worth the hassle. Our "forgetting," however, amounts to repressing it and forcing it deeper inside, where it can do its work in ways that will probably be destructive. In interpersonal relations, we develop elaborate patterns, even rituals, for avoiding conflict. The resulting style is both unassertive and uncooperative. The self is stifled, and the relationship has no generative power at work. Our intergroup relations may include even more formal ways of avoiding open conflict. The structure of the relationship may be such that the group with the most power can make things very difficult for the less powerful group, while the conflict is never allowed out into the open. Avoidance, of course, is sometimes an appropriate choice; we may determine that the issue is trivial and that energy needs to be directed to more important issues. *Temporary* avoidance may allow for a cool-down period which promotes more constructive management of the difficulties. An avoidance process which is actually structural in the relationship, however, points to a second form of response.

2. *Alienation.* This response may take one of at least two different

forms: (a) active alienation and, (b) domination-submission. In *active alienation,* the disagreement is stated, in brief; the heated emotions are vented, hurtful things are said or done, and "that is the end of it." One or more of the parties involved are not afraid to say what they are feeling; they take at least the first step toward a potential resolution by being willing to recognize and express their feelings. Unfortunately, they do not have the skills or commitment to follow through with the work of clearing the emotions between them and proceeding toward a resolution. Thus, the distance is maintained or increased. The fight stays on the level of carefully practiced low blows, and there is no goal of victory for all parties concerned. In active alienation, everyone loses.

The domination-submission model of response is described by David and Vera Mace as the traditional model developed in a male-dominated culture. In a social system where it is assumed that one dominating party will always resolve disagreement or conflict, there must be a submitting party as well. Social and behavioral scientists refer to this as accommodation. In the traditional pattern, the male will be the dominant person. Exceptions to that pattern, of course, have existed in some few cultures or particular individual situations, with the female being dominant. The point is that a role structure in the relationship establishes a pattern in which *one* person or group always decides, and normally will win. The other party, or parties, submit. This pattern prevails in many families, in work settings—in most of our social experience. If this has habit behind it and is accepted by the parties involved, it may not increase the distance; at times, the distance between them may even be decreased out of sheer relief that the matter is resolved. *It is not likely, however, that this type of conflict resolution will increase intimacy.* The sharing of real feelings and exertion of personal vitality and power on the part of both parties is not sufficient to provide the clearing and feeling of openness and equality that builds intimacy.

3. *Shared Management.* This response assumes a recognition of the value of conflict as well as the necessity for collaboration in approaching it. Each party involved has an opportunity to express feelings and to hear—really hear—the feelings of the other. Respect is held for the other and it is recognized that the resolution must be one in which each party has sufficient gain that the *relationship* will win. As Bach and Deutsch put it, "either both win more intimacy, or both lose." There can be no dominance and submission, and certainly no avoidance. Active cooperation is essential. The possibility of compromise is open. The parties must be able to recognize patterns of response that lead to increased alienation, and express that recognition. This response form is essential to a loving relationship.

There are some necessary preconditions to learning shared management and entry into dialogue and discussion. At least three need to be emphasized.

Those committed to shared management recognize both the *reality* and the *value* of conflict in their relationship. Open conflict allows the expression of real differences and of deeper and broader dimensions of each personality (or group identity). It opens the door to breaking down barriers, decreasing distance, and permitting movement toward intimacy. It may sound strange at first, but conflict permits us to share a wider range of emotions and provides an opportunity for greater depth in intimacy. Powell refers to the wisdom from Kahlil Gibran which tells us that "we can forget those we have laughed with but we can never forget those with whom we have wept." I am not, of course, talking about the form of conflict that is expressed in brutality or cruel hostility. Cruelty is a form of conflict in which there is little or no caring or respect for the other. Rather, our attention is given here to our day-to-day experiences in which differences with persons we care about are accompanied by strong emotions, such as anger, resentment, fear, frustration, isolation, competition, and anxiety. In a loving relationship we may choose to face those feelings in such a way that our working with them becomes a contribution to our increased intimacy, rather than weapons in warfare, whether psychological or conventional.

Another precondition is that we know *how* we usually try to avoid conflict. Each of us has our own methods. Some avoidance techniques are undoubtedly necessary for psychological survival and/or daily functioning. When these techniques are general patterns, however, and are used in all our relationships, they assure that we shall not achieve intimacy in any relationship. One of my methods is to avoid contact with the person. Another is to try to control the conversation in order to keep away from the feelings needing to be expressed. What are your ways to avoid conflict with those you care about? One reason that we need to be aware of our avoidance methods is that they often simply add to the conflict, or create new ones. If, for instance, I am controlling the conversation to avoid expression of feelings, I am actually increasing the distance and probably intensifying the tension. I am helping the other person to feel manipulated, frustrated and angry.

A third precondition is the need to recognize the unexpressed presence of conflict within us. My body provides internal messages about such things—I assume that yours does, too. With your hand, touch that part of your body that tells you when you are heating up, or feeling tense or anxious. Is your hand on your chest, your stomach, or, perhaps your temples? Those are some common places to feel tension when a clash is developing. There are others, of course. It helps to be aware of how our physical being is experiencing the situation, even if we are not giving verbal expression to our feelings. Having received the signals, we can exercise some choices about our response to our circumstances. The enhancement of a caring relationship builds upon a collaborative, cooperative approach to the experience of conflict.

Before turning to some specific approaches offered by professionals in conflict management, there is one more idea fundamental to our considerations. A term that has been popular for several years now is one which remains crucial to our thinking about, and acting upon, shared conflict management. The word *dialogue,* although often used and sometimes misused, remains essential to the process of reducing distance and increasing intimacy in human relationships. There is probably no real substitute for the word. Powell uses communication interchangeably with dialogue as the "secret of staying in love." I would suggest, however, that dialogue not only describes a process of human interaction, but also expresses a value regarding our exchanges. Dialogue has two equally important parts: talking and listening. Frankly, most of us are not very skilled at either of these as components of real dialogue, although we may be a bit more competent at talking than at listening. Dialogue requires that we be willing to talk, to say what we are feeling, to be direct with the other person. The hitch for many of us here—especially males—is in knowing what we are feeling, and how to put it into words. Then comes the courage to do so. We need to be as specific as possible in order to be understood as accurately as possible. With this kind of talking, we care about the self and the other at the same time. We care enough to want our own feelings to be expressed, to be heard, and to be understood. We also care enough about the other to want to be sure that they hear things as they really are, trusting in the other's maturity and capacity to make decisions about the appropriate response. We want the other to have the opportunity to respond to what is really there, rather than being misled into responding to non-realities.

Listening is a skill most of us need to learn and practice. What we have probably learned *best* is how *not* to listen to others. Check yourself. How many words are stated by your conversation/discussion/argument partner before you begin formulating your next statement—thus effectively cutting off any real listening to what is being said? It is not unusual to hear from persons who have shared a lot of life together—roommates, siblings, spouses, business partners, and others: "we know each other so well that we can complete each other's sentences." I'm suspicious of that. If those sentences were dealing with any real substance of feelings and individual thought, a check with the partner might reveal that the alleged completion really *wasn't* where the sentence was originally headed! It may be more a matter of arrogance than love for me to be sure I *know* what you are going to say. It is important that *you* have a chance to say it, and to be *heard*. Listening in dialogue involves both listening to and feeling with the feelings of the other. It means listening to *meanings* as well as to words. Listening to the other's meanings, rather than one's own meanings imposed on the other's words, requires especially sensitive listening and feeling—often called "empathy." Special care can be given to listening to the other person's (or group's) meanings because you respect the "otherness" of the partner, rather than requiring the partner to conform to your own world of meanings.

Karl Menninger considers listening to be "one of the most powerful and influential techniques of human intercourse." In his desire to communicate what that can mean, this pioneering psychiatrist turned not to professional journals, but quoted instead from a *Ladies Home Journal* article in November, 1941, by Brenda Ueland:

> Listening is a magnetic and strange thing, a creative force. The friends that listen to us are the ones we move toward, and we want to sit in their radius as though it did us good, like ultra-violet rays. . . . When we are listened to, it creates us, makes us unfold and expand. Ideas actually begin to grow within us and come to life. . . . It makes people happy and free when they are listened to. . . . When we listen to people there is an alternating current, and this recharges us so that we never get tired of each other. We are constantly being re-created.
>
> Now there are brilliant people who cannot listen much. They have no ingoing wires on their apparatus. They are entertaining but exhausting too. I think it is because these lecturers, these brilliant performers, by not giving us a chance to talk, do not let us express our thoughts and expand, and it is this expressing and expanding that makes the little creative fountain inside us begin to spring and cast up new thoughts and unexpected laughter and wisdom.
>
> I discovered all this about three years ago, and truly it made a revolutionary change in my life. Before that, when I went to a party I would think anxiously: "Now try hard. Be lively. Say bright things. Talk. Don't let down." And when tired, I would have a drink of coffee to keep this up. But now before going to a party, I just tell myself to listen with affection to anyone who talks to me, to *be in their shoes when they talk;* to try to know them without my mind pressing against theirs, or arguing, or changing the subject. No. My attitude is: "Tell me more. This person is showing me his soul. It is a little dry and meager and full of grinding talk just now, but presently he will begin to think, not just automatically to talk. He will show his true self. Then he will be wonderfully alive."[6]

Serious participants in interreligious dialogue have learned that we must have the freedom to tell others exactly what we believe, even with the conviction that it is the absolute truth, without demanding that they accept it for themselves. Likewise, the listener wants to hear another person's deepest convictions without assuming that the other is attempting to convert. Each takes the other with total seriousness—and respect.[7] If you and I are in dialogue over your feelings, the statement of your feelings has validity in itself without an additional demand for a specific change in opinion on my part. There cannot be any argument as to the truth, or rightness, or validity of your feelings. They *are* your feelings, not to be judged. The listener doesn't have to experience exactly the same feelings or immediately change to conform to yours. When these assumptions are built into the exchange in communication, real dialogue can take place.

Dialogue and discussion are not the same thing. Discussion is conversation about something—an idea, a topic, a decision to be made, or future course of action. Constructive discussion between persons who care about each other may need to be preceded by dialogue, in order that feelings can be expressed and received before moving into the discussion process. Discussion is important. It is best done rationally, with as much objectivity as possible. It does not ignore or "step on" feelings, but is able to take them into account only when they have been expressed and heard.[8]

At the risk of being simplistic, our approach to conflict between persons or groups who care about each other might proceed from these assumptions:

We are both "right" about some things;

We are both "wrong" about some things;

We see most things differently, because we are different persons with different backgrounds and perspectives;

How we *feel* about a matter is neither right nor wrong—it just *is,* and is important to hear;

We each want to achieve something for ourselves;

We each have much to contribute to a shared solution to our problem, to a shared management of our disagreement;

We both want to reach across the chasm that separates us and increase our intimacy.

Constructive Approaches to Conflict

Since our goal is to decrease distance and increase intimacy, some models for management of conflict especially geared to these purposes are suggested here for your consideration. These models have been rigorously worked out by combining theory development and hours of practice with individuals, couples and groups. The first, designed by David and Vera Mace for the context of marriage, is included here because I think it has broad, general application to any persons who care about each other and wish to gain more unity in any kind of relationship.

One of the basic emotions in conflict, of course, is *anger*. Most of us aren't very good at knowing what to do with our anger. The Maces developed a "Three Step System" as a way to deal with anger in their own relationship.[9] They have elaborated on the system in their communications with thousands of other married persons.

Step One. "We try to acknowledge our anger to each other as soon as we become aware of it. This allows it no time to build up." A precondition to this step is the acceptance of each person's right to get angry; furthermore, it is not assumed that there is any particular guilt or blame to be placed for having the anger, nor is there any blame implied in receiving the anger.

Step Two. "We renounce the right to vent anger on each other." Telling the other that you are angry is not the same as venting it. Since acting out anger would be damaging to their love, one will say to the other, "I'm getting angry with you, but you know that I'm not going to attack you." The partner thus confronted does not "need to go on the defensive, which would result in retaliatory anger and be likely to lead to a fight." It is sometimes necessary to get feelings off one's chest, but the use of someone else for that purpose is anything but constructive. John Powell calls it using the other person as a "garbage dump" for one's own "emotional refuse."

Step Three. "We ask for the other's help in dealing with the anger that has developed." Although recognizing that this approach may seem strange, the Maces insist that it works. "If your partner is angry with you, and appeals to you to help clear it up, it is very much in your interest to respond."

The agreement which is basic to the system includes a commitment to continue "working on each anger situation that develops between us until we clear it up." Sometimes the anger was unjustified, or was based on misunderstanding. It may have, indeed, been justified by provocations beyond appropriate levels of coping. Whatever the stimulus, the Maces found that, in working on it, they had the "opportunity to learn more and more about possible anger-producing actions that can occur between us." This results in gaining "the power, based on accurate knowledge, to avoid major crises."

The Maces seem to say that anger and love cannot coexist, and lovers, therefore, need to develop ways of defusing the anger. The key to their method is that the persons involved do not suppress their feelings, but accept them and resolve them together. That is what moves them toward increased intimacy.

Others are not so sure that anger and love are mutually exclusive. It may be expected that persons who care about each other enough to allow the other a healthy range of individuality will, indeed, experience anger as a necessary and often growthful part of their relationship. The issue at stake is the method for dealing with the anger, or the experience of conflict involved in it.

A somewhat different approach accepts the notion that persons who are close to each other do "fight," and need to learn how to fight "fairly," in order to increase their intimacy. George Bach and several of his colleagues have written about their counseling and research on conflict. With Peter Wyden, in *The Intimate Enemy*, Bach describes ways in which persons "fight" and some of the ways in which they can learn to do their fighting in a fair and constructive manner. (The Maces, incidentally, do not like the term, "fight." It seems to me, however, that what they are describing in their working with anger is quite similar.) In a later book with Ronald M. Deutsch,[10] Bach addresses the interpersonal process which they call "pairing," and provides readers with transcripts of actual sessions in which they help persons to learn constructive forms of pairing. These include ways of fighting fairly with each other. From those discussions, they developed a list of rules for specific conflict situations. Although it is a long list, it is also a keenly interesting and insightful one. Reading through it, you may find yourself pausing along the way to reflect on conflict situations in which you have been involved and how particular suggestions might have affected them.

1. Be specific when you introduce a gripe.
2. Don't just complain, no matter how specifically; ask for a reasonable change that will relieve the gripe.
3. Ask for and give feedback of the major points, to make sure you are heard, to assure your partner that you understand what is wanted.
4. Confine yourself to one issue at a time. Otherwise, without professional guidance, you may skip back and forth, evading the hard ones.
5. Do not be glib or intolerant. Be open to your own feelings, and equally open to your partner's.
6. Always consider compromise. Remember, your partner's view of reality may be just as real as yours, even though you may differ. There are not many totally objective realities.
7. Do not allow counter-demands to enter the picture until the original demands are clearly understood, and there has been clear-cut response to them.
8. Never assume that you know what your partner is thinking until you have checked out the assumption in plain language; nor assume or predict how he will react, what he will accept or reject. Crystal-gazing is not for pairing.
9. Don't mind-rape. Ask. Do not correct a partner's statement of feelings.

10. Never put labels on a partner: neither a coward, nor a neurotic, nor a child. If you really believed that your partner was incompetent or suffered from some hopeless basic flaw, you probably would not be with this person. Do not make sweeping, labelling judgments about feelings, especially about whether or not they are real or important.
11. Sarcasm is dirty fighting.
12. Forget the past and stay with the here-and-now. What either of you did last year or last month or that morning is not as important as what you are doing and feeling now. And the changes you ask cannot possibly be retroactive. Hurts, grievances, and irritations should be brought up at the very earliest moment, or the partner has the right to suspect that they may have been saved carefully as weapons.
13. Do not overload your partner with grievances. To do so makes the other feel hopeless and suggests that you have either been hoarding complaints or have not thought through what really troubles you.
14. Meditate. Take time to consult your real thoughts and feelings before speaking. Your surface reactions may make something deeper and more important. Don't be afraid to close your eyes and think.
15. Remember that there is never a single winner in an honest intimate fight. Both either win more intimacy or lose it.[11]

Why is sarcasm dirty fighting (item 11)? This is an important one to highlight. People who read books usually like words. People who like words are often tempted to *play* with words. I remember, clearly, when I became skilled at sarcasm. It was in junior high school. There were very real social advantages, at that point in my adolescent development, in becoming clever with the use of words, including sarcasm. It got attention, recognition, admiration from some quarters (never mind, in good junior high fashion, those who were hurt by it!). Having developed that skill at a formative time in life, it lingers on, and insists on creeping in at times when it can be most harmful, in letting down my guard during the expression of feelings. It is dirty fighting because it doesn't take the other person seriously. It substitutes some clever twist of words for the reality of the other, and it often intends to hurt. It strikes where the other is vulnerable. Hitting below the belt *is* dirty fighting! It is also unsuccessful. It avoids bringing the conflict out into the open, where it can be managed, or worked on.

Item fifteen also deserves special emphasis. With so much in our social conditioning and training preparing us for competition and winning, the thought of there not being a winner and a loser in this kind of a fight is a foreign notion. Winning is deeply programmed into us. "We're Number One" is not just a chant for sports events; it has specific personal implications as well. Thus, entering into an open conflict with the goal of emerging with two or more winners and no losers may seem impossible to us. It requires a certain revolution in thinking and personal presuppositions, for most of us. It *is* imperative for real intimacy.

Perhaps it is the mutual winning that we experience when we say such things as, "It feels so good when we make up." When each has shared something from the struggle, when there has been a real sharing of dimensions of the personality that may not have been shared before, when there has been an expansion of the types of experience that can be shared, each *has* won. With mutual winning, there is celebration in making up. When there must be apologies, mutual apologies become expressions of intimacy, a deeper feeling of emotional communication, and a stronger way to say, "I love you," even while saying, "I'm sorry."

Bach and his colleagues are not alone in suggesting rules for fair fighting. John Crosby has laid out six basic principles which he calls "ground rules for fair fighting." In Crosby's approach, the theory of "Transactional Analysis" is utilized. Communication, if it is to be growth-producing, must be between "Adult" and "Adult." In "TA" language, it is easy for negative emotions to elicit transactions between "Child" and "Parent," or a variety of combinations of the ego states. Those are parts of our personality which respond to data recorded within us at earlier stages of our lives. Whereas the "Child" is a *felt* way of living, the "Parent" is a *taught* way of living, responding to rules, approval and disapproval. The Adult "gathers and processes data fed through it by the Parent and the Child," and "does reality testing and probability estimating."[12] As Crosby points out, "The challenge in transactional analysis is to pinpoint the origin of a thought, a feeling, or a communication." We can move into our Adult, having located the origin of our feeling, and process what can be done now with it. Thus, the *first* of Crosby's rules is the decision to "negotiate as the Adult rather than as the Child or the Parent."[13] The *second* rule is, "We must avoid statements that leave the other no room to move around." Rather than negotiation, a statement which attacks is an ultimatum demanding counter-ultimatum. Such attacks come from a Parent position, forcing the other into a Child position in defense. The *third* rule is about winning and losing. Since it speaks directly to a number of concerns in this discussion, here is rule three in its entirety:

In our highly competitive society, we are all socialized to winning and losing. But when one wins and one loses, both lose, In an intimate relationship, the after-conflict feelings are crucial. Whoever wins may feel good, or guilty. Whoever loses may feel defeated—stamped down, rejected, manipulated—or strangely, he may feel good because once again he had had it demonstrated that he is a loser or a victim. Because it is the two partners, the winner and the loser, who form the relationship, the relationship also suffers—and usually more than we recognize. Good feelings and bad feelings become enmeshed. Resentment is bound to result—and feelings of hurt and futility.

Once we succeed in dealing with feelings by becoming self-aware and self-disclosing, by leveling and permitting ourselves to accept our vulnerability, then we are able to place the health of the relationship above the individualized fact of winning or losing. When we see clearly that the relationship always loses when winner is pitted against loser, we can begin to commit ourselves to authentic negotiation instead of allowing ourselves to be manipulated into accommodations or frontal attacks.[14]

The *fourth* rule is about saying "yes," when that is meant, and "no," when that is meant. If there is reservation, it should be stated at the time of the response, not later. To give in too early, "premature accommodation," or to falsely represent one's feelings, is dishonest. Growth of the relationship is inhibited, even though we may plead that we are trying to protect the self or other from pain.

Rule *five,* quite simply, is "avoid attack." The best way to assert oneself and avoid placing the other on the defensive is to make "I" statements, taking responsibility for one's own feelings, rather than accusing the other of making one feel or do a certain thing. Closely related is the importance of first focusing on the feelings, and then on the behavior related to it. Crosby's example: "I feel very badly when everything I say is rejected." That leaves the other with considerably more room than, "You put me down. Every time I say something you have some way of canceling it out."[15]

The *sixth* rule calls for a "checking-out technique." It is asking for accuracy of perceptions. Like the Bach and Deutsch approach, this does not want to assume that you know what the other is thinking or feeling until it has been checked out: "if in doubt, ask."

Michael Zwell also has some suggestions for "skills and techniques" to utilize in conflicts which some would call "fighting." You will see that they are, in fact, a useful review of some things that have already been emphasized.

1. Use active listening.
2. Use I-messages.
3. Be specific.
4. Specify points of agreement and disagreement.
5. Watch for fouls or low blows.
6. Exchange listening time.
7. Try reversing roles. Take a few minutes and each play the other person.
8. Go scream into or pound a pillow.

9. Exchange discharge time.
10. Talk and make agreements during times of low conflict.[16]

Zwell's "discharge time" is a particularly creative approach. Discharge refers to the natural forms of relieving distress through physical means—laughing, crying, raging, trembling, and so forth. We don't have to learn these things. We *do* learn ways, however, of expressing our feelings through certain patterned behaviors—slamming doors, telling others to "shut up," and the like. Zwell suggests that a caring person can intervene in another's patterned behavior and encourage actual discharge of the feelings. It may require "active listening," in order to ascertain what is really bothering the person. In the list above, he is suggesting that each party to the conflict support the other in discharge time, during which feelings can be expressed without defensive response, including crying, verbal lashing out, or whatever is needed—except acting out the feelings. Both parties understand that the discharge is needed, and that they can move ahead with more constructive conversation after the exchange.[17]

Some fundamental assumptions reside in each of the approaches to "fair fighting." Perhaps the first is that all parties are committed to the relationship, its maintenance and improvement, more than they are to winning a point or having their own way. At the same time, it is recognized that the strength of the relationship requires that individual identities be strengthened and supported; excessive accommodation by one party for the good of the relationship will not, in the long run, benefit their ties. In addition, feelings are allowed and respected. They are recognized as basic components in the conflict and its eventual management. Each party takes personal responsibility, not expecting the other to second-guess the situation or take the lead in doing something about it. Respect for both self and other must be maintained. Being specific in what is stated, whether about feelings or about what behavior is disturbing or desired, is necessary. Taking time to think is essential, although it must not become an excuse for postponement.

I have a reason for emphasizing the word management in regard to conflict. Although it is common to speak of conflict resolution, the plain fact is that not all conflicts are *resolved,* even in a loving relationship! There are some differences between persons, or groups, that cannot be totally resolved to the satisfaction of everyone involved. Living together in ways that reduce distance and increase intimacy includes the acceptance of some of those differences and working out methods to manage, or live with, them. Irresolvable differences still need to be faced. As Crosby points out, *defused* but unresolved conflict is certainly better than conflict which is not faced. Facing the difficulty defuses it, takes the sting out of it, and reduces or removes the potential for it to be destructive in hidden ways.[18]

Negotiation: "Getting to Yes"

An advertisement in the *Wall Street Journal* proclaimed: "Our idea of a Perfect Merger: Everybody Wins." Although there probably aren't any perfect mergers, it is still possible for everyone to win. It is because of a certain amount of imperfection in all human efforts to reach out to each other that the process of negotiation becomes important. As the Directors of the Harvard Negotiation Project, Roger Fisher and William Ury have responded to the question, "What is the best way for people to deal with their differences?" As they put it, "we have evolved a practical method for negotiating agreement amicably without giving in."[19]

The Fisher-Ury method has been used in a wide variety of settings. It has been utilized in personal conflicts. It was the approach used by President Jimmy Carter in the Camp David talks leading to agreements between Egypt and Israel. Their method is discussed and summarized, in *Getting To Yes—Negotiating Agreement Without Giving In* (1983). This is an excellent, brief, and readable resource if you want to learn some new ways of thinking about, as well as acting upon, techniques for implementing loving concern in interpersonal and intergroup disagreements. Everyone, they insist, is a negotiator in some way:

> Negotiation is a fact of life. You discuss a raise with your boss . . . The United States Secretary of State sits down with his Soviet counterpart to seek an agreement limiting nuclear arms . . . People negotiate even when they don't think of themselves as doing so. A person negotiates with his spouse about where to go for dinner and with his child about when the lights go out. Negotiation is a basic means of getting what you want from others. It is back-and-forth communication designed to reach an agreement when you and the other side have some interests that are shared and others that are opposed.[20]

"Getting what you want . . ." If what you want is intimacy, it is important to recognize that both or all parties to that intimacy have interests that are shared. Finding out what those interests are, and how they can be most constructively shared, will certainly go a long way in deepening the potential for intimacy. Likewise, discovering and confronting opposing interests will lead to the removal of barriers and open new possibilities in the relationship. Thus, even though there may not be any *perfect* merger, it does remain possible to reach an agreement in which everybody wins.

The strategy proposed by Fisher and Ury is an extremely practical one; it is also, in their view, a principled one. That is, it resists arguing over positions; it avoids unwise agreements; it is efficient, because it doesn't get bogged down in the defense of positions; it is wary of an agreement whereby one party wins to the detriment of the relationship. People who care about each other are tempted to use an approach to problems which they call "soft." Others, who are only interested in getting what they want, follow a strategy which is "hard." Their "principled" approach is an alternative to either the "soft" or "hard" approach—it works, they insist, whether one is dealing with one other person on a very friendly basis, or is bargaining with an adversary. The participants are seen neither as friends nor as adversaries, but as problem-solvers, faced with a mutual problem. They are not after an agreement on a position or a victory, but their goal is a wise outcome which can be reached efficiently and amicably. You can see how this works out in this chart:[21]

PROBLEM Positional Bargaining: Which Game Should You Play?		SOLUTION Change the Game—Negotiate on the Merits
SOFT	**HARD**	**PRINCIPLED**
Participants are friends.	Participants are adversaries.	Participants are problem-solvers.
The goal is agreement.	The goal is victory.	The goal is a wise outcome reached efficiently and amicably.
Make concessions to cultivate the relationships.	Demand concessions as a condition of the relationship.	Separate the people from the problem.
Be soft on the people and the problem.	Be hard on the problem and the people.	Be soft on the people, hard on the problem.
Trust others.	Distrust others.	Proceed independent of trust.
Change your position easily.	Dig in to your position.	Focus on interests, not positions.
Make offers.	Make threats.	Explore interests.
Disclose your bottom line.	Mislead as to your bottom line.	Avoid having a bottom line.
Accept one-sided losses to reach agreement.	Demand one-sided gains as the price of agreement.	Invent options for mutual gain.

Search for the single answer: the one *they* will accept.	Search for the single answer: the one *you* will accept.	Develop multiple options to choose from; decide later.
Insist on agreement.	Insist on your position.	Insist on using objective criteria.
Try to avoid a contest of will.	Try to win a contest of will.	Try to reach a result based on standards independent of will.
Yield to pressure.	Apply pressure.	Reason and be open to reasons; yield to principle, not pressure.

The method, as you see above, proceeds from four basic points:

1. Regarding people: Separate people from the problem.
2. Regarding interest: Focus on interests, not positions.
3. Regarding options: Generate a variety of possibilities before deciding what to do.
4. Criteria: Insist that the result be based on some objective standard.

Some of the features of this method resonate with the approaches we have already considered. They insist on openness, in which the feelings of participants are accepted—in fact, the statement of feelings is encouraged as a way of getting to the operating interests in the matter. Participants must take each other seriously, and make an effort to assist the other in making their situation more easily presented and handled. Empathy is basic, leading the parties to become collaborators on solving a mutual problem in a way that is beneficial to all. Trust is not a test for participation, but something that becomes a part of the process of developing a solution. Participants never yield to pressure from the other, but only to principle—the over-arching principle which defines and guides the ongoing relationship.

Since I am especially interested in how we *think about* our relationships with self and others, I am particularly attracted to the comments made by the Harvard Negotiation Project authors regarding *perception*. "Ultimately," they tell us, "conflict lies not in objective reality, but in people's heads."[22] Reality as seen by each party both constitutes the problem and offers a path to solutions. With that in mind, they offer these suggestions:

—Put yourself in their shoes. (Withhold judgment while trying on their views.)

—Don't deduce their *intentions* from *your fears*. (Dismal interpretations tend to short-circuit fresh ideas and changes in position.)

—Don't blame them for your problem. (Even if justified, blaming is counter-productive, because it entangles people with the problem.)

—Discuss each other's perceptions. (Take seriously what is not disagreed upon—it gives you both something to build on.)

—Look for opportunities to act inconsistently with their perceptions. (Sending a different message from what is expected opens up new possibilities.)

—Give them a stake in the outcome by making sure they participate in the process. (Early involvement is more likely to lead to approval of the product.)

—Face-saving: Make your proposals consistent with their values. (Each person needs to be able to reconcile an agreement with past words and deeds.)[23]

In concluding their book, Fisher and Ury have some important observations about winning. What is important to win is a "a better process for dealing with your differences." Recognizing that it is not "easy to change habits, to disentangle emotions from the merits, or to enlist others in the task of working out a wise solution to a shared problem," they aim toward a way to negotiate which "avoids your having to choose between the satisfactions of getting what you deserve and of being decent. You can have both."[24] When both—or all—parties to a conflict can be decent and come up with an agreement which protects what each deserves, a loving relationship is enhanced.[25]

This negotiation model is particularly exciting in its application to conflict between groups. It has been used in labor-management disputes, community agency decisions, landlord-tenant controversies, as well as in a number of international situations. There is no assumption that individuals like each other. An assumption of trust is not essential to its effectiveness—in fact, one of the strong suggestions made by the authors is a reminder that "trust is a separate issue" when one party asserts a lack of trust in the other. The model establishes a different way to play the game from traditional expectations. It keeps the focus on the *interests* of the parties involved, and moves toward as much collaboration as possible where mutuality of interests can be established. Trust, as such, may develop in this process as the parties experience the willingness of the other to take them and their interests seriously. There is an underlying assumption, of course, that there are basic human interests shared by all of us who are different in significant ways. The focus on interests encourages a serious acceptance of legitimate and real differences. What happens in this process is well described by an insight which developed in a somewhat different context. Writing about his research with "Indians and other racial groups" in urban settings, Hoy Steele concluded:

> The roadblocks are many to good relations between people—or peoples— who are different from each other in significant respects. They are particularly formidable and hazardous when those who are involved are representatives of groups characterized by great power inequality or that see each other as threatening or competitive. Perhaps the surprising fact is that good relations exist at all, ever. Those of us who wish to make them more frequent and persistent may be more successful if we hold before us a paradox. Interracial bonds cannot begin without an acknowledgement that real, substantial, and frequently troublesome differences do indeed exist. That is the paradox: by fully exploring our differences we discover our common humanity.[26]

Lovers who find themselves in conflict do not have to take the stance of antagonists. They can, as it were, move to the same side of the table, with the mutual problem in front of both of them, rather than between them. The move from being opponents to collaborators on solving (or managing) something in which both have a stake, is a loving move.

From Hostility to Hospitality

Henri Nouwen speaks of changing our way of being with others from that of hostility, or enmity, to hospitality. Hospitality is the creation of a free space where the stranger can enter, move about, find comfort and warmth, and gain resources for moving on. I find this to be a helpful *symbolic* conceptualization of our concern with conflict in loving relationships. When there is distance between us, we are, indeed, strangers. The space between us feels hostile, and activity may very well be going on within that space which is hostile. The symbol of hospitality suggests turning that space into a receptive area, inviting the guests to reveal the promise carried within them. Parents can do that with children. Children, after all, are not possessions of their parents, but guests who come as gifts and move on in a short time to their own lives. Within that short span of time in which parents create a space for their growth, the space may be one of great tension, full of demands and attempts to establish control. Parents may be preoccupied with creating and maintaining authority and find themselves always in a struggle with a guest reacting to or against that authority. Or, the space may be one of love, of an awesome response to the opportunity to be a part of the shaping and expansion of a young life, and the inevitable conflicts which arise may be approached as learning opportunities for both parent and child. Obviously, it is not as easy as it sounds. I have been there, and am there. How I feel and what I am able to do in the presence of my children, I have found, is greatly altered by bringing together ("symbolizing") attitudes and experiences through the concept of *hospitality.*

This notion of creating a free and friendly space, as Nouwen suggests it, is a good way of describing each of the methods for management of conflict that have been discussed in this chapter. David and Vera Mace are certainly suggesting a change of rules for dealing with anger; at the heart of their method is the welcoming of the partner into a space that wasn't there before, a place that is safe and within which collaboration can be pursued in defusing the anger. The varieties of rules for fair fighting encourage confrontation; the rules for the encounter, however, remove the partners from opponent status and insist on moving the participants into a new arena where options are open and the only victory attainable is one in which both can share. The Fisher-Ury negotiation model is, from the outset, a creation of a free and friendly space. It is soft on people, while being hard on the problem. It insists on visualizing the widest possible range of solutions. It seeks fairness, insisting that there *is* no solution if anyone loses. It offers ways of collaborating, even where there is an apparently hopeless differential of power, or where one side insists on hard bargaining and dirty tricks.

Nouwen says it best:

> Hospitality is not to change people, but to offer them space where change can take place. It is not to bring men and women over to our side, but to offer freedom not disturbed by dividing lines. It is not to lead our neighbor into a corner where there are no alternatives left, but to open a wide spectrum of options for choice and commitment. It is not an educated intimidation with good books, good stories and good works, but the liberation of fearful hearts so that words can find roots and bear ample fruit. It is not a method of making our God and our way into the criteria of happiness, but the opening of an opportunity to others to find their God and their way. The paradox of hospitality is that it wants to create emptiness, not a fearful emptiness, but a friendly emptiness where strangers can enter and discover themselves as created free; free to sing their own songs, speak their own languages, dance their own dances; free also to leave and follow their own vocations. Hospitality is not a subtle invitation to adopt the life style of the host, but the gift of a chance for the guest to find his own.[27]

Remember our friends from chapter one who look upon their differences as alternatives in style, rather than competition. This allows each a hospitable free space in which to move.

Perhaps the ultimate form of hospitality—certainly of conflict management—is the experience of forgiveness. "Repentance and forgiveness," Keen says, "change the fundamental structure of consciousness from antagonism to compassion."[28] An insight of John Powell puts it even more directly: "The most ailing relationships can be restored to health almost miraculously by this simple but sincere request: 'Will you forgive me?' "[29] This is a powerful question. He is not saying that the healing begins when one party initiates the action by pronouncing, "I forgive you." The healing begins by the asking for forgiveness. Also very important is his emphasis that there is no guilt or blame implied in the process. In much of our experience with forgiveness, we may very well be hearing an accompanying message—"in spite of the lousy thing you did to me, I forgive you," or, "even though you wouldn't be tolerated by most people, I'll forgive you." Real forgiveness takes no account of guilt or blame. The basic issue is being included in one's love. As Powell puts it, the questioner is asking, "Will you take me back into your love?"

It is well that Powell considers this action *almost* miraculous. It is not simple, and it is certainly not magical. Forgiveness *is* powerful. Distance is reduced. Energy may be redirected toward intimacy. It takes at least two to do it.

Shared Experiences and Insights

A humorous approach to some of life's nitty-gritty:

> Conflict is when you want to kiss from the right side and so does he.
> It's when your best friend can't understand why you are dating her ex-boyfriend.
> Conflict is when your parents want you in Florida with them, and your boyfriend wants you in Kansas City, and you want to be in Colorado, but you're in Lawrence, Kansas.

A comment on internal conflict which becomes interpersonal:

> What sometimes dribbles from the mouth is not always what pours from the heart.

A painful admission:

> He was writing graffiti on the walls of my heart.

On conflict in values never "resolved":

In a loving relationship, one does not ask one's partner to give up a cherished belief simply because it is not common to the two of them. This is where respect enters in . . . and freedom "to BE." As long as we understand our partner's belief and honestly do not feel that this makes him inferior or diminishes his worth in any way, we have respect. Sometimes, even though we do not share that conviction, we can have only admiration and increased love for our partner *because* of his beliefs and convictions. We respond by honoring them, respecting them, trusting them. In a loving relationship, deep-seated convictions which conflict with our own may take much understanding: many "listening" occasions—for us to understand how they were developed and why they are important to the one we love. Conflict in this kind of situation may be an on-going thing characterized by awareness of differences and constant consideration and acceptance of those differences. This does not mean we embrace the same values; it means we learn to live within them in our partner and honor his judgment in keeping his convictions.

10

Sex and Sexuality in Loving Relationships

Sex, in the Western world, is *contact without harmony.*
—Ashley Montagu[1]

. . . we struggle daily to explore our sexuality and understand what the lifelong task of *becoming a sexual person* means for us living in the radically changing social environment . . . In trying to understand our sexual nature we find ourselves at the hub of a wheel, with dozens of spokes radiating inward to influence our experience as sexual persons. From our conception to our later years, each of us is molded by biological, social, family, cultural, psychological, historical, legal, and religious factors that contribute to our unique sexual being."
—Robert F. Francoeur[2]

"Having sex" is great fun. Most people know that. But "making love" is unutterable joy, for in it there is such a mutual interpenetration of lives that nothing can give greater delight and bring greater fulfillment . . . Love is sharing; love is concern; love is caring. And love includes anguish, quite as much as it provides ecstasy. It is personal meeting. So a penetrating and disturbing question, which might well be asked after every sexual contact of a physical sort, is this: "Now that I am leaving this person, am I leaving a person with whom I have shared something of joy of mutual existence, expressed in physical fashion?"
—Norman Pittenger[3]

Sexuality is our self-understanding and way of being in the world as male and female . . . it is crucial to bear in mind that *sexuality* involves much more than what we *do* with our genitals. More fundamentally, it is who we *are* as body-selves who experience the emotional, cognitive, physical, and spiritual need for intimate communion—human and divine . . . Our human sexuality is God's good gift. It is a fundamental dimension of our created and our intended humanness.
—James B. Nelson[4]

Sexuality and spirituality are not enemies but friends. A development of one does not mean a denial of the other. Both flow forth from the innermost center of human life. Our goal is not to choose between them but to integrate them, to be both spiritual and sexual, holy and sensual, at one and the same time.

—Donald Goergen[5]

Loving relationships demand expression. Caring will be communicated. We express who we are and how we feel through the only instruments available to us—our bodies. Our bodies include minds that think, senses that feel, skin and limbs that touch, and genitals that perform a variety of functions and respond to stimuli. We are, as James Nelson has so brilliantly demonstrated, "embodied," and our "bodies are always sexual bodies."[6] Sex—and sexuality—are therefore central to our consideration of what is involved in being in relationship through love.

Eros, Sex and Romance: Confusion

In an age when sexual appeal is used to sell anything from toothpaste to automobiles, and male briefs are heralded on a huge billboard overlooking New York's Times Square, we can agree with Rollo May that we are living in the midst of a "sexual wilderness."[7] We receive mixed and confusing messages, from early infancy on, about sex and its place in our lives. We hardly have time to begin integrating the sensual pleasures to which we are introduced as a baby before we are increasingly influenced by the assumptions, values, anxieties and distortions of people around us regarding sex, sex roles, and the meaning of spending one's life in the body with which one is born. The child is unlikely to escape an adult somewhere who is bent on letting it be known that curiosity about, or simple enjoyment of, some body parts is dirty. Religious sources will speak of the body as "the temple of God," while those same sources may warn that normal adolescent attention to it is a satanic temptation. Our post-puberty peers press us to respond to growing, changing feelings in our bodies with activity focused on the genitals, while elders concentrate on helping us feel guilty for having and expressing such feelings. As young adults, we find our struggle for identity often tied up in our sexual feelings and behavior. As older adults we find that younger persons around us assume we have neither sexual feelings nor behavior. It is confusing.

From the moment of our conception, sex is involved in our relationships with others. We are recognized and labeled as male or female. Our bodies experience sensations which are transmitted to the person therein embodied, and we have feelings about the self as well as the source of stimulation. In one way or another, this is a sexual experience, and it enlightens us about the relationship with self and with the other. We want to be close to another, to be held, caressed, or hugged. That feels good, and although we may insist that what is being felt is not sexual, our insistence is probably revealing a deep-set conditioning about what sex is and to whom it is appropriate to feel sexually attracted.

Our culture's obsession with romance leads to further confusion. A warm, tingling feeling within us generates our creative energies and heightens the desire to be around another person. We think it is romantic love, especially if the other fits our expectations of a potential, and approved, love/sex partner. On the other hand, we may feel repulsed, and repress the feelings, if the other is judged by voices within us to be inappropriate or a threat to perceptions of the sexual self. In either case, the opportunity for a caring, supportive, self-confirming relationship may be sacrificed to an over-emphasis on love as romantic attraction.

As noted earlier, we are helped by the recognition that sex has been separated from "eros" in ways that are harmful to our culture as well as to our individual selves. That awareness is important to a recovery of a constructive role for sex and sexuality in our loving relationships.

Some ancient Greek writers described a special power working in human beings, as well as in all nature, in their understanding of *eros*. All things are moved toward their potential and purpose by this power. Thus, we can speak of potency or impotence in human beings as expressions of the capacity for erotic love. The common usage of "erotic" in our time, of course, is usually concentrated on matters of sexual arousal. Keen, however, corrects this contemporary notion with the original meaning of *eros*: "to love or desire ardently." Greek mythology provides us some background for this language:

> Plato's myth of the androgyne gives the original meaning of eros. In the beginning, according to Plato, there were three kinds of human beings: man-man, woman-woman, and man-woman. Each unit was joined back to back, had four arms, four legs, and a single head with faces front and back. These hybrid creatures could either walk upright or run cartwheel fashion, but they could never face each other. When Zeus decided to divide and conquer these powerful beings, he split each unit down the middle so that a single person would henceforth be incomplete and would have to search for his or her other half. Thus we are now motivated by eros, by a profound longing to be reunited with our missing complement. Sexual love is only one of the many modes in which eros seeks to reunite us with what is missing.[8]

Passion felt in sexual arousal is certainly a part of eros. Sexual arousal, however, tends to build toward a release of tension, where eros seeks the increase of stimulation. Two lovers who are having a primarily sexual experience may carry their arousal toward the passionate release in orgasm, and then fall asleep, or begin to move away from one another. Partners in erotic passion are more likely to experience the orgasmic release as only one part of a continuing series of stimulating experiences, bringing them closer and closer to each other and to something they experience as beyond themselves. Many have noted that the most exciting phase of genital intercourse is not orgasm but entry.[9] The moment of penetration is the time when the physical separation is no more, and a literal entry of one into another takes place. When eros is present, the entry is not only a physical union, but a psychological and spiritual one as well. The two lovers sense a dropping of barriers, a release of control over self from the other, and a merging of their two beings with nature, and with their fuller purposes as creatures in a universe of powerful meanings and feelings. A push toward a union of sensations and the mutual giving of pleasure is then possible. It may culminate in a release which allows one or both to feel, if only for a split second, a part of all that is—a unity with the other and, at the same time, a unity with all creation. As exciting and tension-releasing as that moment may be, erotic lovers do not stop there. They continue to find ways to celebrate and extend their unity. They enhance each other's desires for self-fulfillment while cementing their mutual passions and goals.

The passion of *eros* is also known in many ways that have little to do with the lover's embrace. One is the intense caring about what happens to another human being, whether it be one's own child or a total stranger who is nonetheless perceived as sharing in our created humanity and thus a significant part of one's self. Another is the joyful merging with hundreds—or thousands—of others to demonstrate a common commitment to social justice. I stood on the steps of the state capitol building, and looked out over the crowd of more than 3,000 students who gathered from campuses all over Kansas in May, 1970, after the American bombing of Cambodia. They had convened in Topeka to petition their governor and state legislature to press the federal government to end its military involvement in Vietnam. They were peaceful, orderly, and quiet. They were also passionate. At the end of the planned, brief program, they stood, spontaneously, their joined hands raised in the air, singing quietly and fervently. Their bodies merged into a message of determination and hope. It was a moment of union achieved around one of the deepest of human dimensions—the communion of hope for rationality and caring in human interaction. As I write these words, many faces cross my memory, and stories come to mind of persons who carried on beyond that day with its intentions and goals. Occasionally a letter arrives, or a person drops by to see me, bringing me up-to-date on ways in which the passion of that day has carried on in individual, particular ways in their lives. These are reminders that eros is deeply related to meanings and values, tied up in a special way with love. It is involved with creativity, our imagining of possibilities within ourselves and specific others.

What does this have to do with sex? Certainly it is not meant to support the absurd racist charges that civil rights demonstrations during the 1950s and 1960s were mere cover-ups for sexual orgies. Those charges were, of course, attempts to discredit those who were confronting white supremacy with the truth of its injustice and inherent immorality. What this *does* have to do with sex is a reminder that our erotic passion includes sex but is also much more. Our sexuality includes what we usually think of as sexual, but much, much more. In our relationship with the self and with others, we are "embodied." In Nelson's words, "we experience the world only through the body-selves . . . The body is the *means* by which I can know objects, persons, and events."[10] Our feelings about the world, about others, are shaped in and through our "bodies-as-selves." With a better understanding of this embodiment, of its part in our sexuality, we are better prepared to participate in loving relationships on all levels.

Sexuality

Sexuality, many would say, is anything having to do with, or leading to, genital intercourse. Others place the term in a much broader context. As one writer put it, "sexuality is not what I have, but what I am."[11] In other words, it doesn't refer to genital activity as much as it does the totality of being. Since I am male, it is my feeling about who I am as a male, accepting my maleness while knowing and accepting those parts within me that feel "female." When we hear someone say, "I feel good about my sexuality," we are probably hearing an expression of self-confidence, comfort with one's body, comfort with the opposite sex, and nonthreatening ability to be affectionate with members of one's own sex. Sexual attraction, even arousal, is part of one's sexuality, but only part of it. Nelson pulls it together for us:

> Our sexuality . . . is at the center of our response to life. It is the way in which we are in the world as embodied selves, female or male, with certain affectional orientations, with qualities socially defined as "masculine" and "feminine." It is a basic way in which we express both our incompleteness and our relatedness. It is God's ingenious way of calling us

into communion with others through our need to reach out and touch and embrace—emotionally, intellectually, physically. Sexuality thus is never accidental or peripheral to our possibility of human becoming. It is basic and intrinsic to that possibility. It is both the physiological and psychological grounding of our capacity of love.[12]

To say that I am male is to describe certain physiological and biological make-up. It involves hormonal and chromosome balances that give my body a certain structure, and appearance, and indicates some things that I can and cannot do. My body can produce a fluid which fertilizes an egg, and thus participate in the formation of new human life. My body cannot produce that egg, nor enclose it while it evolves into its own distinct being. I can impregnate, but I cannot menstruate, germinate, or lactate. In a sense, then, my "maleness" is differentiated from "femaleness" in certain specific ways, and that is a part of my sexuality. At the same time, the mix of hormones, and of chromosomes, produces glandular and other chemical combinations which will vary from person to person and thus the individual experience of *being* male or female will vary. Perhaps it is most accurate to say that we have a male or female gender.

To say that I am "masculine" is to go beyond simple sex or gender formation, and to describe cultural and social preferences, expectations and roles. From the time a newborn human being is observed by parents and others in society, its gender is translated into a myriad of assumptions about what a girl or boy is or should be like. A mother was viewing pictures of her preschool son, trying to select her favorite poses for purchase from the traveling portrait studio. The studio representative, supposedly helping with the selection, exclaimed: "look at those beautiful brown eyes and that hair! Isn't it too bad it's a boy?" Our sexuality is heavily influenced by what others think it *means* to look like a particular sex/gender. Francoeur's words, quoted at the beginning of this chapter, underline the complexity of the way in which each of us is "molded by biological, social, family, cultural, psychological, historical, legal and religious factors that contribute to our unique sexual being."[13] Thus, what we think and feel about sex, specifically, and about ourselves as the particular bodily being we are, generally, is shaped in many ways we usually don't think about. In addition, those influences shift in differing environments. A young woman, for instance, may have been raised in a home which emphasized equality of sexes in all things, including family and societal responsibility. She encounters rather different perceptions, however, in certain legal and business matters, when she steps out on her own. When she marries, she may choose a spouse who sees her as an equal and independent person, but they will have to contend with social systems that assign her status and primary identity to her through her husband. She knows and delights that she is female, but she may resent what her employer prescribes as appropriately feminine attire on the job. She may be considering a career in ordained ministry, but is aware that the God language in her church is always about "He" and "His"—and that the Board of Trustees is made up entirely of men. It can be confusing, to say the least, as well as frustrating.

When we think of sexuality in terms of who we are as male or female, it is easy to fall into descriptions of sex roles: "Women are . . .; Men are . . ." A woman is feminine, and a man is masculine, right? There are traits for each of these, and we have almost unlimited resources telling us what those traits are. You might want to make a list of such traits. Having done so you'll probably recognize that there are items on both lists that fit you at times. At this point in history, we are finding more openness to recognition and acceptance of that reality for each of us. Although sex roles are alive and well in human societies, there are signs that their power is not as influential as it once was. Donald Goergen observes:

> The feminine cannot be identified with woman nor the masculine with man. Each of us is both. My task is not to become a masculine person; it is to become a person, who is in fact a man. Nor is it the nature of a woman to be exclusively feminine; it is the goal of a woman to be a person, a person who is comfortable with her femininity as well as her masculinity.[14]

Sex roles sometimes make things easier in the sense that convenient stereotypes allow us to have clear expectations. The problem is that they often don't really match the way an individual feels—the way we experience ourselves in our inner being—and they often put us in the position of easily being used through the roles. Part of our growth in regard to sexuality is to be able to distinguish how we actually feel from the roles and identities placed on us, and to accept those feelings as an important part of our selves.

The beginning step in integrating our sex and sexuality into loving relationships, is, of course, coming to terms with one's own sexual being. Francoeur's very brief definition of sexuality tells us what we are dealing with: "The combination of our gender and sex, coextensive with personality."[15] For most of us, that involves acceptance. A noted theologian, Paul Tillich, emphasized the significance of our accepting the fact that we are "accepted" by the "ground of our being." Nelson has turned Tillich's language to our concerns of sex and sexuality:

> You are accepted, the total you. Your body, which you often reject, is accepted by that which is greater than you. Your sexual feelings and unful-

filled yearnings are accepted. You are accepted in your ascetic attempts at self-justification or in your hedonistic alienation from the true meaning of your sexuality. You are accepted in those moments of sexual fantasy which come unbidden and which both delight and disturb you. You are accepted in your femininity and your masculinity, for you have elements of both. You are accepted in your heterosexuality and in your homosexuality, and you have elements of both. Simply accept the fact that you are accepted as a sexual person! If that happens to you, you experience grace."[16]

We have seen that our acceptance of who we are depends on many things. Psychologists and educators give us their insights regarding human development. Researchers of brain development are formulating fascinating theories about the imprint of gender formation on the brain and resultant behavior and attitudes. Students of society and culture contribute to the discussion, as do those who insist that in matters sexual, as in all other things, we are shaped by politics and economics. I want to concentrate on certain values as they are transmitted to us through value institutions, because I am convinced they have a lot to do with our attitudes toward love and relationships. The religious values to which we have been exposed, whether we are "religious" or not, are both major influences on and reflections of other basic values transmitted through culture. In looking at the development of religious values regarding sex, we discover a mixed bag, considerably more mixed than we often see. At the same time, we can see tendencies that have had direct influence on our ways of thinking and acting.

Religious Values, Sex and Persons

How does the Bible view sex? It depends. It will depend on where one looks in the Bible, as well as what presuppositions and interpretations one brings to the text. Biblical perspectives deserve careful treatment, and there is a growing, rich literature on the subject. I shall focus here on some general trends and over-arching notions that may enlighten our way of being in relationships.

The Hebrew story of creation found in Genesis 2:5-25 asserts that woman was created as a *companion* for man, in a special relationship with God. (In the first chapter of Genesis, a somewhat different creation story also emphasizes that male and female were created "in the image of God," in the completion of God's creating activity which is judged to be "very good.") The people who passed on these stories of creation understood that one purpose of having two sexes is to know the fulfillment of shared lives. Procreation is not mentioned *at that point* in the story. "Be fruitful and multiply" shortly follows (in the version scholars consider to be the later story), but there is no suggesting that procreation is the *only* or even the *primary* purpose for there being two sexes. Nor is there anything in this story about the nakedness of their bodies which suggests shame (Gen. 2:25).

Throughout the Hebrew scriptures (the Old Testament), genital intercourse is understood as a good thing. Laws about intercourse tend to be stated in relation to property rights of males over females. Adultery, for instance, is often understood as the violation of a man's ownership of a woman. The man's punishment for adultery, therefore, is in relation to his violation of another man's property, which is different from the offense by the woman—who also was more likely to receive more drastic punishment in that patriarchal system. Other admonitions about sexual behavior, such as promiscuity and homosexuality, are normally found in texts emphasizing the importance of being different from neighboring people who do those things. An important factor in group and personal identity, as in the Tribes of Israel, is to have a clear distinction between their behavior and that of other groups around them. This is true in a wide range of activities, including sexual behavior. Perhaps the most important point to emphasize, however, is that sexual experience between male and female is a good thing in the Hebrew tradition. This is expressed in romantic poetry which some folks actually find difficult to accept as belonging in the Bible:

How fair and pleasant you are,
    O loved one, delectable maiden!
You are stately as a palm tree,
    and your breasts are like its clusters.
I say I will climb the palm tree
    and lay hold on its branches.
Oh, may your breasts be like clusters of the vine,
    and the scent of your breath like apples,
    and your kisses like the best wine
        that does down smoothly, gliding over lips and teeth.
I am my beloved's
    and his desire is for me.
Come, my beloved,
        let us go forth into the fields,
        and lodge in the villages;
let us go out early to the vineyards,
        and see whether the vines have budded,
        and whether the grape blossoms have opened
        and the pomegranates are in bloom.
There I will give you my love.

This delightful verse is found in the Song of Solomon (called "Song of Songs" in some versions of the Bible) 7:6–12. The book has a number of passages like this, rich in detail of sensual and romantic pleasure. Who were these two persons so obviously enamored with physical beauty, sexual attraction, and emotional satisfaction? Were they married? To each other? The text doesn't tell us. We do know that fidelity seems to be important in their relationship—the two parties see it as unending. There are traditions that this (and similar literature in religious groups throughout the Middle East) is a love song of a king and his queen. Some rabbis later interpreted it as the relationship of God to the people of Israel, just as later Christians were to interpret it in terms of the relationship of Christ and the Church. There are other traditions as well. However one may choose to *interpret* the text within the context of a particular religious perspective, it is important to see that the inclusion of this poetry in the scripture, without any specifics about the formal relationship of the persons involved, conveys a celebration of sexual, physical love as both beautiful and appropriate. No overt attempt is made in the canon of scripture to put this relationship in a moral context, or to say that it has its fulfillment in procreation, as appears in some forms in later Christian doctrine. It simply recognizes, as does one element of the Creation story, the beauty of companionship of *two persons who are in awe of the God-given intimacy available to them.*

It is not nearly as clear how the Hebrew scriptures viewed sexual love between persons of the same sex, in spite of the fairly rigid tradition opposing homosexuality in both Judaism and Christianity. We know that David and Jonathan shared a deep and loyal love, as did Ruth and Rachel, although no clear suggestion of a sexual relationship is found in the texts. We further know that the attempted gang rape of Lot's male angel guests and the lying of a man with another man, as though he were a woman (as done in the temple worship of "heathen" neighbors and in the licentiousness of some of their communities) were proclaimed "abominations" along with long lists of other actions. We know nothing of sexual relationships between persons of the same sex who were committed to each other in love—there simply was no term for that in the language of the time, even though we know that such was a part of their life. (The term, "homosexual" is an invention of recent centuries, with its broad application to sexual behavior between persons of the same sex, no matter what their relationship).[17]

When looking to the Christian scriptures in the New Testament, we may well ask, "what did Jesus say about sex?" The answer would have to be, very little. He suggested that one's *attitude* toward another is as important as acting out behavior. "Lusting after another" in one's heart, as Jimmy Carter reminded us in the famous *Playboy* article, is equated by Jesus with adultery. He sided with Jewish law, in which he was well trained, where adultery was the major basis for divorce. He did *not* accept the tradition of stoning the adulteress, but stymied the crowd about to carry out that practice by suggesting that "he who is without sin among you cast the first stone." We also know that Jesus was a person with close, intimate relationships with both women and men. His willingness to include women among his close associates was unusual for his time, and his retreat to the home of female friends is a clear indication of an ease and familiarity with them, as well as a recognition of their equality as human beings.

Persons all through history have been fascinated with the total lack of information about the adolescence and young adulthood of Jesus. Was he married or involved in any other kind of sexual relationships? Celibacy was certainly not a virtue in his Jewish background—it was, on the other hand, practiced in the Essene community to which some recent scholars have related him. Was there a romantic, or sexual, tie between Jesus and Mary Magdalene, as suggested in ancient legends as well as recent novels and musicals? What was the nature of the intimacy shared between the men who surrounded Jesus? The answer is, we just don't know. Speculation about such matters remains just that—speculation.[18] For those to whom it is important to ascribe perfection to Jesus and to load perfection with certain kinds of behaviors (or abstinence from behaviors), it has been important to develop doctrine in which Jesus had *no* sexual experience in a genital sense. For others to whom spiritual perfection or maturity has no essential connection with sexual mores or behavior, it has not been important to emphasize Jesus' sexuality.

Some things can be known regarding Jesus' sexuality, if we take seriously Goergen's distinction between "genital" and "affective" sexuality:

> Sexuality has both a genital and an affective dimension. Affectivity and all that it implies is a vital part of sexuality. The affective dimension of humanity consists in all those qualities of gentleness and tenderness which make sexuality truly human. Gentleness and tenderness are rooted in human sexuality. Compassion is a supreme sign of a well integrated sexual life. The Gospels portray Jesus as a compassionate, gentle, loving, tender, and warm person. He touches people—physically, psychologically, and spiritually. He has friends—male and female. One cannot underestimate the importance of John, Lazarus, Martha, and Mary in his life. It is in this sense that his sexuality comes through ... Sexuality is good and exists in the context of relationships.[19]

Since the earliest centuries of the Christian movement, orthodox Christians have insisted, against various detractors, on the full humanity of Jesus. Whatever the Christ-faith may claim about Jesus' divinity, those doctrines that denied Jesus' being "fully human" were soundly rejected. Contemporary Christians are urged by Nelson and others to take his humanness seriously if they are to see their own human embodiment clearly.[20]

The apostle Paul has had a tremendous impact on the theological development of Christianity. His views toward sex are basically a reflection of the particular background in Judaism from which he came, mixed with his own expectation that the present age is about to come to an end and that all behavior should be directed toward preparation for the coming of the new Kingdom of God. His support of the general customs of the time is indicated in his response to questions from the churches. He warns them in his letters to refrain from a wide variety of excesses, including promiscuity (translated "fornication" in many English versions.) He sides with Hebrew law in denouncing certain forms of sexual behavior between persons of the same sex; the texts for these statements need to be examined very carefully for their context and full meaning before Christians draw some of the absolute conclusions heard with regularity in our day. Paul certainly leaned toward genital intercourse as belonging within marriage. His statements about it, however, are part of other discussions concerning the need for discipline and concentration in preparing for the Kingdom. It is difficult to know to what extent his comments also reflect the early church's understanding of appropriate sexual behavior.

When we look at the development of Christian thought and its direct influence on moral perceptions in Western culture, we cannot avoid the impact of St. Augustine. Since the fourth century, his attitudes about sex have been pervasive in the teachings of the Church and, often, in other institutions in society. His own conversion included a strong rejection of the sexual license of his early years. He came to see direct connections between sexual behavior and separation from God, even to the point of transmission of original sin through the act of conception. His attitudes toward women have helped keep them in second-class status in both the Church and the larger society. As Derrick Bailey has noted, "Augustine must bear no small measure of responsibility for the insinuation into our culture of the idea, still widely current, that Christianity regards sexuality as something peculiarly tainted with evil."[21]

It is not unusual in our time to hear comments about "Victorian" or "Puritan" attitudes toward sex which suggest they are primarily responsible for unhealthy repression of sexual development. Although those phenomena have received, in many ways, a rather bad press, and need to be understood more carefully, it is accurate to say that they are also cultural manifestations of certain religious views toward sex. Such views, in turn, had their origins in both cultural conventions and religious commitments. Puritan ideas developed from a portion of Reformation thought that can be traced back to Augustine. It should be kept in mind that the severity of some of their positions is evidence that strong alternative behavior and attitudes were in existence. Otherwise, there would have been no need to be so adamant. Those alternative perspectives and practices existed among folk who were also religious, as well as among those who dissented conscientiously from religion. Thus, such matters as acceptance of genital intercourse before marriage, "free" sex within intentional communities, and same sex genital love expression had origins in other streams of religious tradition. It is accurate, nonetheless, to assert that a major impact of Christian teaching over the centuries has been repression of sexual feelings and expression, and separation of the body from the spirit and soul. Thus, many persons have grown up thinking that sex and anything involving enjoyment of the body, (other than athletics, perhaps) is dirty or bad. This is especially true for women who have been raised in a male dominated church. A woman who is married to a pastor reported that during her pregnancy, a woman in their congregation told her, with some reluctance, that although she wanted to congratulate her on her pregnancy, she had a hard time thinking of "her pastor making babies." Dedicated, spiritual folks, apparently, aren't supposed to use their bodies the way others do!

The Jewish tradition through history has escaped some of the repressive and confusing attitudes experienced by Christians. As Eugene Borowitz points out, "Judaism considers sex God's gift and procreation His command." Marriage is seen as the proper context for intercourse, and it is understood as a religious duty.[22] Although there have been other problems in some streams of Jewish tradition regarding sex, it is probably fair to say that one of the most important Jewish contributions to the Judaeo-Christian ethic is what Borowitz calls the "dignity and nobility of their sexual practices." This is an important resource to a helpful sexual attitude in the transition from the twentieth to the twenty-first century.

The mainstream moral position of both Judaism and Christianity has been that sexual intercourse is to be confined to heterosexual marriage. That position has been strongly disputed in theory, both within and outside the religious communities, and has clearly been ignored in practice—again, both within and outside.

Although all centuries have seen some forms of reaction against the repression of the body and its sexual realities, the twentieth century has produced a reaction which is probably more widespread than previous ones. We now find ourselves in the midst of this reaction, this "wilderness," as we search for values that contribute to a constructive inclusion of our sexual being in our relationships with self and others. One of the symptoms of our difficulty in doing so is the widespread fear of homosexuality—homophobia—in human societies.

A Special Problem—Homophobia (and Heterosexism)

The homophobia upon which the oppression of homosexuals is based is one aspect of the distress our whole culture puts on sex. It is one of the main things keeping men from getting close to and supporting other men, and also keeping women from each other. This attitude is harmful to relationships with members of both the same and the opposite sex, because it places undue reliance on opposite-sex relationships for the fulfillment of our needs. We thus downplay our friendships with members of the same sex and overemphasize those with members of the opposite sex. Neither set of friendships is treated with the respect and care it deserves.[23]

A phobia is a fear. It is irrational; it is excessive, and it is persistent. Obviously, not all opposition to homosexuality is phobic. For some, it is believed as a matter of religious faith or moral assumption that sexual orientations other than heterosexuality are morally deviant. This stance, sometimes referred to as "heterosexism,"[24] may be based on biblical interpretation, moral argument, and/or assertions regarding what is natural. Such views are often a part of a sincerely held belief system, with loving concern expressed for those persons who are seen as deviant. To the extent, however, that such positions are expressed through fears, fears that can be demonstrated to be without logic or empirical evidence, they become phobic. To the extent that the position is sufficiently persistent as to operate as a prejudice—pre-judging persons on the the basis of a behavior, style of dress, or way of speaking— it is phobic. Many human societies, especially those dominated by males, or patriarchal, are homophobic. American society is basically patriarchal and, generally, homophobic. The fear is extensive and its ramifications must, for the most part, be left to the many excellent discussions of the matter in other books. Our concern at this point is to be aware of the reduction of our EQ—Keen's "Erotic Quotient"— which closes us off from a significant portion of our own capacity for loving, as well as leading us to impose restrictions on others.

This issue is charged with considerable emotion, and it is difficult to engage in serious, open discussion in many settings. It especially creates heat in most religious circles these days. We are learning much more about this part of human life, and religious groups are discovering their need to go back and study their Bibles more carefully, their traditions more sensitively, and emerging scientific and historical evidence more openly.

It is unfortunate that a few Bible passages are used uncritically to support a rigid but misdirected opposition to this form of sexual intimacy. Sodom and Gomorrah (Genesis 19) are the great flag words for some religious enthusiasts regarding homosexuality—yet, the references *within* the Bible to the "sin" of those people had little to do with sexual practice. Their abusive rejection of representatives sent to them by God, and their practice of idolatry, injustice, and oppression, was the basis of their trouble with divinity. As suggested earlier, prohibition of same-sex behavior in Hebrew law is much more directly related to idolatrous practices carried on by neighboring peoples who did not recognize Yahweh as the one God.

Jesus had *nothing* to say about the matter, according to the Gospel record.

Paul included homosexuality in his lists of behaviors that persons who want to be included in Christ's Kingdom must refrain from—but there is no evidence that he was referring to intimacy involving persons now considered to be "constitutional" in their attraction to the same sex, or to equal-status adults in a mutual, committed relationship. Nelson has clarified the problem in reading Paul on this matter:

> Paul's words in Romans 1 are usually taken as the strongest New Testament rejection of homosexuality. (Here is the one and only biblical reference to female as well as male same-sex activity.) Paul, however, speaks specifically of same-sex acts that express idolatry and acts undertaken in lust (not tenderness or mutual respect) by heterosexuals who willfully act contrary to their own sexual natures. I am not inferring that the apostle necessarily would have approved of other kinds of same-sex acts. I am simply arguing that it is inaccurate and unfair to interpret his words as directed to nonexploitive and loving acts by same-sex couples for whom mutual homosexual attraction is part of the given of *their* natures.[25]

Norman Pittenger correctly insists that "to use the Bible in the way opponents of all homosexuality tend to do is indeed to *misuse* it."[26] Furthermore, William Sloan Coffin has focused the issue where it belongs for those who are attempting to respond to life in the fullest sense with love:

> How ironic that because of a mistaken understanding of the crime of Sodom and Gomorrah, Christians should be repeating the *real* crime every day against homosexuals! Clearly, it is not Scripture that creates hostility to homosexuality, but rather hostility to homosexuality that prompts certain Christians to retain a few passages from an otherwise discarded law code. The problem is not how to reconcile homosexuality with scriptural passages that appear to condemn it, but rather how to reconcile the rejection and punishment of homosexuals with the love of Christ. I do not think it can be done. I do not see how Christians can define and then exclude people on the basis of sexual orientation alone—not if the law of love is more important than the laws of biology.[27]

The law of love *is* more important than what Coffin calls "laws of biology." In our best moral traditions *love* supersedes all manners of human condition and behavior. The problem of homophobia is, then, a problem for loving in both personal and community contexts. Irrational fears have a direct impact on our own capacity to accept and embrace the natural parts of ourselves that "feel" as though they belong to the opposite sex, due to cultural interpretation and learned sex roles. They make it difficult for us to relate warmly and comfortably with others of the same sex, even within our own families. These fears limit our ability to be expressive with friends of the same sex, especially for males. Our distorted fears force us into placing all our needs for affection on a heterosexual partner, often distorting that relationship. Our power needs are likewise distorted. Having squeezed our sexual feelings and forms of expression into a tighter box, that pressure flows over into the ways in which we express personal power with others. Again, this especially affects men's attitudes toward women. We become victims of cognitive dissonance in such a way that we are not able to accept and celebrate the wholeness of another, and therefore of ourselves.

Community dimensions of homophobia permit us to assume that "they" are not "normal," and are in some way threatening to societal standards. "Straights" can then accept everyday violations of the personal and civil rights of persons who happen to have a same-sex attraction for their most intimate sexual practice. We repeat unfounded and dangerous ideas that further the prejudice already operating: "they" are likely to sexually abuse our children; "they" are bad role models and shouldn't be allowed to be teachers; "they" must be socially and/or psychologically immature or sick. We fall into the trap (characteristic of many forms of prejudice with dangerous social consequences) of joining with a majority definition of a minority, focusing on a particular behavioral trait as an overall personality and character description. One of the more recent historical consequences is reported by Letha Scanzoni and Virginia Mollenkott:

> Not so very long ago, the following statements were made to a national audience:
>
> Homosexuality is that mark of Cain, of a godless and soulless culture which is sick to the core.
>
> The teaching of the youth to appreciate the value . . . of the community, derives its strongest inner power from the truths of Christianity . . . For this reason it will always be my special duty to safeguard the right and free development of the Christian fundamentals of all education.

The first statement comes from a Fascist pamphlet published in Nazi Germany; the second was made by Adolph Hitler in a 1933 edict on the education of German young people. In the name of Christ and moral purity, Hitler later had persons who were suspected of homosexuality either shot without trial or exterminated in concentration camp gas chambers.[28]

Another community dimension of homophobia is a bit more subtle, but nonetheless real. It contributes to a rigidification of sex roles and accompanying mentalities that we now know to have serious political implications, both at home and on the international scene. The "macho" mentality is much more likely to be militaristic, and to deal with others through force rather than negotiation. We who are out of touch with the fullness of our own embodied nature, and that of others who are different from us, are more willing to unleash destructive physical power on others and, ultimately, to bring it down on ourselves.

Many are suggesting ways to deal with our homophobia. Hard work is called for, confronting the realities of the fears and limitations that we have imposed on ourselves and have accepted from others. We may also enter into open and accepting relationships with persons who know and accept the gay or lesbian realities that are a part of themselves. A United Methodist Bishop has been attacked and even charged, unsuccessfully, by other church members with violations of church regulations for appointing a minister who made public his gay reality. The bishop has made it clear that he hears all public utterances and church positions through the ears and eyes of four "cherished individuals, including a member of his own family." These are persons who have a same-sex, rather than other-sex orientation, something which was not learned and practiced, but is "something they are." These are persons who, in spite of messages they hear from others that they cannot be authentic Christians, or even full persons, are seen by the bishop and his wife as being "as close to authentic Christian living as we perceive ourselves to be."[29]

Another approach to dealing with this phenomenon is to *think*—more specifically, to *think about how we've managed to think this way!* Drawing on the "symbolic interactionist" stance, Nelson suggests a crucial rephrasing of the question about the deviancy which is assumed to be involved in same-sex preference. Rather than asking, "how did this person become sexually deviant," we should really be asking, "why is this particular sexual expression considered deviant?"[30] Before I allow myself to relax with the question of how my friend became the way he is, I must ask why I consider the way he *is* to be something to be asked about. If I get serious about that question, as I have, I discover that I go back into a number of messages passed on to me in my early socialization about people who are "queer," "fairy," or "faggot." I think again about whether any recognized abuse of intimacy between persons of the same sex is *morally* different from abuse of intimacy I see around me nearly every day between heterosexuals. I pause with the question of why two persons really caring about each other and expressing that caring with their bodies is unacceptable when they happen to be of the same sex. And the questions go on.

Deviance is often thought of as pathology. Goergen is very helpful in sorting out the supposedly "pathological" elements of a relationship from those that are healthful, whatever the gender of those involved. Healthy personalities, he suggests, are able to integrate both the dimensions of heterosexuality and homosexuality in their affective relationships:

> A person who is exclusively caught up in heterosexuality so that he is unable to relate affectively with members of his own sex has certainly moved in the direction of pathological heterosexuality. His heterosexuality manifests an inability to face his own homosexual dimension. His masculinity may be so insecure that he cannot incorporate homosexuality into his own personal growth. He identifies masculinity with heterosexuality. Many times this person, seen as the epitome of heterosexual masculinity, is unable to be warm and tender even in his heterosexual relationships because he is blocking much of his sexual life. Heterosexual relationships can be pathological just as homosexual relationships can. Health is not a category I attach to heterosexuality and pathology a category I attach to homosexuality . . . It is not homosexuality but *monosexuality* that is pathological . . . A man who is not able to relate tenderly to his own sex is pathologically heterosexual; a man who is not able to relate tenderly to the other sex is pathologically homosexual. Pathology enters when exclusiveness with one sex predominates and impairs our ability to relate to both sexes.[31]

Toward the end of class one day, a number of opinions had been expressed about the legitimacy, morality, and other aspects of homosexuality as opposed to heterosexuality. Several comments were made about what the Bible says. Finally, one young woman who had occasionally expressed herself quietly as a committed Christian, stated: "If two people are together, and are exploiting each other, taking advantage of each other, not caring about each other—the same sex or the opposite sex—that's bad. If two people who really care about each other don't exploit each other, are tender with each other—the same sex or the opposite sex—then, it seems to me, that's good!" With that, the class adjourned.

With that, also, we move on to considerations of sexual expression in loving relationships, wrapping up something of what those expressions might mean, what significance they have, and some factors involved in differing contexts of loving ties.

Sexual Expression in Loving Relationships—Contact with Harmony

Although we might recognize the truth of Ashley Montagu's statement quoted at the beginning of this chapter, we would probably protest that he hasn't described a *loving* relationship when he says, "sex . . . is contact *without* harmony." Sex in a relationship between persons who care about and are committed to each other is precisely contact *with* "harmony." Embodied personalities want contact with others. That contact happens, and is desired, on a wide range of dimensions, including what we have come to understand as "sexual."

Norman Pittenger has suggested some important things about our human nature. First, he asserts, we can be defined or described as a "*lover* in the making." That is, we are created to love. Our "deepest intentionality" is that we shall love, and our humanhood is expressed in our loving. Pittenger also recognizes, as his second contention, that our efforts at loving become frustrated and our usual condition is one of distortion and "twisting," a predicament which he terms as "sin." We can, he asserts as his third point, be *released to love* in the way that we are intended to do. As a Christian theologian, he draws on the Christian symbols of redemption, atonement (at-one-ment) and reconciliation to describe the experience of release and fulfillment.[32] This is possible for us through the availability of "grace"—the *gift* of our being who we are, in relation to the Creator of who we are.

Sexuality is basic to this nature. As part of our fundamental reality, we have sexual feelings and bodies through which those feelings may or may not be expressed. We have experienced a good deal of distortion and twisting of what that means, in our development, but we can also be released from those distortions to express ourselves as whole persons toward other whole persons.

Given what we have been discussing throughout this book, what does this mean for our relationships? I suggest the following:

—Loving sexuality will be expressed with *care* for self and care for another. The well-being, opportunity for growth, and development of both self *and other* will be enhanced and celebrated through the expression.

—Loving sexuality will be expressed with *responsibility.* As Fromm emphasized, responsibility is the ability-to-respond. Our bodies as well from the center of one self to the center of another.

—Loving sexuality will be expressed with *respect*. An independent, integrated person will already respect the self, and will want the same independence and integration for another. This respect prevents the response to the other from falling into domination or exploitation. It longs for and facilitates a mutual celebration of joy about who we are and what we can do.

—Loving sexuality is expressed in the process of *knowing* another, of really entering into the other while remaining open to be entered into. It is sensitive to what another, as well as self, is feeling, desiring, and capable of. It is in awe of what is not yet known, but can be, as contact is allowed and appreciated. It is *communion*.

—Loving sexuality is expressed in *tenderness*. It wants to fathom the depths of shared sensations that are available only to the softest of touch, to the slightest reach, to the tears (whether sadness or joy) of self and/or other. It knows that such contact is easily bruised and broken, and sticks around for the consoling and mending when that happens.

—Loving sexuality is known and expressed in *openness*. Openness to self allows awareness of wide-ranging possibilities waiting to be discovered and explored. Openness to the other encourages and supports that discovery and exploration by the other.

—Loving sexuality discovers and explores *meanings*. Not only are sensations and feelings experienced, but meanings are found in them, and those meanings are related to other facets of one's life, including life-with-others.

—Loving sexuality takes *risks*. Because it is open, it is vulnerable. It knows hurt and pain, and it offers ways to healing. Willingness to embrace accepts the wound that may come, knowing that there is also entrance to deeper intimacy.

—Loving sexuality is an expression of *dignity* and an affirmation of the dignity of the other. It celebrates with the other without possessing the other. It protects the emergence and extension of power.

—Loving sexuality is an expression of personal *power* and a merging of that power with another, with that of the universe. It is an experience, or combination of experiences, of creativity, of potency, of productivity. It passes on power through procreation.

—Loving sexuality is *friendly*. It delights in sharing common humanity, celebrating the differences of the other. It meets the needs and desires of the cherished other. It *trusts* the other because it trusts the self.

—Loving sexuality exists in *community*. In Nelson's words, it "is socially responsible, nurturing the fabric of the larger community to which the lovers belong."[33] It cares about what happens in the larger community, and empowers members to act.

—Loving sexuality *reduces distance and increases intimacy.* Although it takes care not to move too soon to an inadequate and unfulfilling union, it is open to the passion of feeling and allows a framework for feelings to live and to merge.

—Loving sexuality is *androgynous.* It allows the individual to experience and accept the fuller dimensions of both femininity and masculinity within the self, and allows those dimensions to function in interaction with others.

—Loving sexuality is *passionate and compassionate.* It knows and enjoys feeling. It feels with others. It can get worked up and is readily energized for self, for others, and for the total environment within which life is known.

—Loving sexuality is *erotic.* Its focus is, at one and the same time, deep within the self, within the exclusive other, and within sources of life and being that seem to be far beyond the selves, pulling each, together, to enrichment and fulfillment.

—Loving sexuality allows the *child* in each of us to discover and explore. It encourages the *adult* in each of us to integrate experience and meaning, to deepen and mature.

—Loving sexuality opens the human to *other-than-human* reality. The stroking of the pet in one's lap, the walk in the rain, the soaking in of the sunset are gifts to be received and to expand dimensions of the self. The biblical "Song of Songs" celebrates not only the bodies of the lovers, but the pleasures of flowers, trees, fruits, and running water. My pine tree is not mine, but we enter each other in our *mutual lives within nature.*

—Loving sexuality knows *death.* With total giving of the self, there is loss of the self, perhaps even experience of the loss of the other.

—Loving sexuality is *committed.* It takes the self and other seriously, is prepared to take and give time. It gives and is worthy of fidelity.

In each of the above expressions, there may be genital sensations or activity. Or, the experience may be of quite a different kind. The experience may be affectional, reaching to another for whom one cares and in whom one finds meaning. The experience may be passionate, an involvement with others for greater humanization of community and each within the community. It may be fuller identification with nature, with the environment that nurtures and extends and receives life, and also gives reality and meaning to death.

When I know and accept and extend my sexuality, I am more able to surround a child with love. I can more readily reach out to an elder parent. I can touch the sick person with a healing contact. I can share with a friend more openly, creatively, and without judgment.

Genital and affectional sexual expression may have special meaning at the death of a relationship. Gerda Lerner relates in a brief, simple and moving way the importance of the final time of love-making with her dying husband:

> We made love that morning. It was sad and sweet and tender. He did what he could and gave me all his gentle love, his strength and secure trust in himself and in both of us, despite his helpless and crippled body. Amazingly, he spoke to me with his body the way he had always spoken. For the final thirty days of his life he would never again trust himself to let me come that close again. It was his way of saying good-bye, while he still could function with some wholeness. A man giving up his love by loving. That's the way he wanted it. That's the way he went.[34]

Contact with harmony. Through full expressions of sexuality, a relationship based on love is able to break through the jangling disharmonies and distortions of experience and reach toward human fulfillment and spiritual growth.

Shared Experiences and Insights

When I am feeling sexy I feel warm and caring toward others, *touchy*—I want to share the "bubbling over" joy of warmth and love and gaiety that is welling up in me. I feel tall and supple and in tune with my whole body—the image of a beautiful chestnut filly shaking her mane in the wind and sun, kicking up her heels and racing across the meadows comes to mind—I am free and easy and confident in the awareness of myself and confident in the strength and energy and life that is radiating from me to others.

Sexuality is the recipe of the human being. It is the philosophical, religious, and moral ingredient that makes the end product; but it depends on how and to what proportions they are added, and that determines the success or failure of that product. It is how one feels about the creation and how one accepts what has been created: how one feels about being male or female and the role one plays as related to that sex. Culture has already determined who we are and what role we will play, but this is not always the case. We are "normal" if we fall into this category of male and female and "abnormal" if we don't . . . One can deviate from the norm and still be accepted, today.

I sit and reflect on the events of the evening: stroking the new kitten, quieting her unease over her new environment; chopping vegetables, crying over the onion, savoring the aroma of the soup as it simmered; rereading my daughter's letter to me and feeling the warmth of her presence;

recalling the joy and pleasure of the telephone conversation with my other daughter yesterday; sitting down with a warm cup of coffee and conversation interspersed with laughter, and warm, open, caring smiles from my dinner guest that reach from the center of his being to mine; taking comfort in the smiles and warm enfolding arms, taking pleasure in the playfulness of interchanging roles of pursued and pursuer; loving each other with tenderness and passion; cracking my head on the window in the midst of it, leaving a permanent memorial to this man that I love partially because of the affirmation he gives me as a sexual person; discussing together what each of us consider the "role" of the other sex to be over dinner; attending a humanities lecture that fulfilled academic and spiritual needs for both of us in differing ways; saying goodbye while saying hello to new possibilities; . . . realizing once again that all of the above *is* my definition of sexuality today.

I think being in touch with my own sexuality has to do with being in touch with characteristics which I perceive as being masculine as well as feminine. I enjoy being a woman, mother, wife. I enjoy being graceful, intuitive, gentle, protected, submissive; I also enjoy being strong, decisive, purposeful, assertive. I am comfortable as both the hugger and the "huggee." I have stopped being afraid of the sexual feelings I have for my women friends and accepted that they make perfect sense in light of the way I feel about those friends. I have stopped feeling guilty about sexual feelings I have for some men other than my husband. While I don't act on those feelings, they are absorbed into a rich fantasy world which serves to reinforce and reaffirm my sexuality.

11

Loss of a Loving Relationship

Every human relationship is terminal.
To give oneself to a relationship in love is to assure the experience of loss.

Inevitable Change

The physical presence of each party to a relationship must, at some time, come to an end—normally, not at the same time. The termination may happen because physical functioning has ceased. It may come because one person makes the choice to be removed from the relationship, or at least from immediate physical presence. Communication may end, by choice or by the tragedy of illness or injury. However it happens, there will be a termination. Relationships end and there is loss. *The only way to avoid loss is to avoid loving.* Such a choice leads to an even bigger loss: life without love.

Loss is a change. In many instances, it is a very serious kind of change, perhaps traumatic. Change implies a form of continuation, with a difference in direction. When we experience loss, our life continues, but it takes a different direction from what it was before the loss. Our response to the change of loss may be, over a period of time, the development of "scar tissue." Such tissue, in a physical sense, is often stronger than the original tissue. It is also often harder, and it may be difficult to have the flexibility that was once there without a stressful reminder of the change. A part of us is gone. In many ways, we may be better off, but we are also different; there has been a change.

We experience loss of a relationship in a variety of ways. Physical death is one, and may be the first that comes to mind when "loss" is mentioned. There are many other loss experiences that are significant for us. Divorce happens to increasing numbers of persons, and the termination of relationships often goes far beyond the two persons ending their marriage. Relatives may no longer speak to, or have any interaction with, one (or sometimes *both*) of the parties. Couple-related friendships often are not sustained. Contact with parts of one's own personal history, when tied to the former partner, may be impossible to maintain. An established pattern of behaviors between parents and children is altered. Breaking up a romantic relationship is a very real form of loss, often accompanied by a great deal of emotional pain. A decision not to be friends any more is a loss, even if the quality of the friendship was not desirable. Separation by moving to another geographical location may occasion considerable grief.

When a child matures and leaves home, the parents experience loss— and eventually the child learns that she or he has, also. The loss of a job may terminate relationships on several levels: self-esteem is damaged, meaningful relationships with other persons are severed; in many cases, the relationship of the person with the *work* itself is actually broken. The loss of money, however we may express scorn for attachment to material things, can be extremely traumatic.

Loss of the relationship with the *self* happens in many ways. Sometimes it is just growing up, and leaving behind aspects of the self that are enjoyable and attractive. Mental breakdown, personality change, and serious changes in lifestyle involve varying levels of loss. The loss of a limb or other part of one's body may also bring a dramatic change in self-relation.

Abortion is the loss of a relationship that might have been and never will be. It also involves, in many cases, a change in self-perception.

Rape sometimes shatters a woman's confidence in who she is and how she can relate to others.

Getting married is a loss of singleness, a way of relating to self and to others. It is, indeed, a dramatic change which we usually overlook in the excitement of the moment—the reality of the loss later affects us in ways often not recognized. Becoming single again after many years of marriage may include, as a friend put it, the loss of a dream, a hope of happiness in a loving relationship, a sense of identity and self-worth.

A particularly striking form of loss is suicide. Self-destruction is an expression, in many cases, of complete loss of relationship with the self, the absence of self-love. It may also be the negation of relationship with anyone or anything else. A young friend of mine who took his own life often insisted that he "always maintained a policy of complete control over" his own life. Letting anyone else in, to any significant degree, was too much of a threat to that control. The demand for final authority over all aspects of his life ultimately limited his sharing of his own depths with others—perhaps with himself.

Some forms of loss are more subtle. An unusual quality of loss was described by a young woman as "the loss of a thing never had." By that, she meant a strongly hoped-for relationship that never was realized other than in her dreams and expectations. The person was there—the desired relationship was not. We also experience the loss of something that has been and is no more—and would not be wanted even if it remained. Anxiety remains, however, about what will replace it.

We know the *pain* of loss. Many of us are afraid to love, to really risk ourselves in a giving, committed relationship, because the potential loss is perceived as too painful. Our reaction to a loss may be the decision, at least for a time, not to enter into such a relationship again, fearing that the pain would be too much to experience once more. *Not to risk loss is not to love.*

Understanding Loss: We Go Through Stages

It hurts to lose a relationship. Although it won't make it hurt any less, understanding what is going on will help us to grow through it. Perhaps the best description of the loss experience is that developed by Elisabeth Kubler-Ross. Working for many years with dying patients, she researched and recorded how they responded to their experience. A result of her research is a description of the "stages of dying."[1] In recent years, her analysis has become quite familiar to those involved with death and dying—it has also been recognized, increasingly, that these stages are experienced as one goes through the loss of any relationship. Just as the dying person may go through these stages, persons who know and love the dying person will go through similar stages during and after the time of death. Furthermore, counselors who work with divorce situations have found this description to be an accurate portrayal of what many persons go through in that type of loss. Persons who lost their jobs in the surge of unemployment in the late 1970s and early 1980s have often found themselves going through these stages as well.

Following are the stages identified by Kubler-Ross. It should be noted that one does not necessarily move neatly from one stage to the next. One may also return to a previous stage after seeming to have left it. These "stages" do, however, describe what is experienced, in significant ways, by many who grieve a loss.

1. *Denial.* The person who learns that she or he is going to die often responds with, "No, not me." Surely there is a mistake. This is a typical reaction, Kubler-Ross says, and necessary: it helps to cushion the impact of the new awareness. Loved ones who learn of the impending death, or are told of a sudden death, have a similar reaction. A young man, upon learning of his brother's death in an accident, "couldn't believe it." After staying up all night in "disbelief and shock," he met the sunlight of the new day with the feeling of having wakened from a bad dream, "hoping and praying that it had been a nightmare and nothing else." Similar words are spoken by those who confront a broken relationship. "Divorces don't happen in our family . . . he doesn't really mean it." Our denial capabilities are energetic, and familiar. Such things happen to others, not us; this person is too young, has too good a future, or has lived too good a life, for something like this to happen. Reality eventually sinks in, and we then know anger.

2. *Anger.* For the terminally ill, this stage is marked by resentment over dying while others remain alive and healthy. There may be *rage* over the seeming arbitrariness of the "death sentence." Someone else may be blamed for the predicament.[2] It is not unusual, in the case of death or dying, to make God the special target for the anger. After all, God is supposed to be in control and must be allowing, if not ordering, this to happen. Sometimes others are shocked at this outrage toward divinity, but Kubler-Ross considers it permissible as well as inevitable. "God can take it," she adds. This anger and rage needs to be ventilated, and those who are with the person(s) experiencing it must allow the anger to come out.

Those experiencing the loss of another may well be resentful and feel guilty. "If I had just insisted on him going to the doctor earlier . . ."; "If we hadn't taken that trip . . .:" "I've probably been too busy, and now we're not going to have that vacation . . ." With separation or divorce we hear, "If I'd only been willing to . . ." or "Why was I so blind and stupid not to see it, when others knew what was going on?" With a job loss, we can rage, "How can they lay me off and keep so many of those people who are goofing off half the time!"

Sometimes the viciousness, even violence of our anger at such a time is incomprehensible and frightening to others around us. Bruce Fisher, writing about divorce and the rebuilding process, recognizes that "divorce anger is the extreme rage, vindictiveness, and overpowering bitterness" felt at the end of a relationship.[3] We have normally not experienced this special kind of anger before, and "many of our married friends do not understand it unless they have ended a love-relationship."[4] The depth of the anger may frighten the person feeling it. It can also lead to actions which we are actually glad that we took!

During this time we need ways to express our confused, disorganized feelings. We may also need to be alone, even though that tends to confuse others who care about us.

3. *Bargaining*. With denial, we say, "no, not me." With anger, we cry, "why me?" The third stage brings us to "yes me, but . . ." In Kubler-Ross' description, the patient accepts the fact of death but attempts to strike bargains for more time. There is a strong tendency to try to bargain with God, even for those who never "talked with God" before. This may involve a promise to be good, or to do something specific in exchange for another week, or month, or year of life. The content of the promise itself is irrelevant, because most are not kept. There is an attempt to see some kind of fairness in this situation, to exercise a tiny bit of control in circumstances that now seem totally beyond one's control. Our bargaining is also a way, according to Kubler-Ross, to cover our guilt. In other kinds of endings, (such as divorce), one wants, in Virginia Satir's words, "to look at the ledger to see that things are equal."[5] We have begun to accept the reality of the situation, but hope to improve any piece of it that is possible.

4. *Depression*. Now we say, simply, "yes, me." No more lashing out, no more bargaining—there is no energy for that. The mourning of past losses, things not done, wrongs committed, overtake the depressed person. Then comes a state of "preparatory grief," getting ready for the arrival of death. At this point, the dying person grows quiet and doesn't want visitors. Others have a hard time with this apparent rejection. Kubler-Ross sees this as a sign that unfinished business with significant others in the person's life has been finished, and a necessary detachment must take place. The young man who lost his brother described his depression stage: "I couldn't comprehend what life would be without his smiling face. I understood what was happening but I couldn't cope with being without my older brother."

In many losses, depression centers around blaming ourselves, even hating ourselves. There may be a strong sense of failure. A young woman mourning her father's death reported that "I really get mad at myself when I get depressed because I am just feeling selfish." Another said about her loss, "I ran away from it, I cried a lot, I tried being brave and cooked steaks and went to movies, and finally I began to sit down with the grief. I'm still sitting and I still don't understand it at all." From depression we begin to move toward acceptance.

5. *Acceptance*. For the dying person, this is a time of quietly letting go, a way of saying, "my time is very close now, and it's all right." The denial, anger, and depression are over. There is no need to try to gain more time. All is going to have to be left behind, and separation takes place. At this point, the person doesn't want many visitors and usually is not interested in much talking. Assurances that things will get better

are meaningless. Many seem to have very little feeling at this point, although Kubler-Ross sees it as a time of "victory." For those who have time to prepare for it, the final passage, which must be done alone, is anticipated. Family members who can't accept that and insist on finding new ways to prolong the experience in the name of hope are not very welcome. Both the situation and the self are accepted. It is time to move on.

The young man who reached the stage of acceptance of his brother's death discovered that another important thing happened at the same time. The accident had involved extreme negligence by the driver of a truck in which the brother was killed. He hated that driver—he wanted to kill him! When he reached the point of acceptance, however, the brother found that he was also forgiving the driver. Many persons who work through their divorces have found that *forgiveness* emerges with full acceptance.

For many, the acceptance of the end of a love-relationship comes with being able to say, "it's over," and mean it. It *is over*. He, or she, is not coming back. I can't depend on her, or him, for what I used to expect. I can't project my feelings onto someone else any more. That person is gone, the relationship is finished—and I am still here. I can let go, as Bruce Fisher puts it, of the "emotional corpse" which I have been carrying around with me. And—I'm relieved. Is it OK to feel relieved? The worst is over. The rest of my life lies ahead. A friend said it this way:

> I realize I have the freedom to do whatever I want and my future depends on my attitude. I felt if I could keep my head on straight and never lose my sense of humor I could survive divorce. I live in the present and always look to the future and only look back to learn from the past. This is my beginning.

The relief is not without mourning. One whose marriage of many years came to a painful end had this insight: "I can't say that I was too relieved to mourn. I did mourn, for the lost life together. But I had mourned for so long, and so long ago, the loss of his love, that when the separation came it brought with it more hope than despair."

Hope? Is there hope in the midst of the death of a relationship?

6. *Hope.* Persisting through all these stages, Kubler-Ross found, is a sense of hope. "Even the most accepting, the most realistic patients left the possibility open for some cure, for the discovery of a new drug,"[6] or the success of a research project on a life-saving treatment. This is a process that runs through each of the described stages for most patients. The hope provides a feeling that there is meaning in the suffering:

> It gives the terminally ill a sense of special mission in life which helps
> them maintain their spirits, will enable them to endure more tests when
> everything becomes such a strain—in a sense it is a rationalization for their
> suffering at times; for others it remains a form of temporary but needed
> denial.
>
> No matter what we call it, we found that all our patients maintained a little
> bit of it and were nourished by it in especially difficult times.[7]

When there is a temporary need for denial, in order to regain
strength to go on, the hope may be for a cure. At other points, it is a
way of infusing meaning into the experience, perhaps a sense of having
a special role in life that is played out through this lonely struggle. The
hope may also provide a way of maintaining coveted communication
and sharing with other persons.

Linda knew that her cancer was terminal when she appeared in my
course on "The Loving Relationship." The following Christmas she
wrote me a note. In the class she had learned a lot about herself, she
said, and it had helped her to reveal herself to others more easily. She
felt that she was more able to reach out to others "with concern and
love." The experience of many around her was that she was already
doing that—perhaps the course experience stimulated her to be more
conscious of it. The word "hope" appeared several times in her note,
each in a different, but very meaningful way. She was "hoping" to be
accepted into a graduate program in social work in a nearby university,
a program that she chose because it would offer her the most career
options! "I do *hope* that you and your family have a joyful and peaceful
Christmas." She said that she would be "getting in touch again to let
you know how things are going," and, with recognition of my "busy
schedule," "I *hope* you'll drop me a note." Her hope included the
possibility of a career for herself in which she could be of even more
help to others; it included reaching out to me; she hoped to continue to
be in touch with me, and to hear something from me. She was not able
to contact me again, at least by letter. Five months later, the notice of
her death, hundreds of miles away, appeared in our local newspaper.
The paper took note of the fact that she had refused to let her cancer
and chemotherapy crush her spirit, and that she had shared her experiences in seminars and speeches throughout the community. The newspaper had interviewed her a year previously, and quoted from that
article: "I know I may die sooner than I would expect . . . but I no
longer emphasize dying . . . I emphasize living." Her letter to me was,
on the one hand, a way of "finishing unfinished business," expressing
thanks for something that was meaningful to her. It was also a way of
reaching out in hope, concentrating on the rich possibilities of life as

long as they were there to touch and to think about.

Una Loy Clark has provided important insights into the hope which carried her famous husband, Dr. Barney Clark, through his days with an artificial heart. Although the implantation of the plastic organ appeared to be a success, what followed was anything but a comfortable life for Dr. Clark. Pain, seizures, further operations, and difficulties unrelated to the heart left her with the observation, "I cannot tell you how he did it." Convinced that the heart was going to be an important discovery in medicine, Clark's purpose was to "gain satisfaction knowing he had participated in an experiment that someday will be very beneficial to people."[8]

Just as these kinds of hope are important for persons with terminal illnesses, one who faces the end of any love relationship may find hope for new meaning in the midst of pain and expectation of new possibilities in the future. My friend who experienced more hope than despair in the eventual separation from her husband was able to hear others confirming her as a person in new, growth-producing ways. One of her children made a poster for her that likened her to daisies that "bloom where they find room." A friend commented on her capacity to "live with courage and dignity in an intolerable situation." These new perspectives, she said, freed her to hope again. They helped her to open new avenues in herself for exciting, productive aspects of living that she had not previously anticipated.

We Need to Grieve

It is one thing to be able to understand the loss. We are helped by seeing the stages through which most of us seem to move. It is quite another thing to actually get through those stages, and get on with life. The key is *grief*.

It *hurts* to lose a relationship. If we don't feel the hurt, it is a sign that we are repressing it in some way, perhaps because of the message so often given us, "you must be strong." Strength seems to imply that we don't cry, or in any other way allow our emotions to show—to do so would demonstrate that we are weak. Many of us know better than that, but for some, especially males in Western culture, there is still a lot to be learned about the false separation between being strong and showing feelings.

"I hurt" is another way of saying "I grieve." Much of the self has been invested in the relationship; to have the relationship end is to extract something from the self, and that hurts! You know what that kind of hurt feels like. You probably experienced deep loneliness and disappointment as a child, and have buried that someplace inside, allowing it to surface on rare occasions, if at all. Growing older, you have extended yourself to others, or have basked in the gift of a relationship into which you were born, and have lost it. If you let yourself feel what is inside you at that time, you are grieving. The grief process must be entered, and worked through, if you are not to remain stuck at one of the early stages described by Kubler-Ross, thus prevented from really moving on to more loving, productive possibilities. Growth through the loss of a relationship means we have to do our "grief work."

A trip to the library or a good book store will reward you with a number of recent books with suggestions for helping with grief work. It is interesting to see how many of these methods closely parallel Kubler-Ross' five stages of dying—some, in fact, specifically utilize that outline. Similar ideas in a somewhat different approach are the "Stages of Grief" worked out by Robert Kavanaugh.[9] The first stage, *shock,* is much like Kubler-Ross' "denial." The sufferer receives the first impact of loss and has not yet marshalled coping mechanisms for it. In the second stage, *disorganization,* there is overlap of denial and anger. It is a time of confusion, in which one may do things that are out of character. There is a real need to express feelings. Crying and talking take place without concern for objective rational judgment. In the third stage, *volatile emotions* are let out. The helplessness, hurt, and resentment may explode in ways that are difficult for others to understand and accept. The griever may also need to be alone. Next comes the *guilt* stage, which was also recognized by Kubler-Ross. The feelings may or may not be well-founded, but they are nonetheless felt deeply and expressed: "If only I had . . .;" "I should have . . ." *Loss and loneliness* is the next stage, in which it is recognized that the relationship now gone was unique and cannot be duplicated. A student poet who graced one of my classes, cries out,

> I want sweet nectar I can drink
> to cool my thirst for you;
> Give me, but soon, a monstrous cotton ball
> to fill this cavity within my gut.

As the grief work goes on, a stage of *relief* is reached. The bad part is over; the dying person is at peace, or the separated one is, in fact, gone. No more heavy medical bills; no more moment-by-moment trauma; no more suffering with the pain of the departing or the anticipation of what is to come. The tension of that period can now be left behind. In the *re-establishment* stage, there is recovery, self-improvement, the development of and acting on new perspectives. As one has put it, "This is my beginning."

There is nothing automatic about going through these stages. Many get locked in to one stage or another, and may stay there for years. For some it is denial, for others anger and volatile emotions. Others may move back and forth between stages, but never reach acceptance and re-establishment. Further, there is no guarantee that once we reach acceptance we will not occasionally fall back into earlier stages. To get through our grief stages, we need the help of another or others. Each of us has the opportunity to be of help to others in their grief, if we understand what we are doing.

A teacher of pastors who regularly give counsel to those in grief has provided an excellent description of the "needs of the bereaved," with important insights into ways of helping those needs to be met. David Switzer pinpoints the functions of *communication* in the dynamics of grief.[10] We may be aided in our being with others—or recognizing some of our own needs—through the following points made in his analysis of those dynamics:

1. *Release of negative emotions.* In his research of the literature on psychiatric counseling and theoretical studies of grief, Switzer found a universal emphasis on the necessity of "working through negative emotions, such as hostility, hate and guilt." We may feel, while in this circumstance, as though we want to perform emotionally charged acts. Anger and "volatile emotions" are at work. Talking with another may become a substitute for performance—or provide insight into the performance—and allow understanding and acceptance of the feelings. Other persons who know how to listen, quietly and with some empathy, are needed for the facilitation of this necessary action. It is not easy—in some relationships, the expression can be quite threatening to the listener. In my telling you how terrible I feel, I may get carried away and make *you* the "whipping-post" for my feelings—or, it can seem that way to you. You will need to understand that, if the venting of my feelings is to be complete—and healthy.

2. *Affirmation of one's self.* Whether the loss was a job or a love partner, one may be left with the feeling, "everything I thought I was, is now gone." Closely related to the first need, this step allows the person to affirm positive attitudes toward the self. Anxiety over the loss may threaten and disrupt one's selfhood. Communication of these feelings, with another, will help to reestablish the selfhood. As James Kavanaugh put it, a friend will "remind me of another day when I was beautiful."[11] The friend is there, doing the reminding, also affirms that I am now, and can be in the future, beautiful. I may be that daisy, blooming where I can find room, and I may need to see my daisy-ness in your eyes.

3. *Breaking libidinal ties.* Widely recognized, according to Switzer,

is the need to free one's self from the "bondage to the deceased, breaking the ties, the removing of the libido from the lost loved object . . .
grief is the conflict between uncontrollable desire for the loved person
and recognition that the person no longer exists."[12] Another way of
saying this has to do with "letting go": if I let go of my attachment to
the person with whom my relationship has died, I can move toward the
next step in which that other person is allowed to live on within me in
some growthful, healthy way. This is especially difficult in the case of a
terminated relationship—the separation of lovers, the ended friendship,
the divorce. In such cases, the person is still physically alive and may
be present, but the emotional attachments are, at least partially, dead.
Bruce Fisher gives a graphic illustration of how difficult this is:

> Imagine your hands clasped together with the fingers intertwined, and then
> imagine pulling those hands apart while you continue to clasp . . . It in-
> volves the painful letting go of all the strong emotional feelings for that
> other person.[13]

The libidinal ties are those having to do with identity, dependency,
definition of self in relation to others. They also represent affectional
and sexual needs. The importance of really letting go of these ties
before moving on to Switzer's next step is dramatized by Fisher's advice to divorced persons: if you wish to remain friends, don't try to be
friends until *after* you've completed your letting go of the other. The
anger, frustration, and other emotions that must surface if one is to
grow and move on are held back until one breaks those ties. The letting
go will not necessarily mean completely giving up any attachments to
the lost person or object. As pastoral counselors have noted, the attachments need to be "sufficiently altered to permit the grieving person to
admit the reality of the loss and then live without constant reference to
it."[14]

In a male-dominated society where women are socialized to be dependent on men, there are particular issues for women in breaking
these ties. The woman who is not able to establish an adult-adult relationship with her father may find that it is too painful to let go of her
little girl-daddy relationship with him. A woman who has seen her
husband as her father has to deal with a very complex set of losses
when her marriage ends. A woman who invests her dependency needs
in her eldest son may face a trauma when her son marries. Each of
these has at least one relationship she must allow to die within her own
needs before she can move on. Likewise, men have related but different
dependency needs whether focused on mother, or some fantasy about
women perpetuated through the male culture. The dependency relation-

ship will have to be let go. Only when those ties are broken, is it possible to move fully into the next step.

4. *The resurrection of the deceased within the self of the bereaved.* Basic to Switzer's analysis of grief is his observation that, "when the other dies, the self is perceived as threatened with death by the loss of the other." When someone especially close to me dies, I may fear that I too shall die—or at least that the self that I have enjoyed in relation to this other is going to be lost. The security of the self need not be destroyed. What can happen through a healthy grief process is that "the other which is within one can be reaffirmed as living as a part of one's self."

In chapter one, we met the Little Prince and his fox friend, as well as the family of Gramp. In each of these stories we find colorful illustrations of Switzer's point. In *The Little Prince,* after the Prince has tamed the fox, the time comes for them to part. In the taming process of establishing ties, the fox pointed out to the little boy that the boy's hair is the same golden color as the wheat in the fields. Although the fox has no use for wheat, he will think of the boy when he sees the golden wheat. When the Prince announces that he will leave, the fox admits that he will be sad. Even though he will cry, and experience grief, it was worth it to establish the tie—it has done something important for the fox. The little prince will live on in the fox, especially when the fox sees the color of wheat fields. The fox's own existence is not threatened by the other's absence—the prince is not external to him, but is with him in a way that lives on as a part of his own self.

Four-year-old Hillary was very close to her grandfather, and was with him throughout his "deterioration" and death. Gramp Tugend had introduced to his family an interesting array of characters which he called "chillysmiths, rupes, Michigans, and bugeyes"—all to Hillary's delight. She spoke of them often after Gramp's death.

Hillary had a mobile of fish hanging in her room. When asked by an adult why she remembered Gramp's imaginary characters so vividly, she retorted: "They're not imaginary, they're real. They're not pretend. They moved over to our house." Then, confiding in conspiratorial tones, she explained: "They tied strings together and made themselves into a mobile in my room. They look like fish now. They remind me of Gramp."[15] Something created and enjoyed by Gramp, shared between grandfather and grandchild, had now become a part of the enjoyment-world of the young girl, given new shape by her within her own context.

5. *Renewal of relationships.* It is necessary for the bereaved to "cultivate other personal relationships, to renew and deepen other old relations and to establish new ones." Switzer here asserts that the most active power in dealing with the anxiety of grief is the love that we

experience in relations with others. We experience this love through various means of communication, whether verbal or nonverbal. Many of the most important forms of communication are nonverbal, including the simple quiet presence of certain persons while we experience grief-anxiety. Bereaved persons have often reported that they can remember nothing, or little, that some of their visitors *said*—but it was extremely important that they were *"just there."*

In Gerda Lerner's moving account of her experience with her husband's death, she relates the ways in which he said goodbye just before his death. "To friends," she said, it was "sometimes an embrace, held just a trifle longer, a handshake with a deep, meaningful look." Nurses who came to see him received "a special smile and a handshake." "His sweetest, most giving farewell," she says, was to his daughter. Gerda Lerner and their daughter sat by Carl Lerner's bed while he was "supposedly semicomatose, heavily drugged with morphine." As they sat, he opened his eyes and detached his hand from his daughter, who had been holding it:

> Slowly, gently, like a blind person, he touched the outlines of her face with his fingertips, her chin, her nose, her lips. Finally he put his hand back into hers and closed his eyes. The gesture brought tears to her eyes and to mine, it was so delicate and exquisite and it seemed to spring from an assured knowledge of what she most needed. It was a perfect gift.[16]

Switzer also insists that the powerful affective content of words in verbal communication will be essential to the renewal of old relations and development of new ones. The willingness to say the simple messages are a big step: "Thank you," "I need you," "I'm okay now," "It's good to see you—you've been such a good friend, and knowing you were there has been a great help." Those who care about the grieving person will perform a significant role in maintaining communication that encourages them to reach out.

6. *The rediscovery of meaning.* For this concept, we are best helped by turning directly to Switzer's words:

> We cannot really exist as fully human without a sense of coherence, purpose, values, and an understanding of our own roles in the larger life about us. When all of this is challenged by the death of someone who has been involved in the production of meaning in our lives, there is the sense of threat, the rise of anxiety which we call grief. The rediscovery of meaning brings with it the reduction of anxiety, in this instance, the healing of grief, since it was the loss of meaning which contributed to the rise of anxiety in the first place. The rediscovery of meaning, then, is to be seen as a process taking place on two levels. One is the emotional and relational: release of negative emotions, affirmation of oneself, the breaking of old emotional

ties, the experience of the new life of the deceased within one's own life, the renewal of relationships. The other level is that of conceptualizing the process taking place, putting these experiences into meaningful symbols, verbalizing, which itself becomes reinforcing to the entire process.[17]

My poet friend *conceptualizes* and *symbolizes* her loss. In one of her poems, she speaks of herself as being "full, and empty—a cavity and a lump in the same space." She also sees herself as a "storm," as "the silence of Sahara at the end of a tired wind." Still, she affirms strongly, "I am complete—a person—with or without you." With that recognition, she would "crawl into a silent place" deep inside herself, and do her healing, "a tissue at a time." That completed, she anticipates that she would then "emerge, prepared to give my love anew." Some of us can do our own "symbolizing" (pulling meaning together), and others of us need the help of others. We all have to have meaning (May's framework of "intentionality") within which to reach out again in love. We can ask for help in reshaping that meaning. And we can offer help to each other. That is part of the meaning.

Although Switzer's dynamics are focused on the loss experienced with death, his insights are equally relevant in other types of losses. We often are not aware that we do actually mourn and grieve, for instance, when a friend of many years moves to a new home 1,000 miles away. Even though we can "reach out and touch" by telephone, it is not the same kind of touch. We mourn the loss of the physical presence, the immediate availability of the other person. Another may be just blocks away, but has *emotionally* moved away, leaving a hole in our way of life. The loss of a job may bring on depression because the job is the major source of self-esteem.[18] Words and other forms of communication will help us to work through that grief in the processes described by Switzer and others. Likewise, we can be aware of the need of someone we love to be helped through listening and talking—and being there when she or he is experiencing loss.

No matter how much it is affirmed that death—and loss—are a part of life, we are generally conditioned to see them as a threat to life, and are usually not taught well to cope with such experience. The cultural patterns in much of contemporary North American society, in fact, tend to so gloss over death that its reality is avoided. The institutionalization of death has changed experience markedly from times in which families prepared the body for burial, dug the grave, built a casket or prepared a shroud, and personally placed the body in the ground. Now we turn the body over immediately to a mortician. If we see it again, it is only after it has been made as attractive as possible. We conduct the funeral or memorial service and burial in such a way that little emphasis is placed on the finality of the death. Thus, we avoid the reality that must be faced if adequate grief work is to be done. We try to hide death from children and children from death—except in the gross expressions of television drama. Even the death of close relatives is something from which, in many families, children are excluded. It is no wonder, then, that we have great difficulty entering into grief and assisting each other in grief.

It need not be that way. Mark Jury comments on Hillary's response to Gramp's death:

> In the months following Gramp's death, we kept a wary eye on Hillary, wondering if the experience had caused her any harm. But today she shows a tolerance and acceptance of aging and death that are enviable to any one who had such matters treated as mysterious and forbidden during their own childhoods.[19]

One of my aunts died, in her mid-eighties, after a long, struggling illness. My sister's two young sons attended the funeral, the only young children there. After the service, my nephews rode in the car with their grandparents and their uncle for the fifty-mile drive to the burial. After about ten minutes, Matt's four-year-old voice came from the back seat: "Too bad she died." My mother, sister to the great-aunt he was mourning, replied that she felt badly that she was dead, but she was glad that she didn't have to be sick any more. About ten miles later, the voice again came from the back seat, in the same words, "too bad she died." Again, grandmother agreed, but spoke of the long life and her sister's readiness to give up her life. At the next two ten-minute intervals, the same comment came and was met with further assurances. By the time our journey had concluded, it was quite clear that the young child and his grandmother had been very consoling to each other. Each had listened to the other's feelings, and had spoken from the context of their own experience. The rest of us in the car had benefited, as well.

"When we shy away from death, the ever-changing nature of things," Peck tells us, "we inevitably shy away from life."[20] Letting ourselves feel our loss, however painful, is a reminder of our full involvement in life and total commitment to it. The refusal to grieve is avoidance of that depth of involvement. In being open to grief and the healing that can come from it, we are able to move on even more fully to love.

Moving On With Love

Bruce Fisher has developed a very helpful approach to "moving on" from the experience of divorce. He presents it as a matter of stacking up rebuilding blocks, working through stages from the initial, devastating experience of loss through a reorientation of self to new capacities for relationship and an exhilarating feeling of freedom. The blocks are shown in his own chart:[21]

The REBUILDING BLOCKS

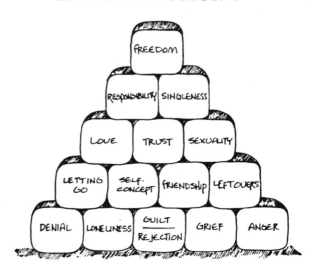

As you look at his blocks for moving along the trail of rebuilding to new self-confidence and freedom, you will notice that the five foundation blocks are similar to the processes of grief as described by Kubler-Ross, Kavanaugh, and Switzer. The next level involves doing work on oneself, to let go of the relationship and begin to restore personal resources for growth. This includes restoration and reshaping of self-concept, being open to friendship, and recognizing and dealing with the leftovers from the terminated relationship which will get in the way of future ones. The third tier of blocks are central to the matters which we've been discussing throughout this book. Nearing the end of the trail, in the top three blocks, Fisher suggests that responsibility includes adults being adults with each other; singleness is an okay state and the person who has previously seen that as the opposite of his or her reality now accepts it as a good; freedom is the perch from which to fly, like a butterfly, into new possibilities. Anyone who has entered into the pain of ending a relationship, whether as dump-er or dump-ee, will find Fisher's insights helpful. They are garnered from his experience in workshops and counseling with many persons in divorce circumstances, and offer step-by-step approaches to measuring one's progress.

The foundation row of blocks represents a process that is also seen in Abraham Maslow's hierarchy of needs discussed in chapter eight. There are certain dependency needs, Maslow shows, which must be taken care of, and internalized, before we can move on to other levels of maturity and self-actualization. The first five blocks in Fisher's chart all relate to deficiency needs—those ways in which we are dependent upon others for our self-perspective. With the second tier, we are taking responsibility for those needs ourselves, and are beginning to increase our capability to open up, with new levels of maturity, to the possibilities for relating in love with others. Approaching the top of the trail, as Fisher describes it, we are taking responsibility for self-definition and gaining control over the meeting of our needs required, in Maslow's understanding, for self-actualization. Then there is *real* freedom to love and capacity to receive love.

The loss of a love relationship may be painful, discouraging, depressing, and may leave us for some time in a state of despair. It will pass. It is not the end of love, nor the end of life. It is change. With help, it can be growth.[22] The nature of love is such that loss/growth opens possibilities for new and greater love. The risk is worth it.

Shared Experiences and Insights

A person does not prepare for something like this. There is no book for a person to read and no lecture for a person to take notes on and come out of it "prepared" for a death. The best lesson is experience.

By helping his family, it made me a lot stronger.

The loss of my husband's love was one of the most painful and difficult losses of my life. For years I was paralyzed by feelings of guilt and failure in this—my most intimate relationship. But I was able to let go, to survive, and even to have hope that something better was possible some day, because of significant people who were loving enough themselves to be able to affirm me and to help me see that there was hope, at a time when I could not help myself.

The cohesiveness of our family greatly increased due to (my brother's) death. The love is more evident, but the display of such love is still lacking. Closer contact is kept with each other, but sharing of emotions and beliefs is still minimal. Just being together at the funeral home made each other realize the love in our family and how much the other family members really did mean. This instilled within me the want to be more open with my family and to display the love I have toward them.

. . . my education still posed a threat and even though he reluctantly "permitted" me to attend school he was baffled by the changes he saw in me. My attitudes toward religion, sex roles, personal freedom were altered. One day he said with sadness (without anger for once) that this simply wasn't the same marriage commitment we had both originally agreed to. He is correct.

A message from parents to their missing/runaway child:
What you don't realize is that everything around us becomes a form of torture, the ringing of the telephone, the noise outside the house. We hear automobiles slowing down in front of the house more often and each time we think somebody is bringing you home. We hear car doors closing all times of the day and night. Our ears have become fine tuned instruments to automobile noise. Each person who walks on the porch has your footsteps, and whenever we see bushes around the window moving in the wind, we think you are running by a window and up to the porch. Our whole life is filled with expectancy and dread.

What really hurt me was coming to terms with my loss of self-esteem. I've never been very confident, but I was really entered into a crisis situation when I discovered that someone I felt very deeply about had no feelings for me. That was hard. The best a comforter can do in such a situation is be there when needed, and be respectful of one's need to be alone. As in any loss trauma, there is no easy cure. It must be ridden out.

I still feel that part of my life is missing. It just is not right for me to be going on without him. It seems like a part of me died in his room that day . . . I expect my hurts to diminish as I learn to turn loose of what I still want to hold tight. I never deserved such love but I got used to it. I never deserved such beauty but I luxuriated in it. It was all too brief but oh, was it good!

My friends really have helped me by treating me as a "normal" person. This is really important to me because I want to be treated the same as everyone else. Even though my father's death has changed my life in many ways, I am still me. I have just grown in a new and special way.

12

Loving the Enemy

You have learned how it was said: "you must love your neighbor" and hate your enemy. But I say this to you: love your enemies and pray for those who persecute you; in this way you will be sons of your Father in heaven, for he causes his sun to rise on bad men as well as good, and his rain to fall on honest and dishonest men alike. For if you love those who love you, what right have you to claim any credit? Even the tax collectors do as much, do they not? And if you save your greetings for your brothers, are you doing anything exceptional? Even the pagans do as much, do they not? You must therefore be perfect just as your heavenly Father is perfect.

Matthew 4:43–48 (*The Jerusalem Bible*)

Love your enemies. Isn't that going a bit too far? How can you possibly have a loving relationship with someone who wants to hurt you, or believes something totally different from you, or—is someone you hate?

Our discussion of relationships so far has concentrated on those we normally consider loving: self, family, friends, lovers, marriage partners. Even those we work with, or who share our community, may be seen as possibilities, so long as loving doesn't require us to *like* them. We've also looked at some problems and issues that arise in these relationships. Now, let's *test* our loving attitudes and skills.

Enemy Love as a Test of Loving Relationships

A different way of thinking about, and doing, our loving interactions with others was suggested by Jesus of Nazareth in his teaching about love, recorded in the New Testament. The passage quoted above is taken from what is usually called The Sermon on the Mount. This collection of teachings is considered to be at the heart of Jesus' sayings to groups who gathered in various places during his brief but busy ministry. New Testament scholars agree that this passage is absolutely central in Jesus' interpretation of love. It is fundamental in *his* understanding of the way in which God relates to human beings and expects persons to relate to each other.

Jesus' reference to "you must love your neighbor" is from the Hebrew law, and his listeners would likely have recognized it (Lev. 19:18). They would have also been familiar with the second part of his reference to early teachings, "hate your enemy," although that was not a part of the written law. The hate language is an English translation of an Aramaic way of saying, "There is less obligation to love one's enemy," or, "you do not have to love your enemy." There appeared to be an updated understanding and elaboration of the law which distinguished the obligation toward the nearby neighbor, a member of one's group, from expectations regarding the enemy. Jesus urged moving beyond that distinction. Why? Because that is what it takes to be like God. The expression, "sons of your Father in heaven" is a reference to those who would be like God. If you love your enemies (and a way to do it is to actively pray for those who would punish you for your faith), you are being like God. This deity doesn't distinguish between those who are bad and good, honest and dishonest, in providing the life necessities of sun and rain. Neither, says Jesus, will those who are trying to be God-like in their lives.

The listeners aren't allowed even a moment's comfort. What's the big deal, he asks, in loving those who already love you? Anyone can do that, even the tax collectors! Now, that stings! After all, the Romans recruited a few folks from among the locals to collect the taxes for support of the Empire, and those who took the jobs were deeply despised for selling out to the occupying power in this way. Knowing of their contempt for such a person, Jesus got his point across most effectively by pointing out that even *those* people can love folks who are close to them. The pagans, those who don't claim to give loyalty and obedience to the God known to his listeners, can do that much. Any who would try to be like God, which is what God's people are supposed to be doing, must go *beyond* what all the others can do.

The English translation of this text offers us a momentary respite, in calling the listeners to be perfect. No one, we can respond with relief, is perfect. The original language of the text, however, doesn't really refer to perfection as we think of it. Rather, it uses words that refer to actualization of what we are intended for. The intent of the passage is to reflect what one will do if one is *mature* in relationship with God. In this sense, one is "perfect" if one fulfills or completes the purpose for which one is created and placed in the world.[1] It is also helpful to note that a similar account, in the Gospel according to Luke, concludes with emphasis on mercy, rather than perfection: "Be merciful, even as your Father is merciful."[2] Clearly what is called for here (and expected!) is indeed within reach of mere mortals.

The real test, then, of our skills for loving, is our ability to love the enemy. Granted, there is often *nothing simple* about loving the family member, the chosen life partner, or the friend. We have already explored some of the difficulties and opportunities for that. At the same time, we are directly challenged, in a very meaningful way, with the message that has confronted members of the Christian community, at least, for twenty centuries: If you are really *serious* about being a lover, direct your energies toward loving your enemy. OK, let's get serious about that. Who is the enemy? What does it really mean to love this enemy?

Who Is the Enemy?

Many discussions of how to deal with the enemy, of "turning the other cheek," identify the enemy in national, political, or military terms. The enemy is whoever Washington tells us is a threat to national security, or is the target of our military support to an ally nation. On the other hand, it is not unusual for someone to answer the question of "who is your enemy?" with the response "I'd have to say that, number one, perhaps my worst enemy is myself." There are many ways in which that assessment has meaning, and we have examined some of those in previous chapters. For now, however, let's assume that the enemy is an *other*—an individual, or a group. Certain characteristics usually apply to our experiences of enemy. I will suggest some of the more typical characteristics—you may be able to think of more.

An enemy is someone (or a group) we *dislike*—or, someone who dislikes us. This dislike may be rooted in a wide variety of sources. We may not like the way such persons behave or talk. We may not like their values. We may not like what we see of their culture. They may dislike our insensitivity to their concerns or way of doing things. Dislike is sometimes the basis of enemy status. On the other hand, you may object that this is too mild a term for what we experience as enemy feelings.

An enemy is someone (or a group) we *hate*—or who hates us. This is a stronger emotion, and we often know when we feel it. Or do we? Actually, many of us are sure, for religious or moral reasons, that we don't hate anybody and are therefore not aware of hatred that we carry around within us and let out in unrecognized ways. Recognized or not, that hatred places the other in enemy status. Sometimes we are taught to hate. Wartime training to kill enemy soldiers usually includes a process of learning to hate.

An enemy is someone (or a group) we *fear*—or who fears us. Fear is a common basis of enemy status. The fear may be founded on some actual experience, or it may be totally irrational. If I am walking down a street in an unfamiliar city, and find myself approached by a group of young men talking in a language I do not know, I may fear them. I feel certain they are talking about me, and are plotting how they are going to relieve me of my money—or something worse. So far, that fear has each time proven unfounded. Whether real or irrational, such fear is functional and powerful. One of the best ways to place persons in enemy status is to convince self or others that there is reason to fear them.

An enemy is someone (or a group) *from whom we anticipate harm*—or who anticipates harm from us. We may or may not fear those we expect to harm us, but the knowledge (or perception) that they may harm us leads us to consider them as enemies. We may insist that we have no intention to harm someone else, but they may see sufficient evidence in our behavior to expect it from us, no matter what we are saying. Harm may be wrapped in diverse packages. It may be significant personal inconvenience, or a forced change in our way of life, or mental, emotional or bodily damage. As long as we perceive the possibility of some form of harm, we are likely to see the source of harm as enemy.

An enemy is someone (or a group) we *see as a competitor for something we want*—or who sees us as such a competitor. Adolescents sometimes refer to a peer as "my enemy." On further inquiry, it may be determined that each wants the same boyfriend or girlfriend. They are competitors for something (or someone) perceived as having high value. Athletic competitors over time are often called enemies. The language and behavior usually seems friendly enough, but it may not take much of an incident to turn a situation into a nasty scene. Two small towns may be rivals, and the annual football game, or some other competitive event, may be a time for the release of a great deal of feeling. The game may go well, but others may decide to have a fight after the game and find the opportunity to do so. Damage may be done to local businesses or public places. There is often a narrow line between "rival" and "enemy" circumstances, depending on the intensity of the values for which they are competing—values which may be rooted in a history no longer a part of the consciousness of the current competitors. On another level, nations who might control the flow of oil over which *we* want to maintain control are a threat to our accustomed consumption of gasoline and other petroleum products so much a part of late twentieth century living. Competitors in this sense easily become enemies.

An enemy is someone (or a group) *we don't know or understand*—or who doesn't know or understand us. When persons or groups do not know each other's languages or customs, it is easy to misinterpret intentions and values. Groups who have set out to be reconcilers between warring or hostile nations have learned that an important step is to help the two groups get to know each other, to understand each other as human beings, as groups with vested interests. Getting persons together to carry on discussions, do work projects together, and share customs and values, may lessen tensions and establish bases for conflict resolution. Persons with common knowledge and understanding are much less likely to think of each other as enemy.

An enemy is someone (or a group) we *have learned from others to distrust*—or who have learned from others to distrust us. A song from the musical "South Pacific" proclaims that "you have to be carefully taught." We learn from others to distrust those who are of a certain skin color, speak a certain language, claim a particular ideology or political loyalty. We may not have any basis in our own experience for such distrust, but we learn from others that such persons, usually easily stereotyped, simply are not to be trusted. It is not hard to think of them as enemy.

An enemy is someone (or a group) we *have learned from experience to distrust*—or who have learned from experience to distrust us. In this instance, we actually experience events or interactions that lead us to distrust a specific person or group—or they us. The experience may or may not have been discussed or carefully examined. It is, however, a part of our experience and something about which we and/or they have feelings.

A person, or a group, can be placed in enemy status. What I mean by *enemy status is to be placed outside the normal bounds of human interaction,* our human framework of contacts. At minimum, enemies are "them," or "they"—not we or us. Once placed in enemy status, a person or group is not treated as we would expect to be treated in normal circumstances. Normal human assumptions do not apply.

Allow me now to suggest a way of looking at "enemy" that may not have occurred to you before. I offer it because it may open up new possibilities in our thinking about the way we relate to persons beyond the usual boundaries of interpersonal affectionate feelings. I believe that as individuals and as a society, we place in enemy status most (if not all) persons who are *involuntarily institutionalized.* This includes persons who are:

—hospitalized against their will
—committed to mental hospitals involuntarily
—placed in nursing homes or homes for the aged when they don't wish to be there
—imprisoned or sent to detention or "half-way" houses
—those who are conscripted (drafted) into military service

All these persons have been placed outside what has been "normal" for human interaction for them, and continues to be normal for the society as a whole. Their situation is not just exceptional, in the sense that they have circumstances in their lives which require special and unusual treatment. They are, in reality, *excluded.* In some cases, we do not trust them; we may fear them, or anticipate harm from them; we no longer know them, and increasingly do not understand them. We do not treat such persons as we would like to be treated, or as we would expect to be treated in *any* circumstances. We may ignore the treatment they get, treatment which may actually go against our values for appropriate treatment for *any* person. We may simply *ignore them.* Thus, it is not unusual to hear someone in an institutionalized condition say, "I feel as though I'm some kind of enemy."

We even go so far as to structure our lives in such a way that persons outside our normal bounds of human contact are simply not visible. Freeways and public transportation systems taking persons to and from their homes in the suburbs are usually designed so that one can ignore the people living outside the rapidly moving window. Persons entering a subway station downtown in one of our major cities were asked to draw a map of the city and its surrounding area. Most of them were able to draw the central city, some neighboring areas, and their own suburb. Very few included a large area beginning just two blocks from the subway station in which minority persons are crowded into substandard housing and face enormous social and economic problems. They were simply left off the map, invisible. They were not included in the normal bounds of contact; they had enemy status. It is no wonder such people feel as though they are enemies. They are. It is a short next step to a sense of deprivation described by William Gaylin:

> It is when deprivation is seen as stemming from indifference to us or, worse, contempt for us as individuals, that we feel isolated and alienated. It is when we feel that society does not represent an extension of ourselves; when we are found "not acceptable" into this symbolic family setting; and

when we are made to feel like the "other"—then we will surely see those privileged and secure representatives of the society and the society itself as alien and other to us.[3]

"Alien and other" is enemy status. The experience is, as Gaylin describes it, one in which "the person now feels so 'other' that he is no longer within the framework of identification necessary for introjection of a value system."[4] This total dissociation, involving the experience of being unaccepted, disapproved, and unloved, is dangerous. The enemy then rejects the self or, in a desperate attempt to maintain some identity, rejects the alienating community. The cycle is then complete, and the behavior which goes on between declared enemies becomes the norm.

Thus, an enemy is not only the Soviet Union, or Cuba, or the peasants in any number of countries around the world who become labeled "Marxist-Leninist guerillas," in their revolts against the regimes which our leaders in Washington have chosen to support. The enemy is also the man you grew up with who is now serving time in the state prison, the woman down the block who was put away in the state mental hospital, and your great-uncle who was pronounced incompetent and was moved from his home of many years to a nursing home. The enemy is your cousin who was drafted to serve in Vietnam, and has been drifting, unable to get his life together, since he returned.

How do we go about loving these enemies? What does it *mean* to love an enemy? Before turning to specific responses to those questions, let's look at some resources for insight into our problem.

Resources for Loving the Enemy

The account with which we began this chapter comes from Christian scripture. It is clear that the command to love the enemy is central in that tradition. A number of biblical scholars are agreed that, in these accounts in Matthew and Luke, what is being reported is unquestionably characteristic of the teaching and preaching of Jesus. The command to love enemies comes directly from Jesus himself. Attached to this command is a theological basis: such behavior is a part of the very nature of God. It means looking at other persons in the way God looks at human beings. As Victor Furnish explains:

It is Jesus' commandment to *love* the enemy which most of all sets his ethic of love apart from other "love ethics" of antiquity, and which best shows what kind of love is commanded by him. To love God means not only to be obedient to God's commands, as a son obeys his father, but to be *like* him in loving even those who despise us, just as God loves those who have turned against him . . . it is clear that the *command* to love does not involve simple sentimental affection. But it is equally clear that this command involves one's *affirmation* of the other (even the enemy), and that it is therefore something deeper than a merely grudging acknowledgment of his existence . . . it is precisely a certain inner attitude which God requires. Thus, to love means to show *goodwill* toward others, and that presents us at once with an understanding of love as something sensitive and concretely responsive to other persons and their needs.[5]

The kind of love held by God for human beings is generally identified as *agape* love—totally unconditional. Anders Nygren, the Swedish theologian who wrote the first extensive study of agape in the twentieth century, emphasized that God's agape love is unmotivated and spontaneous. Jesus' acceptance of that perspective on the part of God led him to proclaim that human love for neighbor, and thus enemy, should likewise be unmotivated and spontaneous. "There is no occasion to look behind our neighbour's actual condition for any hidden valuable quality that will explain and justify our love for him. God's love is explanation and sanction enough."[6] Gene Outka, who has gone beyond Nygren in a more recent and monumentally thorough study of agape, notes that such love does not depend on the attractiveness of the other:

The love in question does not arise from and is not proportioned to anything a given neighbor individually possesses or has acquired. It is based neither on favoritism nor instinctive aversion. Its presence is somehow not determined by the other's actions; it is independent both in its genesis (he need not know who I am) and continuation (he may remain my enemy). One ought to be "for" another, whatever the particular changes in him for better or for worse.[7]

What does such love look and act like? In the Christian Gospels, the answer to that question is given in Jesus' parable of the Good Samaritan. That particular story was told in response to the question, "who is my neighbor?" The neighbor in the story, it turns out, is an enemy. The history of Jewish-Samaritan relations would have made a strong case against the Samaritan's aiding the man in the ditch. The man was treated the same way one would treat a family member or a best friend. As Pheme Perkins puts it, "Certainly this parable deals with the problem of love of enemies at its very roots. It deals with those enemies created and reinforced by the social groups of hostile neighbors—neighbors whose hostilities are grounded in religious differences."[8] The enemy is neighbor, another human being whose humanity cannot be ignored, especially at a time of need.

These insights point to an interest in and concern for others on grounds considerably different from what is conventionally thought to be love. No blood ties, no physical or personality attraction are involved. What *is* involved is common humanity, common creaturehood or, in an older language, common "sonship." The power of the Spirit of God is present when this kind of love is active.[9] Is the purpose to convert the enemy into a friend, and ally? This is an important question, because such a goal was assumed in other traditions about loving the enemy. Several of the Greek philosophers suggested that love of the enemy, conducted actively enough, would convert the persecutor or antagonist. Others argued that nonretaliation toward an aggressive enemy would establish one's moral superiority, encouraging others to change.[10] The ancient Hebrew teaching that one should return a stray ox or ass to one's enemy, or assist "one who hates you" with a burden (Exod. 23:4–5) is not clear in its motivation. Later rabbis were led to ask "why do this?" In the Talmud, the answer was given which supports the personal virtue stance: such action will "crush your evil inclination," helping to make you a person more likely to do God's will. A later addition to the Talmud, the Tosefta, answers the "why" with the assertion that it will "crush the enemy's evil inclination, and change the enemy into a friend." Thus it is heroic to change one who hates into a lover, by loving him.

No such presuppositions, it seems, were operating in Jesus' commandment to love the enemy. According to Furnish,

> It presupposes only God's own mercy and love toward his enemies, and one's responsibility to be thus disposed toward his own enemies. There is nothing here about "making the enemy into a friend." Loving him is not proposed as a means of transforming him or of dissolving the issues which may have generated the enmity in the first place. Though such issues remain standing, they are now approached, from one side at least, in ways directed by love. Thereby the whole *relationship* between us is changed, although the enemy remain "the enemy."[11]

Love of enemy changes the *relationship*, whether or not it changes the *enemy*. What will go on in the relationship is directed by love, at least from one direction, and that clearly redirects the relationship. Closely related to this understanding is the conviction of the early Christian community that they are gathered together as "friends of God," and there is power in what exists through their community. Thus, when those groups encountered open persecution, hostility, and aggression, they focused upon including their persecutor(s) in their community of those who were awaiting an overwhelming change in history. They chose to relate to their abusers as though they were "fellows," members of the same loving community. From one side, therefore, the dynamics at work are quite different, and thus the relationship is altered. Vengeance and retaliation are not seen as available to the loving community. The "radical extent of Christian love" included giving generously to any who begged and seeking no recovery of stolen goods. Love "busies itself with doing good."[12] A significant phrase in Christian theology is "agape creates fellowship." When such love is directed to enemies, says Nygren, "It creates fellowship even where fellowship seemed impossible."[13] It is action, not merely reaction. In theological understanding, sin is brokenness, separation between created humans and their God. Enemy status is likewise brokenness of relationship, separation between beings who have a common source of life and growth. "Just as God's love is for sinners, so the Christian's love is a love for enemies. God's love for sinners and Christian love for enemies are correlatives."[14] This approach emphasizes *serving* the enemy, *affirming the person* who is in enemy status. *Ignoring* the enemy person is excluded, Furnish shows:

> To affirm the other person, even when he is my enemy, necessarily carries with it the acknowledgment that his finite presence to me as "an other," his finite existence, is caught up and bound up with my own finite existence. Just as Jesus' commandment excludes my *hating* him, so the facts of human existence along with the positive command to *love* him exclude my ignoring him. That would be only another form of seeking his annihilation. To affirm him in the love Jesus commands means to be constructively and compassionately extended to him.[15]

Even though the earliest Christian communities saw their task as loving-as-God-loves, it did not take long for them to become more evangelical in their intent. Their love is to be active, reaching out, resisting evil, never being subordinate. Luise Schottroff finds in the Letter to the Romans and in 1 Peter a more political approach. It calls for a practice which "overcomes evil with good," conquering the enemy and leading them to a way of life which participates in the Christian hope.[16]

Throughout the succeeding centuries, Christians have held a wide variety of perspectives regarding the application of the love commandment within the historical realities of war and peace, and church-state relationships. The strong pacifist commitment of the "believers' churches," particularly within the Anabaptist tradition, would require Christians to refuse participation in violence and coercion, even when ordered by the state. More dominant Christian traditions have allowed members to participate in war under various conditions. There is, however, a general consistency of recognition that, whatever the enmity between states and the demands that war may place on citizens, individual relationships remain under the rule of Jesus' commandment.

Martin Luther, who did not hesitate to urge the German princes to use their swords against the rebelling peasants, nonetheless retained a biblical perspective: "Even one who has done me some sort of injury or harm has not shed his humanity on that account or stopped being flesh and blood, a creature of God very much like me; in other words, he does not stop being my neighbor."[17]

History has, of course, shown a considerable inconsistency between the principle of enemy-love and some of the behavior of nations, groups, and individuals. Mohandas K. Gandhi and his development of the life of Satyagraha represents, dramatically, the reassertion of Jesus' teaching in the twentieth century. Gandhi lived and taught a way which would intervene in the patterns of violence, hostility, and repression practiced by persons of all religious faiths and political commitments. Gandhi set out to resist evil through "soul-force," or nonviolence. At the heart of this commitment is love for the enemy.

The term *Satyagraha* was coined by Gandhi to describe what he was leading Indians to do in South Africa, in opposition to a repressive system. It means, literally, "clinging to truth." Sharatan Kumarappa, editor of one of Gandhi's most important books, explains: "as Truth for Gandhi was God, Satyagraha in the general sense of the word means the way of life of one who holds steadfastly to God and dedicated his life to him. The true Satyagrahi is, accordingly, a man of God."[18] Gandhi's own words are:

> Its root meaning is holding on to truth, hence truth-force. I have also called it Love-force or Soul-force. In the application of Satyagraha I discovered in the earliest stages that pursuit of truth did not admit of violence being inflicted on one's opponent but that he must be weaned from error by patience and sympathy. For what appears to be truth to the one may appear to be error to the other. And patience means self-suffering. So the doctrine came to mean vindication of truth not by infliction of suffering on the opponent but on one's self.[19]

Where did Gandhi get his ideas? Fundamental are the *Gita* ideal of the *Karmavogin,* and Jesus' Sermon on the Mount. Gandhi also credited the writings of Thoreau and Ruskin as being influential—he was also especially appreciative of the work of Tolstoy. Application of the ideas in the practical situations where he worked—South Africa and India—were his own.[20] Gandhi was convinced that the world is based on what he understood as truth, or love, even though the records of history say little about it. History, rather, is written about events that *intervene in* the normal ongoing life of love:

> The fact that there are so many men still alive in the world shows that it is based not on the force of arms but on the force of truth or love. . . .

Thousands, indeed tens of thousands, depend for their existence on a very active working of this force. Little quarrels of millions of families in their daily lives disappear before the exercise of this force. Hundreds of nations live in peace. History does not and cannot take note of this fact. History is really a record of every interruption of the even working of the force of love or of the soul. Two brothers quarrel; one of them repents and re-awakens the love that was lying dormant in him; the two again begin to live in peace; nobody takes note of this . . . History, then, is a record of an interruption of the course of nature. Soul-force, being natural, is not noted in history.[21]

Soul-force, dependent on truth, is most basic to human nature, and is lived in much of our daily lives without thinking about it. On the other hand, evil is active in the denial of truth, and serious discipline is required for the resistance of evil. "Ahimsa," literally nonviolence, is a renunciation of the will to kill or damage others. It is a rejection of the inner violence of the spirit. Tolstoy was considered by Gandhi to demonstrate the greatest nonviolence of the age. After noting Tolstoy's approach, Gandhi said, "True Ahimsa should mean a complete freedom from ill will and anger and hate and an overflowing love for all. For inculcating this true and higher type of Ahimsa amongst us, Tolstoy's life with its oceanlike love should serve as a beacon light and a never-falling source of inspiration."[22] Gandhi considered it impossible that anyone would totally attain such a state in this life; nonetheless, one's life should be given to it. The goal is clear: "Truth is my God. Nonviolence is the means of realizing Him."[23]

Nonviolence, to Gandhi, is anything but passive. For that reason, he was displeased with what he saw of nonresistance movements in Great Britain, Africa, and India in the early years of his career. Truth does not surrender to evil and violence. Love is a strong force, "the strongest force the world possesses and yet it is the humblest imaginable."[24] Such a force appeals to the reason and conscience of the opponent. If necessary, it takes suffering on to oneself. Conversion of the opponent to a status of ally and friend is the motive. Such a moral appeal is more effective than one based on threat of injury or violence. Gandhi believed that violence never overcomes evil. Rather, "it suppresses it for the time being to rise later with redoubled vigor. Non-violence, on the other hand, puts an end to evil, for it converts the evil-doer."[25] To Gandhi, it is much better to *die* in defense of Truth than to *kill* in its supposed defense; entry into violence is rejection of Truth, and an expansion of the realm of evil. Furthermore, nothing has been done to enhance the possibility of promoting a relationship of love with the enemy. Truth is attained only by "loving service of all." Active opposition to evil systems is a way of serving. It has the opportunity to reform the evildoers, and reaffirms the power of love and truth for all to see.

In the work of both Jesus and Gandhi, it is clear that the placing of others in enemy status is a denial of one's own, as well as the enemy's, being and Truth. Martin Luther King Jr. was greatly influenced by both the work of Gandhi and the Gospel messages fundamental to his own Christian faith. King's overriding goal was the "Blessed Community," in which the boundaries of interaction are pushed out to include all. King's efforts in the Civil Rights movement always kept the strategies for direct action focused on the evil being done—segregation in the work place, in public accommodations and services, unjust laws and practices which denied opportunities to the poor and to racial minorities. He did not allow individuals, however repressive their actions, to be the target of hatred and revenge. As he confronted those in power structures with the injustice for which they were responsible, he always tried to appeal to what he knew to be a "need to belong to the best in the human family," rather than the distorted attitudes which appeared to dominate their actions. To King, "The end is redemption and reconciliation. The aftermath of nonviolence is the creation of the beloved community, while the aftermath of violence is tragic bitterness."[26]

King credited Gandhi with helping him to see the extensive possibilities of Christian teachings:

> As I delved deeper into the philosophy of Gandhi my skepticism concerning the power of love gradually diminished, and I came to see for the first time its potency in the area of social reform. Prior to reading Gandhi, I had about concluded that the ethics of Jesus were only effective in individual relationship. The "turn the other cheek" philosophy and the "love your enemies" philosophy were only valid, I felt, when individuals were in conflict with other individuals; when racial groups and nations were in conflict a more realistic approach seemed necessary. But after reading Gandhi, I saw how utterly mistaken I was.
>
> Gandhi was probably the first person in history to lift the ethic of Jesus above mere interaction between individuals to a powerful and effective social force on a large scale. For Gandhi love was a potent instrument for social and collective transformation. It was in this Gandhian emphasis on love and nonviolence that I discovered the method for social reform that I had been seeking . . .[27]

Like other Christian theologians, King sees agape love as essential to formation of human community. Agape does not distinguish between friend and enemy—it loves the other for the other's sake, not for any reciprocal benefit. It responds to the other's need to be relieved of tensions, insecurities and fears. King's elaboration of agape love is instructive:

Agape is not a weak, passive love. It is love in action. *Agape* is love seeking to preserve and create community. It is insistence on community even when one seeks to break it. *Agape* is a willingness to go to any length to restore community. It doesn't stop at the first mile, but it goes the second mile to restore community. It is a willingness to forgive, not seven times, but seventy times seven to restore community. The cross is the eternal expression of the length to which God will go in order to restore broken community. The resurrection is a symbol of God's triumph over all the forces that seek to block community. The Holy Spirit is the continuing community creating reality that moves through history. He who works against community is working against the whole of creation. Therefore, if I respond to hate with a reciprocal hate I do nothing but intensify the cleavage in broken community by meeting hate with love. If I meet hate with hate, I become depersonalized, because creation is so designed that my personality can only be fulfilled in the context of community. . . .

In the final analysis, *agape* means a recognition of the fact that all life is interrelated. All humanity is involved in a single process, and all men are brothers. . . .

Love, *agape,* is the only cement that can hold this broken community together."[28]

King echoes an affirmation of Gandhi, as well as most of the Christian tradition: love is *the* reality; it is the power of life in the world, and it is the power of the universe. To go against *agape* love is to go against the power that undergirds all of life. One's loving relationship with the enemy is an expression of that power. It is a way of taking part in the restoration of community.

How Do We Love the Enemy?

Having examined some of the more familiar resources for loving the enemy, we can return to the question of *how* we do it. Keeping in mind the characteristics of the enemy outlined earlier, the following must be done.

1. To love an enemy means seeing that person as a *person.* In hostility between groups, we are prevented from seeing individuals as persons. A man may not be known to us as "John Jones," but rather "one of those Joneses." Jesse Jackson is not seen as a "candidate for nomination for President," but as "a *Black* candidate . . ." Those who are, or have been institutionalized, carry a label. Mrs. Baxter down the street is not just Mrs. Baxter . . . she is Mrs. Baxter, *the former mental*

patient. Willie Smith is an "inmate," a "convicted burglar." When he is out, looking for a job, he is an "ex-con."

The language and symbols of war try to keep us from seeing persons as persons, and they are often very effective. I was seven when the United States entered the Second World War. As a child, one of my favorite games was playing *war.* My brother and I, along with any neighborhood kids we could gather, would fight Germans or "Japs." As Anglo-Saxons of Dutch-German-English descent, we called Germans, "Germans." We called Japanese "Japs," as did most of the people around us. This fit well with the fact that our farming neighbors of recent German descent may have been looked at a bit suspiciously, but they were not shipped off to detention centers, as were the Japanese on the West Coast. On Saturday afternoons, we went to the movies and watched Marines and Commandos shoot "Japs" out of the trees. When we played war we shot Germans around the corner of the house or garage, but we shot "Japs" out of the trees. The impression we had from movies and from the propaganda machinery of the government was that Japanese were not really human. Later, when I went off to college, I had a roommate from Japan. I spent months mentally taking the tail off him! The symbol system of the war period had been very effective in creating an image of him as a monkey-like animal, rather than a person like me. Loving an enemy means seeing that person as a *person.*

2. To love an enemy means to see the other person as one who is *loved.* Loved by other human beings, this person is special, valued in unique ways that are not significantly unlike the ways in which caring persons love me. The enemy is a person loved by God, the universal power of life and love. This power has given life and love to both the other and to me from the same sources. Whatever I may think of the enemy, due to my fear, my distrust or my ignorance, other human beings impart dignity to this person, as does our common source of life. I have to honor and respect their love.

3. To love an enemy means to *care about what happens* to that person and to others who love that person. There are things that could be done to that person, even by people representing me, that I don't believe should happen to anyone. Those who are outside the normal bounds of human interaction can have unconscionable things done to them, whether intentionally, unintentionally, or by the functioning of a system or institution. Furthermore, there are others who care about that person. I know a man whose younger brother was murdered in a distant city. When he traveled there to attend the trial of those accused of the murder, he surprised some around him by spending part of his time making sure that the families of the accused were receiving pasto-

ral care and support. As a pastor himself, he knew that was important. As one who had suffered great pain in the death of his brother, he was sure that the families of those accused must also be suffering in the face of the horrible act done by their loved ones, the harm done to others by someone they care about. In many prison settings, family members of inmates must undergo considerable indignity just to have an occasional visit with their loved one. They may be subjected to a strip search. A wife and mother may be told, after waiting for two hours, that she must keep her children quiet in the visiting room or they will have to leave, just as her husband is finally ushered in. Lovers may be prohibited from touching each other. By the time one or both parties to the visit get over their anger and frustration about the procedures prior to their visit, their precious time may have ended without any constructive conversation. In spite of their desires and intentions, the weekly or monthly attempt at a visit may actually contribute to the further breakdown of their family and marital ties. Although it is easy and usually more comfortable to ignore what is happening to enemies, loving requires awareness and concern.

4. To love an enemy means to *probe the sources* of our dislike, our hatred, our fear, our distrust, and our competition to find out what is originating from within the self. There are, of course, many circumstances in which we are given reasons for our feelings by actions of the other. It is still important to probe our *own* feelings, to discover what there is in *us* that contributes to feelings of hatred or fear. Distrust often has something to do with our own perspective of insecurity and a disproportionate view of the powers of others. Our own needs for competition, fed by a highly competitive society, lead us to push for some of our selfish desires or to compete with others' selfish desires in ways that assure enemy relations.

We do not enjoy this kind of probing. We have many internal mechanisms preventing us from doing it. William Sloane Coffin points out that "while love seeks truth, fear seeks safety. And fear distorts the truth not by exaggerating the ills of the world (which would be difficult), but by underestimating our ability to deal with them."[29] We can probe, and once we find what is going on within us, we usually have the ability to work with it, as well as to deal with our external problems—if we let ourselves do it.

Try a little probing just now. Think of a person, or group, you consider to be enemy. Try to identify what is involved—hatred, fear, competition, whatever. Now, go into the sources of those feelings as best you can. What are some ways you can take care of some of those feelings, yourself, without projecting them on an "enemy?"

5. To love an enemy means to *affirm* the personhood of the other, and recognize their rights. To be "constructively and compassionately

extended" to the other is involved in affirming the enemy.[30] What that extension means is spelled out by Gene Outka:

> I said that agape enjoins one to identify with the neighbor's point of view, to try imaginatively to see what it is for him to live the life he does, to occupy the position he holds. Clearly the other's right to assume a point of view different from one's own is also affirmed, and the agent honors his own freedom by not confusing identification with a compulsion to adopt the other's stance, to share his particular likes and dislikes. Such identification is taken nonetheless to imply that some minimal consideration is due each person which is never to be set aside for the sake of personal gratification or long-range social benefits. He is never *merely* a means or instrument. To ignore him completely or treat him as a pure social functionary, for example, is not permitted on any grounds. A further inference often drawn is that, in one's behavior toward another, one should be influenced more by the immediate and reasonably foreseen effects on him than by the more remote and grandiose goals of the society at large. If through no fault of his own an individual ceases to be a public asset, he should still receive equal consideration. And those who believe that his nature and destiny exceeds any political or secular definition of it—that a political and secular account cannot say all there is to say, or indeed even the most essential thing—will have especially powerful reasons to resist a social productiveness criterion of human worth. One is enjoined to honor from first to last the space he occupies and time he has.[31]

Many of those confined in institutions are considered socially unproductive. The fact that they are not making contributions to society, according to some forms of measurement, seems to justify allowing inhuman things to happen to them, or excluding them from benefits or pleasures. Outka says *no,* and he is joined by all who insist that love is affirmation, for the enemy as well as for others. By definition, those placed outside normal bounds of social interaction require special attention to see that they are, indeed, being affirmed, that their space and time are honored.

Living in a loving way with another or others, according to David Viscott, requires the recognition of the rights of each other. The rights which he identifies need also to be considered when we are thinking of the enemy. They are, he says, the right:

—to grow,
—to be oneself,
—to be loved,
—to privacy,
—to be trusted,
—to be respected,
—to acceptance,

—to be happy,
—to defend yourself.[32]

Let's get serious about loving the enemy, and ask what it means to guarantee these rights in specific instances in which persons are placed outside the normal bounds of human interaction.

Does it make sense to suggest that the 84-year-old lady in the nursing home, who seems not to remember her daughter's name or her grandson's recent visit, has a right to *grow*? If so, how is it done? What does it mean for her to grow?

Okay, so the 25-year-old mentally retarded man who has strong sexual feelings and seems to function much of the time on a pre-adolescent level, has a right to be himself. What does that mean? When? Where? With whom? Those who care about him are confronted by others who would rather just not have him around. How is this enemy loved?

The young woman who had been sexually active with her fiance, and plans to be married, is in prison. How is her right to be loved recognized? What form can that love take? What barriers to her being loved can be permitted? Is it possible for her prison experience to return her to a positive marriage relationship?

Two years after celebration of their Golden Wedding anniversary, a man loses his wife of fifty-two years. Too frail to take care of himself, he is placed in a senior citizens' home residing in a 12' by 14' room with a male roommate he has never seen before. What does it mean for him to have privacy? How will that be managed?

The thirty-year-old mental patient has tried, on three occasions, to commit suicide. What does it mean for her to be trusted? With what? Around whom? Under what conditions?

The Vietnam veteran has not left the Veterans' Administration Hospital for three years. On his more coherent days he may talk calmly of his assignments to assassinate village leaders. Other days find him surly, unkempt, and often hostile. How shall he be respected? Who will do the respecting, and in what ways?

The man convicted of murder eighteen years ago is released from prison and returns to his home community. How can he be accepted? By whom? What risks are implied in the acceptance?

The woman grieving the deaths of four of her family members in a violent accident is hospitalized, seemingly unable to cope with the situation. Others have found it impossible to deal with her despondency and thorough depression. Whose responsibility is it to support her right to be happy?

You learn to your surprise and horror that your closest relative is going to court to have you declared incompetent. If the effort succeeds, you will no longer have control over your money, where you live, where you can go, how you will get there, eventually over what you will eat or wear. How do you defend yourself? Who could you count on to help you?

Loving our enemy, in these instances, will have to begin with bringing this person within the boundaries of our interactions. Keen writes of bringing the enemy "within the circle of co-promise, conversation, and compassion." Our ability to do this is centered in *metanoia,* a little known term which is actually the opposite of paranoia. It involves our "flexibility to adopt many different perspectives," our capacity to turn around, to repent, to see the shadows within ourselves and own them, in order to be open to the other.[33]

Perhaps best known throughout the world for bringing the "other" from outside our normal bounds of human interaction into the circle of compassion is Mother Teresa of Calcutta. Through her efforts, persons left dying on the streets are brought to a quiet place to be attended and treated with dignity and love in their final hours, rather than being totally alone and ignored, their humanity denied.

I consider it *deeply* meaningful and important that the one United States citizen to be honored in this century by making his birthday a national holiday is one who demonstrated the power of loving his enemies. Martin Luther King Jr. insisted on encountering the enemy with active, outgoing love, rather than giving in to the perpetuation and multiplication of hatred, fear, distrust, and competition. He reduced or changed the enemy status by changing his own view of self and the other. With greater self-respect, what he often called "somebodiness," there was no need to accept the definition of self imposed on him and his people by the majority. With greater self-trust, it is possible to trust others. With more understanding of what is bothering others, there is less need to hate or fear. Being able to face the anger, fear, and hatred of others with secure selfhood and a commitment not to respond with violence, King, liked Gandhi, found it possible to change the extent and power of enemy relations. In his last book, these words are recorded:

> We can no longer afford to worship the God of hate or bow before the altar of retaliation. The oceans of history are made turbulent by the ever-rising tides of hate. History is cluttered with the wreckage of nations and individuals who pursued this self-defeating path of hate.[34]

Yet to be documented, as this book goes to press, is the training in nonviolence that led to the astonishing replacement of the Marcos regime in the Phillipines by Corazon Aquino and her followers. Cardinal Sin and many others were involved in widespread training in the principles and strategies of nonviolent change led by persons from the International Fellowship of Reconciliation. History will likely record the establishment of a new society based on capacities for community-building, rather than destruction.

Loving the enemy, like other forms of loving relations, does not come easily. It is a challenge. As a test of our loving skills, it is also a test of will. It offers the choice of participation in the power which creates and nourishes life at its fullest. The alternatives are not worth choosing.

Epilogue

It was midevening when she came to talk with me. She turned to me as a campus pastor, my vocation at the time, and as a friend. We had talked before, but I sensed right away that this conversation would be more urgent and intense.

More than twenty years have passed, and I don't remember all that we talked about. I *do* remember that we talked long into the night and the early morning hours. She was quite depressed, convinced that she was a person no one could love—and that she could not love herself. Her descriptions of her relationship with others, especially with men, were descriptions of failure and disappointment. Every experience she had been through with a male was a bad one, beginning with her father. She could think of nothing good to say about herself and was convinced that no one could really love her—certainly, not a man. Through the hours of our talking, I tried to listen closely, accepted her and her interpretations of her experience, and occasionally shared some of my own feelings and experiences. Finally, after yet another expression of her conviction that she was not loved by anyone, we sat silently for a few moments. In that silence, it occurred to me to say quietly to her: "You *know* that *God* loves you."

An amazing thing happened. She had been sitting upright in her chair, looking tense and frightened. In the moments after those words, her face and body began to relax. She sat back in her chair. I could see and feel the tension and fear drain from her. Slowly a smile came over her face. Then came her question: "Why don't more ministers say that from the pulpit?" Not quite prepared for that question, I remember pondering a bit and then suggesting that most ministers *do* say that. I knew her pastor in a local church in which she was quite active, and was sure that he said things like that. Perhaps, I said, she hadn't been able to hear it when it was said; maybe it wasn't said in ways that she could hear.

I've thought about that conversation over the years, and its meaning has changed as I've grown in understanding and perceptions of the meaning of relational love. It seems clear to me that she came at a time of extremely low self-esteem. She desperately needed affirmation. She needed to be with someone who cared about her, and about whom she cared—something she could sense in spite of her insistence that she was not worthy of love nor capable of giving it. As a person with deeply held religious convictions, the *idea* that she was loved by God was not foreign. The truth, the reality of that love had to come to her through another person. Given the content of what she was telling me, along with what I knew of her theology, the message in this particular situation was aided in being conveyed by one who was male. The fullness of the message, however, was not in those few words. They were the culmination of several hours of sharing between two human beings. We might have been able to say to each other, in Beverly Wildung Harrison's words, "You are merely passing on the power of love, gifting me as others have gifted you."[1]

Certainly, the inter-relationship of the love of self, other, and a shared transcendent meaning (as I presented early in this book) was important in what happened. Likewise, the separation and alienation from both self and others was an intense reality from which she was trying to reach out, and close the gap she had been experiencing. What had to happen for her—and for any of us—was a moment of mutuality, of shared vulnerability, of acceptance and respect that encouraged and empowered her self-acceptance and self-respect. That is something that happens in relationship. My friend wanted to know about such love being proclaimed from the pulpits. Obviously, such love can be, and is, *proclaimed* from pulpits and *taught* from lecterns. It is, however, something that is primarily *done between persons*.

A magnificent book has appeared since I completed all but the finishing touches on this manuscript. Beverly Wildung Harrison's *Making the Connections* (1985) would have found its way into earlier pages in this book had it been available. I trust that those who know her work will recognize that at least some of my basic assumptions and goals are similar to hers. In addition, I would remain open to the critique of her profound feminist analysis on what undoubtedly remains of masculine patriarchal rationality and dualism in my work.

It would be my hope that the reader of this book, in Harrison's words, "experience the power of love as the real pleasure of mutual vulnerability, the experience of truly being cared for or of actively caring for another."[2] Such mutual love, she insists, is so radical "that many of us have not yet learned to bear it." Much of the baggage of our cultural and religious heritage—passed on in masculine categories and experience—limits our capacity for giving and receiving—and for "expressing solidarity and reciprocity with the excluded ones" with whom we share our existence.

Loving relationships as presented in this book are not sentimental, gooey, clinging attachments. Such relationships require the courage of openness and demand justice in all connections. Such love, as we have said, is risky, even dangerous. In the words of Harrison:

> Those touched by the power of such love tend to develop a reluctance to accept anything less than mutuality and self-respect, anything less than human dignity, anything less than authentic relatedness. It is for that reason that such persons become powerful threats to the status quo. As women have known, but also as men like Martin Luther King Jr., and Archbishop Oscar Romero understood, as any must know who dare to act deeply and forcefully out of the power of love, radical love is a dangerous and serious business. Without blessed persistence, without the willingness to risk, even unto death, the power of radical love would not live on in our world.[3]

But we *can do it!* We have the power both to build up and destroy the dignity of self and others, as May recognizes in what he calls the "daimonic." We can actively pursue works of love and we can actively go about the obliteration of pockets of concern for humanity in our world. I would affirm with Harrison that "it is still within the power of love, which is the good news of God, to keep us in the knowledge that none of us were born only to die, that we were meant to have the gift of life, to know the power of relation and to pass it on."[4]

Accept the gift. Cherish it, enliven it in your own special way. And pass it on.

Notes

1. What do Loving Relationships Look and Feel Like?

1. Antoine de Saint Exupéry, *The Little Prince*, translated from the French by Katherine Woods (New York: Harcourt, Brace & World, Inc., 1943), p. 78.
2. Ibid., p. 83.
3. Ibid., pp. 83–84.
4. Ibid., p. 84
5. Ibid., pp. 87–88
6. Mark Jury and Dan Jury, *Gramp* (New York: Grossman Publishers, 1976), p. viii.
7. Ibid., p. 26.
8. Ibid., p. 59.
9. Ibid., p. 62.
10. Ibid., p. 88.
11. Ibid., p. 132.
12. Ibid., p. 144.
13. Ibid., p. viii.
14. Ibid., p. 152.
15. Ibid., p. 113.
16. Studs Terkel, *Working* (New York: Avon Books, 1972), pp. 390, 391, 394.
17. Although the description was originally given several years ago, it has recently been updated with them.

2. Thinking About Loving Relationships

1. Eric Fromm, *The Art of Loving* (New York: Harper & Row, 1956), p. 17.
2. Theories about this aspect of our nature are numerous and, to say the least, diverse. I have found a good deal of meaning and help in Fromm's approach to the problem, and his thinking is taken seriously in my own approach throughout this book.

3. Rollo May, *Love and Will* (New York: W.W. Norton & Company, Inc., 1969), pp. 29–30.
4. Ibid., pp. 289–290.
5. Sam Keen, *The Passionate Life* (San Francisco: Harper & Row, 1983), p. 200.
6. Ibid., p. 194.
7. See Willard Gaylin, *Caring* (New York: Alfred A. Knopf, 1976).
8. Michael Zwell, *How to Succeed at Love* (Englewood Cliffs, NJ: Prentice Hall, Inc., 1978), p. 5.
9. M. Scott Peck, *The Road Less Traveled* (New York: Simon & Schuster, 1978), p. 301.
10. I am aware that for some feminist scholars, what I describe is a *male* experience. They argue that women experience a *need to separate* rather than overcoming separateness, and thus my conceptual framework would be of little value. Other feminists, however, do not agree with some of the basic psychological premises in that argument.
11. This translation is from *The Jerusalem Bible.*
12. In reading these accounts, it is clear that even though the neighbor love command came from a different portion of the law (Lev. 19:18), Jesus knew that his listeners were quite aware that it was also commanded. There are various translations of this text in different versions of the Bible, with the wording varying from "you shall love your neighbor as yourself" (the *Oxford Annotated Bible, Revised Standard Version*), to "you shall love your neighbor as a man like yourself" (*The New English Bible*).
13. Victor Furnish, drawing on the work of Rudolf Bultmann, finds the love of neighbor to be as much an act of obedience as the love of God, in the response that the believer is to make to God's sovereign claim. See Victor Paul Furnish, *The Love Command in the New Testament* (Nashville: Abingdon Press, 1972), p. 63.
14. Ibid., p. 50.
15. Pheme Perkins, *Love Commands in the New Testament* (New York: Paulist press, 1982), p. 4.
16. Erich Fromm, in *The Art of Loving,* characterizes unconditional love as "mother's love" and conditional love as "father's love." He traces these distinctions very aptly through various phases of Biblical teaching. His approach on this, however, requires a careful recognition that he is speaking "traditional" cultural roles, and not necessarily ideologically conditioned ways of loving. One of my students responded to the power of unconditional love by writing that she had set that as her goal for loving. In a class project, she expressed her goal this way:

    Let me learn to love unconditionally!
    Let me not love because of what I will get in response.
    Let me not try to love people
      because it is the good thing to do.
    Let me just love because I have love to give.
17. William Silverman, *Rabbinic Wisdom and Jewish Values* (New York: Union of American Hebrew Congregations, 1971), p. 33.

18. John Powell, *The Secret of Staying in Love* (Niles, IL: Argus Communications, 1974), p. 28.
19. Keen, *The Passionate Life*, p. 163.
20. This essential interaction of loving relationships is described in the "message of the World Council of Churches" from its Sixth Assembly:

> . . . life is God's gift. Life in all its fullness reflects the pattern for our life, a gift filled with wonder and glory, priceless, fragile, and irreplaceable. Only when we respond in a loving relationship with God, with one another and with the natural world can there be life in its fullness.

> "Life Together—WCC Sixth Assembly Message" (New York: Ecumenical Press Service, August 10, 1983).

21. Since I tend to side with those who emphasize that love is active, or an activity, I find it more helpful to think of love in verb than noun form. Perhaps the most accurate synonym for "loving" is "caring." A little book which describes some fundamental aspects of loving in clear and useful ways is Milton Mayeroff's *On Caring* (New York: Harper & Row, 1971). Mayeroff uses the language of "caring" throughout that volume, but much of what he says could easily be termed "loving."
22. Peck, *The Road Less Traveled*, p. 81.
23. Fromm, *The Art of Loving*, p. 18.
24. Peck, p. 82.
25. Ibid., p. 285.
26. What empowers the individual to take hold of such power is what Peck calls "grace"; although a psychiatrist by profession, he argues basic theological assumptions in his discussion of "grace" as the source of love's power. In this definition, we once again have the circle of relationships with self, other, and God in the consideration of love.
27. Harry Stack Sullivan, *Conceptions of Modern Psychiatry* (New York: W. W. Norton & Company, Inc.), quoted by Powell, *The Secret of Staying in Love*, p. 44.
28. Morton Kelsey sums up these attempts at definition, especially in relation to the interactional framework which I propose for our understanding of relationships:

> The love that we are talking about refers to that complex of emotions, attitudes, movements of will and actions in which we reach out to others in a caring, concerned manner, desiring to let other people know that we care about them and wish to facilitate the achievement of their potential. My love is never complete until the other person feels more loved by me. Love is my total behavior (emotions, feelings, and actions) directed toward making another person feel cared for by me and by the Divine Lover who is at the heart and center of the universe.

> See Morton T. Kelsey, *Caring* (New York: Paulist Press, 1981), p. 15. As will be seen, especially in my discussion of "community," I am not convinced that loving behavior requires that the other "feel more loved" by me.

29. Henri J. M. Nouwen, *Reaching Out* (Garden City, NY: Doubleday & Company, Inc., 1975), p. 81.
30. Elaine Walster and G. William Walster, *A New Look At Love* (Reading, MA: Addison-Wesley Publishing Co., 1978), p. viii.
31. Clyde Hendrick and Susan Hendrick, *Liking, Loving and Relating* (Monterey, CA: Brooks/Cole Publishing Company, 1983).
32. C.T. Onion, Ed., *The Oxford Universal Dictionary on Historical Principles,* 3rd Ed. Rev. (London: Oxford University Press, 1955), p. 1695.
33. Fromm, *The Art of Loving,* p. 22.
34. Milton Mayeroff, *On Caring* (New York: Harper & Row, 1971), p. 5.
35. Ibid., pp. 10–11.
36. Fromm, *The Art of Loving,* p. 23.
37. Ibid., p. 94.
38. Howard Thurman, *Disciplines of the Spirit* (New York: Harper & Row, 1963), p. 124.
39. Fromm, of course, is not original with these ideas. His treatment of them, is quite helpful—not only in my own thinking, but for many others who have studied his "art."
40. Fromm, *The Art of Loving,* p. 107.
41. Ari Kiev, *Active Loving* (New York: Thomas Y. Crowell, Publishers, 1979), p. 29.
42. Gaylin, *Caring,* p. 63.
43. Ibid.
44. Leo Buscaglia, *Love* (Thorofare, NJ: Charles B. Slack, Inc., 1972), p. 109.

3. Friendship: A Loving Relationship

1. Robert Brain, *Friends and Lovers* (New York: Basic Books, 1975), pp. 264–265.
2. Francine du Plessix Gray, "Friends: A New Kind of Freedom for Women" *Vogue,* (August, 1978), pp. 191, 257.
3. See the treatment of this dialogue from Plato's *Lysis,* in Gilbert Meilander, *Friendship—A Study in Theological Ethics* (Notre Dame: University of Notre Dame Press, 1981), pp. 36–37.
4. Muriel James and Louis Savary, *The Heart of Friendship* (New York: Harper & Row, 1976), p. 70.
5. Gail Hamilton, 1977.
6. Andrew M. Greeley, *The Friendship Game* (Garden City, NY: Doubleday & Company, Inc., 1970), pp. 25–26.
7. Ibid., p. 27.
8. Martin E. Marty, *Friendship* (Allen, TX: Argus Communications, 1980), pp. 7, 8, 11, 14, 17, 26.
9. Greeley, *The Friendship Game,* pp. 27–28.
10. Marty, *Friendship,* p. 226.
11. Greeley, p. 30.

12. Gerald Philips and Nancy Metzger, *Intimate Communication* (Boston: Allyn and Bacon, 1976), pp. 401—403.
13. James and Savary, *The Heart of Friendship,* pp. 34—43.
14. Ibid., p. 20.
15. Fritz Perls, *Gestalt Therapy Verbatim* (Lafayette: Real People Press, 1969), p. 4.
16. For more complete description of the "Third Self" and its applications, see James and Savary, pp. 14—32.
17. Keen, *The Passionate Life,* p. 214.
18. Ibid., p. 216
19. Margie Adam, "Sweet Friend of Mine" (Labyris Music Company, 1976, recorded on "Margie Adam. Songwriter." Dixon, CA: Pleiades Records, 1976).
20. Sharon S. Brehm, *Intimate Relationships* (New York: Random House, 1985), pp. 347—351. She draws on a 1982 study by P.H. Wright for the "side-by-side" and "face-to-face" descriptions. The photographs are found on p. 349.
21. Ibid.
22. Ibid., p. 346.
23. Greeley, pp. 163-164.
24. James Kavanaugh, *Will You Be My Friend* (Los Angeles: Nash Publishing, 1971).

4.   Commitment in Living Together

1. For a slightly different slant on this idea, see Letty Cottin Pogrebin, *Family Politics* (New York: McGraw-Hill Book Company, 1983), pp. 221-224. She considers it to be "more sensible if both men and women were free to have lots of sex with or without love before they marry—and no affairs after."
2. Keen, *The Passionate Life,* p. 106.
3. Bernard I. Murstein, *Love, Sex and Marriage through the Ages* (New York: Springer Publishing Company, 1974), pp. 31-32.
4. For fuller treatments, see Murstein, *Love, Sex and Marriage through the Ages;* James A. Mohler, *Dimensions of Love* (Garden City, New York: Doubleday & Company, Inc., 1975); and M. C. Dillon, "Romantic Love, Enduring Love and Authentic Love," in *Soundings* 66 (Summer, 1983): 133-151.
5. Murstein, p. 3.
6. Rick Masten, *Dragonflies, Codfish & Frogs,* (Carmel, CA: Sunflower Ink, 1979), p. 60.
7. Fromm, *The Art of Loving,* p. 74.
8. Dillon, "Romantic Love, Enduring Love and Authentic Love," p. 148.
9. Patricia Ferris McGinn, "Love, Work, and Family: Perspective on the Two-Career Marriage," in *Criterion,* University of Chicago Divinity School, 22 (Winter, 1983): 8.

10. Ibid., p. 9.
11. Ibid.
12. Ibid., p. 10.
13. Ibid., p. 11.
14. Dillon, pp. 138—139.
15. Elizabeth Achtemeier, *The Committed Marriage* (Philadelphia: The Westminster Press, 1976).
16. Ibid., p. 44.
17. Carl Rogers, *Becoming Partners* (New York: Dell Publishing Co., 1972), p. 158.
18. Achtemeier, *The Committed Marriage,* pp. 48—49.
19. Rogers, *Becoming Partners,* p. 8.
20. Daniel Maguire, "The Morality of Homosexual Marriage," in Robert Nugent, ed., *A Challenge to Love* (New York: The Crossroads Publishing Company, 1983), p. 124.
21. Ibid.
22. For further study of this complex issue, the resources following are recommended. Each has good additional bibliographies. Jack Babuscio, *We speak for Ourselves, Experiences in Homosexual Counseling* (Philadelphia: Fortress Press, 1977); John Boswell, *Christianity, Social Tolerance and Homosexuality* (Chicago: University of Chicago Press, 1980); Victor Paul Furnish, *The Moral Teaching of Paul* (Nashville: Abingdon Press, 1979), Ch. 3; James B. Nelson, *Embodiment—An Approach to Sexuality and Christian Theology* (Minneapolis: Augsburger Publishing House, 1978), especially Ch. 8; Robert Nugent, ed., *A Challenge to Love—Gay and Lesbian Catholics in the Church* (New York: The Crossroads Publishing Company, 1983); Norman Pittenger, *Time for Consent—A Christian's Approach to Homosexuality* (London: SCM Press, 1976); Letha Scanzoni and Virginia Ramey Mollenkott, *Is the Homosexual My Neighbor?—Another Christian View* (San Francisco: Harper & Row, 1978); Richard Woods, *Another Kind of Love— Homosexuality and Spirituality* (Garden City, NY: Doubleday and Company, 1978); Robin Scroggs, *The New Testament and Homosexuality* (Philadelphia: Fortress Press, 1983).

5. Loving in and Through Community

1. Søren Kierkegaard, *Works of Love,* p. 18, quoted in Furnish, *The Love Command in the New Testament,* p. 210.
2. See Perkins, *Love Commands in the New Testament,* p. 23.
3. George Webber, *God's Colony in Man's World* (Nashville: Abingdon Press, 1960), pp. 93–94.
4. Fromm, *The Art of Loving,* p. 110.
5. Adolfo Perez Esquivel, *Christ in a Poncho,* trans. by Robert R. Barr (Maryknoll, NY: Orbis Books, 1983), pp. 136–137.

6. Erich Fromm, *The Revolution of Hope* (New York: Bantam, 1968), p. 143.

7. James Baldwin, *The Fire Next Time* (New York: Dell Publishing Co., 1962), p. 141.

8. See James Sellers, *Warming Fires* (New York: The Seabury Press, 1975).

9. Keen, *The Passionate Life,* p. 108.

10. Furnish, p. 213.

11. Martin Luther King Jr., *Where Do We Go From Here?* (New York: Harper & Row, 1967), p. 187.

12. Ibid., p. 188.

13. Ibid.

14. Reinhold Niebuhr, *Moral Man and Immoral Society* (New York: Charles Scribner's Sons, 1932), pp. 276–277.

15. Ibid., p. 57.

6. Loving Relationships With Nature

1. A symposium on "Humanity and Nature" at Boston University, in April, 1983, brought scholars together to pursue these and other questions. See David Newell, "An Exploration of Rights and Values," and George Steiner, "What Thou Lovest Well Remains," in *Bostonia,* 57 (July/August, 1983): 17, 20. Susan Griffin, not included in that symposium, argues in her writings that there is a clear societal hostility toward nature, and that the source of this hostility is in the patriarchal organization of society. Man-the-controller, who has insisted on controlling both woman and nature, has succeeded in establishing an antagonistic relationship with both. Further, man often identifies woman and nature with each other. Her insights are very important for an understanding of what has happened in our capacity for loving relationships. See *Woman and Nature* (New York: Harper and Row, 1978) and *Pornography and Silence* (New York: Harper and Row, 1981).

2. The Findhorn Community, *The Findhorn Garden* (New York: Harper and Row, 1975), p. 127.

3. Ibid., p. 140.

4. Viktor Frankl, *Man's Search for Meaning* (New York: Washington Square Press, 1963), pp. 62–63.

5. Loren Eiseley, *The Immense Journey,* (New York: Random House, 1957); Vintage Books, 1959), pp. 190–192.

6. Ibid., p. 193.

7. Ibid., p. 175.

8. Peter Singer, *Practical Ethics* (Cambridge: Cambridge University Press, 1979), p. 49. See also Singer's *Animal Liberation* (New York: Random House, 1975).

9. Tom Regan, *All That Dwell Therein* (Berkeley: University of California Press, 1982), esp. pp. 75–98.

10. Christopher Stone, quoted in Newell, "An Exploration of Rights and Value," *Bostonia* 57, (July/August, 1983): 18.
11. Christopher Stone, "On the Moral and Legal Rights of Nature," in *Bostonia* 57 (July/August, 1983): 32.
12. Regan, *All That Dwell Therein.*
13. Frankl, *Man's Search For Meaning,* p. 110.
14. George Steiner, "What Thou Lovest Well Remains," p. 24.
15. Flo V. Menninger, *Days of My Life* (Richard R. Smith, 1939), p. 81, quoted in Karl Menninger, *Love Against Hate* (New York: Harcourt, Brace and World, Inc., 1942), p. 264.

7.   The Struggle With Self

1. Sam Keen makes this point in commenting on a "limited supply of affection" in *The Passionate Life,* p. 57. He asserts that "to the degree that we are arrested at this point of development, the needy child will dominate our motivations."
2. John Powell, *Why Am I Afraid To Love?* (Niles, IL: Argus Communications, 1972), pp. 101, 104.
3. Ibid., p. 105.
4. Kelsey, *Caring,* p. 58.
5. Ibid., p. 59. Kelsey develops an insight which he admittedly borrowed from C. J. Jung, *Modern Man In Search of a Soul.*
6. Ibid., p. 61.
7. Elaboration on these suggestions is found in Ibid., pp. 62–65.
8. May, *Love and Will,* p. 123. Page references to this book are from the original edition; pagination in paperback editions vary.
9. Ibid.
10. Ibid., p. 125.
11. Peck, *The Road Less Traveled,* p. 277.
12. Ibid., p. 122. Quoting Rilke, "Letter 74, Briefe aus den Jahren 1907 bis 1914."
13. Ibid., pp. 146–147.
14. Keen, p. 164.
15. See Genesis 32:22–32. May's discussion is in *Love and Will,* 168–170.
16. See Mark 5:1–20 and Luke 8:26–39. There is a story of two Gadarene "demoniacs" in similar circumstance in Matthew 8:28–34, but the Matthew story concentrates on the miracle of demon departure and does not treat the matter of naming and confrontation.
17. Kelsey, p. 18.
18. See May, pp. 170, 177.
19. Clark E. Moustakas, *Loneliness and Love* (Englewood Cliffs, NJ: Prentice-Hall, 1972), p. 20.
20. Ibid., p. 56.
21. Ibid., p. 49. Moustakas draws on Paul Tillich, the philosopher and theologian, for this view.

22. Ibid., p. 146.
23. Henri Nouwen, *Reaching Out,* pp. 25–26.
24. Ibid., p. 46.
25. Ibid., p. 223.
26. Ibid., p. 267.
27. Frankl, *Man's Search for Meaning,* p. 104.
28. May, p. 156.

8. Power and Dignity in Loving Relationships

1. I am indebted for this idea of freedom within intimacy as a dance to Pat Cayton Kehde, who studied with me while pursuing a graduate degree in Speech Communication and Human Relations.
2. David Viscott, *How to Live With Another Person* (New York: Pocket Books, 1976), p. 32.
3. Kiev, *Active Loving,* p. 144.
4. Viscott, *How to Live With Another Person,* p. 46.
5. Ibid.
6. Ibid., p. 76.
7. Ibid., p. 127.
8. Mayeroff, *On Caring,* pp. 78–79.
9. George Bach and Ronald Deutsch, *Pairing* (New York: Avon Books, 1970), p. 26.
10. John Crosby, *Illusion and Disillusion* (Belmont: Wadsworth Press, 1976), p. 49.
11. Nancy Friday, *My Mother/My Self* (New York: Dell Publishing Co., 1977), pp. 391–392.
12. Crosby, *Illusion and Disillusion,* pp. 49–50.
13. Mayeroff, p. 20.
14. Ibid.
15. Ibid., pp. 20–21.
16. Henri J. M. Nouwen, *Intimacy* (San Francisco: Harper & Row, 1969), p. 23, reminds us: "We probably have wondered in our many lonesome moments if there is one corner in this competitive, demanding world where it is safe to be relaxed, to expose ourselves to someone else, and to give unconditionally."
17. Gordon Clanton and Lynn G. Smith, "The Self-Inflicted Pain of Jealousy," *Psychology Today* (March, 1977), p. 82. Excerpted from Clanton, Gordon and Lynn G. Smith, *Jealousy* (Englewood Cliffs, NJ: Prentice-Hall, 1977).
18. Ibid., p. 80.
19. Keen, *The Passionate Life,* p. 62.
20. Rainer Maria Rilke, *Letters To A Young Poet,* translated by M. D. Herter Norton (New York: W.W. Norton & Company, 1934), quoted by Powell, *The Secret of Staying in Love,* p. 66.
21. Gaylin, *Caring,* p. 63.

9. Conflict in Loving Relationships

1. David and Vera Mace emphasize this lack of preparation in our culture, and our need to learn coping methods, in *How To Have A Happy Marriage* (Nashville: Abingdon, 1977).
2. I am indebted to Professor Gene Reeves of Meadville Theological School in Chicago for his comments on harmony and contrasts in regard to prayer as a work of art; they were presented at the annual meeting of Collegium, An Association for Liberal Religious Studies, October 14, 1983.
3. Powell, *The Secret of Staying in Love,* pp. 145–146.
4. Peck, *The Road Less Traveled,* p. 153.
5. Moustakas, *Loneliness and Love,* p. 66.
6. Menninger, *Love Against Hate,* pp. 275–276.
7. See Robert McAfee Brown and Gustave Weigel, *An American Dialogue* (Garden City, NY: Anchor Books, Doubleday & Company, Inc., 1961). Especially the "conditions for fruitful dialogue," pp. 26–34.
8. John Powell is especially helpful in distinguishing "dialogue" from "discussion." Emotional clearance, he says, must precede the sharing of ideas, preferences and intentions in rational discussion. See *The Secret of Staying in Love,* p. 73.
9. Mace, *How To Have A Happy Marriage,* pp. 113–114.
10. George Bach and Ronald M. Deutsch, *Pairing* (New York: Avon Books, 1970).
11. Ibid., pp. 202–204.
12. Crosby, *Illusion and Disillusion,* pp. 148–149. Transactional Analysis is an extremely helpful tool for self-understanding, and for learning about our communication with others. It is treated extensively in a number of sources. For starters, try: Eric Berne, *Games People Play* (New York: Grove, 1964); Thomas Harris, *I'm OK—You're OK* (New York: Harper and Row, 1967); Muriel James and Dorothy Jongeward, *Born To Win* (Reading, MA: Addison-Wesley, 1971).
13. Ibid., p. 156.
14. Ibid., p. 157.
15. Ibid., p. 158.
16. Zwell, *How To Succeed At Love,* pp. 182–186.
17. See Ibid., especially Exercise 20 on pp. 185–186. Crosby also has some very helpful suggestions for encouraging children and youth to use "discharge" of their feelings. pp. 269–270.
18. Crosby, p. 160.
19. Roger Fisher and William Ury, *Getting To Yes* (New York: Penguin Books, 1983), p. vi.
20. Ibid., p. xi.
21. Ibid., p. 13.
22. Ibid., p. 23.
23. Ibid., pp. 22–30.
24. Ibid., p. 154.

25. Conflict resolution and management is a specialty of its own within the social and behavioral sciences. Two sample sources are: Kenneth Thomas, "Conflict and Conflict Management" in Marvin Dunnette, Ed., *The Handbook of Industrial and Organizational Psychology*, Vol. II (Chicago: Rand McNally, 1975). This article includes a two dimensional model of conflict handling behavior, the Thomas-Kilmann Conflict Mode instrument. A standard source is Robert Blake and Jane Mouton, *The Managerial Grid* (Houston: Gulf Publishing, 1964). In addition, many methods of conflict resolution have been devised by specialists in counseling loving partners, and a perusal of bookstore shelves will locate several of these. In a recent contribution, Nathaniel Branden has worked out a "sentence-completion" technique which can be done face-to-face with a counselor present, in groups, or alone with pencil and paper. See *If You Could Hear What I Cannot Say* (New York: Bantam Books, Inc., 1983).
26. Hoy Steele, "Bonds Between Indians and Other Racial Groups in an Urban Setting," in Rhoda Goldstein and Wendell James Roye, *Interracial Bonds* (New York: General Hall, Inc., 1979), p. 51.
27. Nouwen, *Reaching Out*, p. 51.
28. Keen, *The Passionate Life*, p. 150.
29. Powell, *The Secret of Staying In Love*, p. 147.

10. Sex and Sexuality in Loving Relationships

1. Ashley Montagu, comments on the "Donahue" television show, August 16, 1979.
2. Robert F. Francoeur, *Becoming a Sexual Person—A Brief Edition* (New York: John Wiley & Sons, 1984), pp. 499, vii.
3. Norman Pittenger, *Time for Consent—A Christian's Approach to Homosexuality* (London: SCM Press, Ltd., 1976), p. 104.
4. James B. Nelson, *Embodiment—An Approach to Sexuality and Christian Theology* (Minneapolis: Augsburg Publishing House, 1978), pp. 17–18, 272.
5. Donald Goergen, *The Sexual Celibate* (Garden City, NY: Image Books, 1979), p. 265.
6. Nelson, *Embodiment*, p. 36.
7. May, *Love and Will*, p. 39 ff.
8. Keen, *The Passionate Life*. p. 4.
9. Both Fromm and May, as psychotherapists, report that this observation has often been made by their clients, and they emphasize the recognition of the power of this experience in the total movement toward union.
10. Nelson, *Embodiment*, p. 20.
11. An idea increasingly expressed this way, this particular summary was provided by Father Bill Trienekens in *Marriage Encounter* (December, 1979), pp. 27–28.

12. Nelson, *Embodiment,* pp. 104–105.
13. Francoeur, p. vii.
14. Goergen, p. 68.
15. Francoeur, p. 520.
16. Nelson, *Embodiment,* pp. 78–79.
17. See the excellent treatment of the history of religious attitudes toward homosexuality in John Boswell, *Christianity, Social Tolerance and Homosexuality* (Chicago: The University of Chicago Press, 1980).
18. The idea that Jesus and Mary Magdalene had a sexual tie is not just the invention of twentieth-century novelists; legends in varying Christian groups even suggest that the two were eventually married and produced children. The contemporary rock musical "Jesus Christ Superstar," with its sensitivity to Mary's deep affection for Jesus, has its roots in many traditions and legends inside and outside of Christianity. Some have also asked about the nature of the obviously close and intimate relationships Jesus had with the men who surrounded him. Sexual love between males was not unknown at that time, and close affectional ties between men were certainly accepted.
19. Goergen, pp. 38–39.
20. Nelson, *Embodiment,* p. 77.
21. Derrick Bailey, *Sexual Relation in Christian Thought* (New York: Harper and Brothers, 1959), p. 59. Quoted in Goergen, *The Sexual Celibate,* p. 55. For a much more thorough treatment of these issues, see Bailey and Goergen, as well as Nelson, *Embodiment.*
22. Eugene B. Borowitz, *Choosing a Sex Ethic—A Jewish Inquiry* (Washington, DC: B'nai B'rith Hillel Foundations, published by Schocken Books, 1969), p. 31.
23. Zwell, *How to Succeed at Love,* p. 256.
24. This term was used by Stephen Reid, an Old Testament Scholar at Pacific School of Religion, in an address reported in *The United Methodist Reporter,* March 14, 1986, p. 3.
25. James B. Nelson, *Between Two Gardens*—Reflections on Sexuality and Religious Experience (New York: Pilgrim Press, 1983), p. 115.
26. Pittenger, *Time for Consent,* p. 84.
27. William Sloane Coffin, *The Courage to Love* (San Francisco: Harper & Row, Publishers, 1982), p. 43.
28. Letha Scanzoni and Virginia Ramey Mollenkott, *Is the Homosexual My Neighbor?—Another Christian View* (San Francisco: Harper & Row, 1978), p. 1.
29. From *The United Methodist Reporter,* (May 28, 1982), p. 3. Bishop Melvin Wheatley was cleared by the national denomination's Committee on Investigation of charges that he was in violation of certain traditions and standards when he appointed a young clergyman to a church position with the knowledge that he was an "avowed and practicing homosexual." Since the minister was an ordained member of the denomination's Annual Conference system, the bishop was actually required by the church's *Discipline* to provide him a position. Bishop Wheatley has consistently dissociated himself from public positions of

denomination members or hierarchy who suggest that homosexuality is
a sin or a violation of acceptable standards of Christian behavior.
30. Nelson, *Embodiment*, p. 30.
31. Goergen, p. 79.
32. Pittenger, p. 28.
33. Nelson, *Embodiment*, p. 118.
34. Gerda Lerner, *A Death of One's Own* (New York: Harper & Row, 1980),
     p. 257. We have a growing literature on the problems of the "sexually
     disenfranchised," as Nelson refers to them. The assumption that persons
     who are dying, who are ill or injured in hospitals, are placed in nursing
     homes, are retarded or physically impaired, do not have sexual feelings
     and/or the right to express those feelings is being examined. Fortunately,
     our human community seems to be in the process of moving toward
     recognition of these realities and trying to make some changes.

11. Loss of a Loving Relationship

1. Elisabeth Kübler-Ross, *On Death and Dying* (New York: The Macmillan
    Company, 1969). The stages discussed here are described by Kübler-
    Ross in chapters 3–8. Also of value is her book, *Death—The Final Stage
    of Growth* (Englewood Cliffs, NJ: Prentice-Hall, Inc., 1975). A brief
    form of the stages is found on p. 10, in a summary article by Hans
    Mausch.
2. Virginia Satir describes this phenomenon in her introduction to Bruce
    Fisher, *Rebuilding—When Your Relationship Ends* (San Luis Obispo,
    Impact Publishers, 1981), p. 2.
3. Ibid., p. 71.
4. Ibid.
5. Ibid., p. 2.
6. Kübler-Ross, *On Death and Dying*, p. 139.
7. Ibid.
8. Associated Press, "Memories of a Man—And His Heart," *Kansas City
    Star,* September28, 1983.
9. Robert Kavanaugh, *Facing Death* (Los Angeles: Nash Publishing, 1972).
10. David K. Switzer, *The Dynamics of Grief—Its Source, Pain and Healing*
     (Nashville: Abingdon Press, 1970).
11. James Kavanaugh, *Will You Be My Friend?*.
12. Switzer, *The Dynamics of Grief,* p. 198.
13. Bruce Fisher, *Rebuilding,* p. 89.
14. Kenneth R. Mitchell and Herbert Anderson, *All Our Losses, All Our
     Griefs* (Philadelphia: The Westminster Press, 1983), p. 96.
15. Jury and Jury, *Gramp,* p. 152.
16. Gerda Lerner, *A Death of One's Own,* p. 267.
17. Switzer, pp. 203–204.
18. This and similar problems in coping with losses are discussed by Gaylin in
     Caring. See Chapter X, esp. p. 158.

19. Jury, p. 151.
20. Peck, *The Road Less Traveled*, p. 134.
21. Bruce Fisher, *Rebuilding*, pl 4.
22. An excellent recent treatment of loss experiences is found in Ann Kaiser Stearns, *Living Through Personal Crisis* (Chicago: The Thomas More Press, 1984). Experienced in both clinical psychology and pastoral counseling, Stearns provides rich insights into facing losses and moving into new growth and freedom. Also helpful in personal grief work is Judy Tatelbaum, *The Courage to Grieve—Creative Living, Recovery and Growth Through Grief* (New York: Harper & Row, Publishers, 1980). A thorough discussion of these concerns is given in Richard A. Kalish, *Death, Grief and Caring Relationships*, 2nd. ed. (Monterey, CA: Brooks/Cole Publishing Company, 1985).

12. Loving the Enemy

1. See William Barclay, *The Gospel of Matthew*, 2 vols, Rev. Ed. (Philadelphia: The Westminister Press, 1975), 1: 177.
2. See Luke 6:27—28, 32—36.
3. Gaylin, *Caring*, p. 163.
4. Ibid.
5. Furnish, *The Love Command in the New Testament*, p. 66.
6. Anders Nygren, *Agape and Eros*, translated by Philip S. Watson (Philadelphia: The Westminister Press, 1953), pp. 99—100.
7. Gene Outka, *Agape: An Ethical Analysis* (New Haven: Yale University Press, 1972), p. 11.
8. Perkins, *Love Commands in the New Testament*, pp. 63—64.
9. Ibid., p. 125.
10. Furnish points out that Epictetus, the Cynic philosopher who live about A.D. 50—138, including loving one's enemies in his description of the ideal "moral man." This ideal person "must needs be flogged like an ass, and while he is being flogged he must love the men who flog him, as though he were the father or bother of them all." This type of love is perceived in the model of family love, including affection, both fraternal and paternal. The verb form of love used here is the word *philia*, fraternal love, rather than *agape*. See Furnish, p. 49.
11. Furnish, p. 67.
12. Furnish describes this aspect of the Luke account, Ibid., p. 56.
13. Nygren, *Agape and Eros*, p. 102.
14. Ibid.
15. Furnish, pp. 66—67.
16. Luise Schottroff, "Non-Violence and the Love of One's Enemies," in Reginald H. Fuller, Ed., *Essays on the Love Commandment* (Philadelphia: Fortress Press, 1978), pp. 23—24.
17. Quoted by Outka in *Agape: An Ethical Analysis*, p. 257.

18. Mohandas K. Gandhi, *Non-Violent Resistance* (New York: Schocken Books, 1961), pp. iii.
19. Ibid., p. 6.
20. Ibid., p. iii.
21. Ibid., pp. 16–17.
22. Louis Fischer, Ed., *The Essential Gandhi* (New York: Vintage Books, 1962), p. 207, quoting from D. G. Tendulkar, *Mahatma,* Vol. II, p. 418–420.
23. Ibid., p. 199, quoting from *Young India,* Jan. 8, 1925.
24. Ibid., p. 206, quoting from *Young India,* July 14, 1927.
25. Gandhi, *Non-Violent Resistance,* p. iii.
26. Martin Luther King Jr., *Stride Toward Freedom* (New York: Harper and Row, 1958), p. 102.
27. Ibid., pp. 96–97.
28. Ibid., pp. 105–106.
29. Coffin, *The Courage to Love,* p. 60.
30. See Furnish, p. 67.
31. Outka, pp. 311–312.
32. Viscott, *How to Live With Another Person,* pp. 33–47.
33. Keen, *The Passionate Life,* pp. 146–150.
34. King, *Where Do We Go From Here: Chaos Or Community,* p. 222.

Epilogue

1. Beverly Wildung Harrison, *Making the Connections—Essays in Feminist Social Ethics,* edited by Carol S. Robb (Boston: Beacon Press, 1985), p. 20.
2. Ibid., p. 18. Harrison comments that "I shudder to think how many times during my years of theological study I came upon a warning from a writer of Christian ethics not to confuse real, Christian love with 'mere mutuality.'" She assumes that such writers have simply not yet experienced mutual vulnerability in its pleasure and its power. She is especially critical of Anders Nygren (see p. 271, note 27) in his treatment of agape love, for deprecating mutuality in love. Her comments suggest that his interpretation of agape as the supreme form of love seems to qualify our human experience of mutuality. On that grounds, she would undoubtedly raise some questions about my use of Nygren in Chap. 12, and would likely insist that some of the historical considerations of agape love do not adequately instruct us on the mutuality and justice necessary for the love relationship with an "enemy." I am especially indebted to her editor and my treasured colleague, Carol S. Robb, for refusing to leave me satisfied with my treatment of this matter.
3. Ibid., p. 19.
4. Ibid., p. 20.

Selected Bibliography

Achtemeier, Elizabeth. *The Committed Marriage*. Philadelphia: The Westminster Press, 1976.

Augsburger, David W. *Cherishable: Love and Marriage*. Scottdale, PA: Herald Press, 1971.

Augsburger, David W. *When Caring Is Not Enough: Resolving Conflicts Through Fair Fighting*. Scottdale, PA: Herald Press, 1983.

Bach, George and Ronald Deutsch. *Pairing*. New York: Avon Books, 1970.

Bane, Mary Jo. *Here to Stay—American Families in the Twentieth Century*. New York: Basic Books, Inc., 1976.

Barbeau, Clayton C. *Joy of Marriage*. Minneapolis, MN: Winston Press, 1976.

Borowitz, Eugene B. *Choosing a Sex Ethic—A Jewish Inquiry*. Washington, DC: B'nai B'rith Hillel Foundations, published by Schocken Books, 1969.

Brain, Robert. *Friends and Lovers*. New York: Basic Books, 1975.

Branden, Nathaniel. *If You Could Hear What I Cannot Say*. New York: Bantam Books, Inc., 1983.

Brehm, Sharon S. *Intimate Relationships*. New York: Random House, 1985.

Buscaglia, Leo. *Love*. Thorofare, NJ: Charles B. Slack, Inc., 1972.

Buscaglia, Leo. *Loving Each Other—The Challenge of Human Relationships*. New York: Fawcett Columbine, 1984.

Carmody, Denise Lardner and John Tully Carmody. *Becoming One Flesh—Growth in Christian Marriage*. Nashville: The Upper Room, 1984.

Clanton, Gordon and Lynn G. Smith. *Jealousy*. Englewood Cliffs, NJ: Prentice-Hall, 1977.

Clinebell, Howard J. and Charlotte H. Clinebell. *The Intimate Marriage*. New York: Harper & Row, 1970.

Coffin, William Sloane. *The Courage to Love*. San Francisco: Harper & Row, Publishers, 1982.

Crosby, John. *Illusion and Disillusion—The Self In Love and Marriage*. Belmont: Wadsworth Press, 1976.

Eiseley, Loren. *The Immense Journey.* New York: Random House, 1957; Vintage Books, 1959.

Faber, Adele and Elaine Mazlish. *Liberated Parents and Liberated Children.* New York: Avon Books, 1975.

Faber, Adele and Elaine Mazlish. *How to Talk So Kids Will Listen & Listen So Kids Will Talk.* New York: Avon Books, 1982.

Fisher, Bruce. *Rebuilding—When Your Relationship Ends.* San Luis Obispo: Impact Publishers, 1981.

Fischer, Luis. Editor. *The Essential Gandhi.* New York: Vintage Books, 1962.

Fisher, Roger and William Ury. *Getting To Yes—Negotiating Agreement Without Giving In.* New York: Penguin Books, 1983.

Ford, Edward E. and Steven Englund. *Permanent Love—Practical Steps To a Lasting Relationship* (A Reality Therapy Approach to Caring). Minneapolis, MN: Winston Press, 1979.

Francoeur, Robert F. *Becoming a Sexual Person—A Brief Edition.* New York: John Wiley & Sons, 1984.

Fromm, Erich. *The Art of Loving.* New York: Harper and Row, 1956.

Furnish, Victor Paul. *The Love Command in the New Testament.* Nashville: Abingdon Press, 1972.

Gandhi, Mohandas K. *Non-Violent Resistance.* New York: Schocken Books, 1961.

Gaylin, William. *Caring.* New York: Alfred A. Knopf, 1976.

Gilligan, Carol. *In A Different Voice.* Cambridge, MA: Harvard University Press, 1982.

Ginott, Haim G. *Between Parent and Child.* New York: Macmillan Publishing Co., Inc., 1965.

Goergen, Donald. *The Sexual Celibate.* Garden City, New York: Image Books, 1979.

Greeley, Andrew M. *The Friendship Game.* Garden City, NY: Doubleday & Company, Inc., 1970.

Griffin, Susan. *Woman and Nature.* New York: Harper and Row, 1981.

Harrison, Beverly Wildung. *Making the Connections—Essays in Feminist Social Ethics.* Ed. by Carol S. Robb. Boston: Beacon Press, 1985.

Hendrick, Clyde and Susan Hendrick. *Liking, Loving and Relating.* Monterey, CA: Brooks/Cole Publishing Company, 1983.

Hettlinger, Richard. *Your Sexual Freedom—Letters to Students.* New York: Continuum, 1981.

Huddleston, Mary Anne, Ed. *Celibate Loving—Encounter in Three Dimensions.* New York: Paulist Press, 1984.

James, Muriel and Louis Savary. *The Heart of Friendship.* New York: Harper & Row, 1976.

Jury, Mark and Dan Jury. *Gramp.* New York: Grossman Publishers, 1976.

Kalish, Richard A. *Death, Grief and Caring Relationships.* Second Edition. Monterey, CA: Brooks/Cole Publishing Company, 1985.

Kavanaugh, James. *Will You Be My Friend?.* Los Angeles: Nash Publishing, 1971.

Keen, Sam. *The Passionate Life.* San Francisco: Harper & Row, 1983.

Kelsey, Martin T. *Caring.* New York: Paulist Press, 1981.

Kiev, Ari. *Active Loving.* New York: Thomas Y. Crowell, Publishers, 1979.

King, Martin Luther, Jr. *Stride Toward Freedom.* New York: Harper and Row, 1958.

King, Martin Luther, Jr. *Where Do We Go From Here: Chaos or Community.* New York: Harper and Row, 1967.

Lederer, William J. and Don D. Jackson. *The Mirages of Marriage.* New York: W.W. Norton and Co., Inc., 1968.

Lerner, Gerda. *A Death of One's Own.* New York: Harper & Row, 1980.

Mace, David and Vera Mace. *How To Have A Happy Marriage.* Nashville: Abingdon, 1977.

Marty, Martin E. *Friendship.* Allen, TX: Argus Communications, 1980.

Masters, William H. and Virginia E. Johnson. *The Pleasure Bond.* New York: Bantam Books, 1978.

May, Rollo. *Love and Will.* New York: W.W. Norton & Company, Inc., 1969.

Mayeroff, Milton. *On Caring.* New York: Harper & Row, 1971.

Meilander, Gilbert. *Friendship—A Study in Theological Ethics.* Notre Dame: University of Notre Dame Press, 1981.

Menninger, Karl. *Love Against Hate.* New York: Harcourt, Brace and World, Inc., 1942.

Messinger, Lillian. *Remarriage—A Family Affair.* New York: Plenum Publishing Corp., 1984.

Mitchell, Ann. *Children in the Middle—Living Through Divorce.* New York: Methuen, Inc., 1985.

Mitchell, Kenneth R. and Herbert Anderson. *All Our Losses, All Our Griefs.* Philadelphia: The Westminster Press, 1983.

Molton, Warren Lane. *Friends, Partners and Lovers—A Good Word About Marriage.* Valley Forge, PA: Judson Press, 1983.

Molton, Warren Lane. *Spheres of Intimacy—How Lovers Stay Close.* Kansas City, MO: Piñon Press, 1982.

Moustakas, Clark E. *Loneliness and Love.* Englewood Cliffs, NJ: Prentice-Hall, 1972.

Murstein, Bernard I. *Love, Sex and Marriage through the Ages.* New York: Springer Publishing Company, 1974.

Nelson, James B. *Between Two Gardens—Reflections on Sexuality and Religious Experience.* New York: Pilgrim Press, 1983.

Nelson, James B. *Embodiment—An Approach to Sexuality and Christian Theology.* Minneapolis: Augsburg Publishing House, 1978.

Noddings, Nell. *Caring—A Feminine Approach to Ethics and Moral Education.* Berkeley: University of California Press, 1984.

Nouwen, Henry J. M. *Reaching Out.* Garden City, New York: Doubleday & Company, Inc., 1975.

O'Neill, Nena. *The Marriage Premise.* New York: M. Evans and Company, Inc., 1977.

Outka, Gene. *Agape: An Ethical Analysis.* New Haven: Yale University Press, 1972.

Peck, M. Scott. *The Road Less Traveled.* New York: Simon & Schuster, 1978.

Perkins, Pheme. *Love Commands in the New Testament.* New York: Paulist Press, 1982.

Philips, Gerald and Nancy Metzger. *Intimate Communication.* Boston: Allyn and Bacon, 1976.

Pittenger, Norman. *Time for Consent—A Christian's Approach to Homosexuality.* London: SCM Press, Ltd., 1976.

Pogrebin, Letty Cottin. *Family Politics.* New York: McGraw-Hill Book Company, 1983.

Powell, John. *Why Am I Afraid To Love?* Niles, IL: Argus Communications, 1967.

Powell, John. *The Secret of Staying in Love.* Niles, IL: Argus Communications, 1974.

Robinson, Bryan E. and Robert L. Barret. *The Developing Father.* New York: The Guilford Press, 1986.

Rogers, Carl. *Becoming Partners.* New York: Dell Publishing Co., 1972.

Rubin, Lilian B. *Intimate Strangers—Men and Women Together.* New York: Harper & Row, 1983.

de Saint Exupéry, Antoine. *The Little Prince.* Trans. Katherine Woods. New York: Harcourt, Brace & World, Inc., 1943.

Scanzoni, John. *Sexual Bargaining—Power Politics in the American Marriage.* 2nd Ed. Chicago: The University of Chicago Press, 1982.

Scanzoni, Letha and Virginia Ramey Mollenkott. *Is the Homosexual My Neighbor?—Another Christian View.* San Francisco: Harper & Row, 1978.

Scroggs, Robin. *The New Testament and Homosexuality.* Philadelphia: Fortress Press, 1983.

Shields, David L. *Growing Beyond Prejudices—Overcoming Hierarchical Dualism.* Mystic, CN: Twenty-Third Publications, 1986.

Silverstein, Shel. *The Giving Tree.* New York: Harper & Row, 1964.

Simons, Joseph. *Living Together—Communication in the Unmarried Relationship.* Chicago: Nelson-Hall Publishers, 1978.

Smedes, Lewis B. *Forgive and Forget—Healing the Hurts We Don't Deserve.* San Francisco: Harper & Row, 1984.

Stearns, Ann Kaiser. *Living Through Personal Crisis.* Chicago: The Thomas More Press, 1984.

Switzer, David K. *The Dynamics of Grief—Its Source, Pain and Healing.* Nashville: Abingdon Press, 1970.

Tatelbaum, Judy. *The Courage to Grieve—Creative Living, Recovery and Growth Through Grief.* New York: Harper & Row, Publishers, 1980.

Terkel, Studs. *Working.* New York: Avon Books, 1972.

Viscott, David. *How to Live With Another Person.* New York: Pocket Books, 1976.

Walster, Elaine and G. William Walster. *A New Look At Love.* Reading, MA: Addison-Wesley Publishing Co., 1978.

Weber, Eric and Steven S. Simring. *How to Win Back the One You Love.* New York: Bantam Books, 1984.

West, Uta. *If Love is the Answer, What is the Question?.* New York: McGraw-Hill, 1977.

Willimon, William H. *Saying Yes to Marriage.* Valley Forge, PA: The Judson Press, 1979.

Zwell, Michael. *How to Succeed at Love.* Englewood Cliffs, NJ: Prentice Hall, Inc., 1978.

Index